MW00811982

Structuring the State

Structuring the State

THE FORMATION OF ITALY AND GERMANY AND THE PUZZLE OF FEDERALISM

Daniel Ziblatt

PRINCETON UNIVERSITY PRESS

PRINCETON AND OXFORD

© 2006 by Princeton University Press
Published by Princeton University Press, 41 William Street, Princeton, New Jersey 08540
In the United Kingdom: Princeton University Press, 3 Market Place, Woodstock,
Oxfordshire OX20 1SY

Library of Congress Cataloging-in-Publication Data
Ziblatt, Daniel, 1972–
Structuring the state: the formation of italy and Germany and the
puzzle of federalism / Daniel Ziblatt.
p.   cm.
Includes bibliographical references and index.
ISBN-13: 978-0-691-12167-3 (cloth : alk. paper)
ISBN-10: 0-691-12167-2 (cloth : alk. paper)
1. State, The—History—19th century. 2. Germany—Politics and government—
19th century. 3. Italy—Politics and government—19th century. 4. Federal
government—Germany—History—19th century. 5. Federal government—
Italy—History—19th century. 6. Comparative government. I. Title.
JC201.Z53 2006
320.443′049—dc22   2005043378

British Library Cataloging-in-Publication Data is available

This book has been composed in Galliard

Printed on acid-free paper. ∞

pup.princeton.edu

Printed in the United States of America

1   3   5   7   9   10   8   6   4   2

CONTENTS

FIGURES AND TABLES

FIGURES

TABLES

PREFACE

ONE of the major contributions of scholarship in comparative politics is the insight that political institutions endure and shape life for citizens and groups in unexpected and important ways. We also have come to learn that the present shape of political institutions is tightly linked to their past. As a result, exploring *where political institutions come from* has become a crucial area of research. From this research, we know that political institutions are unfortunately not simply the product, in a mechanical fashion, of particular societal "needs" at particular moments. Instead, political institutions sometimes emerge unintentionally out of periods of intense political conflict among actors who have a multitude of goals that are only distantly related to the function we think the institutions now fill. If we want to know how to change institutions, we must be attuned to the fact that there is frequently a mismatch between the initial aims of institution-builders and the contemporary value we attach to them.

This book explores these themes by examining the development of the state and federalism in nineteenth-century Italy and Germany. The adoption of federalism in nineteenth-century Germany and its failure in the same period in Italy has shaped life in both countries in very decisive ways. With this contrast in mind, the original conception of this book was to explore the hypothesis that important differences in contemporary Italy and Germany might be rooted in their unique paths of nation-state development. While that idea remained a proposition that motivated the research, a more fundamental puzzle captured my attention: why was Italy formed as a unitary state and Germany a federal state? I believe the answer to this question has crucial implications for understanding the violently turbulent twentieth-century political histories of Italy and Germany. But beyond that, by exploring this question, we can also come to some surprising conclusions about how political institutions are created and change. This book finds that institutional continuities shape the state-making strategies of even the boldest political leaders such as Bismarck and Cavour, to whom we normally attribute Machiavellian far-sightedness; the institutional slate is never wiped clean, even in founding moments. Additionally, the book finds that the purposes of state-builders may have very little to do with the benefits and drawbacks we associate today with particular institutions such as federalism; the much touted "market preserving" and "democracy preserving" functions of federalism played only minor roles in the story of federalism's origins. Instead, in Germany in 1871, federalism was adopted partly with the aim of institutionalizing an indirect monarchical check on the new national parliament that was to be elected via universal male suffrage. In Italy in 1861, by contrast, despite support for federalism, a national parliament was coupled with a unitary structure of governance, and mass participation was directly limited via a highly restricted franchise. In both cases, national unification was undertaken by political leaders with the aim of projecting greater geopolitical weight for their states on the European stage but doing so while assuring that the new political entity would remain at least partially in the hands of monarchical leaders. In Germany, federalism assured this goal; in Italy, a unitary state with direct restrictions on mass political participation served the same purpose. To explain why federalism was the vehicle of national unification in Germany, while it failed to take root in Italy, is the main task of this book.

The argument I offer and the book itself grew out of a dissertation that was completed at University of California, Berkeley, in December 2002. My greatest intellectual debt at Berkeley was to my dissertation committee: Ken Jowitt (chair), Andrew Janos, Chris Ansell, and Gerald Feldman. As imaginative intellectuals and careful scholars, they remain my role models. In addition to their support, this project has benefited from the close reading and advice of three scholars who have provided generous, thorough, and useful feedback at different stages: Margaret Lavinia Anderson, Gerhard Lehmbruch, and Raymond Grew. While I was in Berkeley, a group of friends and colleagues were key to the completion of the project: Nick Biziouras, Winson Chu, Ken Foster, Vanna Gonzales, Laura Henry, Jon Hoffman, Marc Morje Howard, Wade Jacoby, Sabine Kriebel, Dan Kronenfeld, Jonah Levy, Conor O'Dwyer, John Sides, Lisa Swartout, and Harold Wilensky. While in Italy, I benefited from always reliable help from Sergio Fabbrini and Nicola Pasini. In Berlin, my research was supported by the Social Science Research Council's Berlin Program for Advanced German and European Studies. In the final stages of the project, I benefited from generous feedback from Barry Weingast and support from all my friends at the Naval Postgraduate School in Monterey, California. Since my arrival at Harvard in the fall of 2003, my intellectual home has become the Minda De Gunzburg Center for European Studies. Here, the manuscript—in its various forms—has benefited from the help, feedback, and encouragement of Anna Grzymala Busse, Cindy Skach, Dirk Bönker, Paul Pierson, Torben Iversen, Peter Hall, Grzegorz Ekiert, Will Phelan, and Eric Nguyen. At Princeton University Press,

Chuck Myers and Richard Isomaki have been crucial in assuring that the book was finished on time. Finally, I know I would not have made it this far without Suriya Sangsub.

Above all, however, this book—especially in its earliest stages—reflects long conversations and always encouraging support from my father, David Ziblatt. This book is dedicated to my mother and my father.

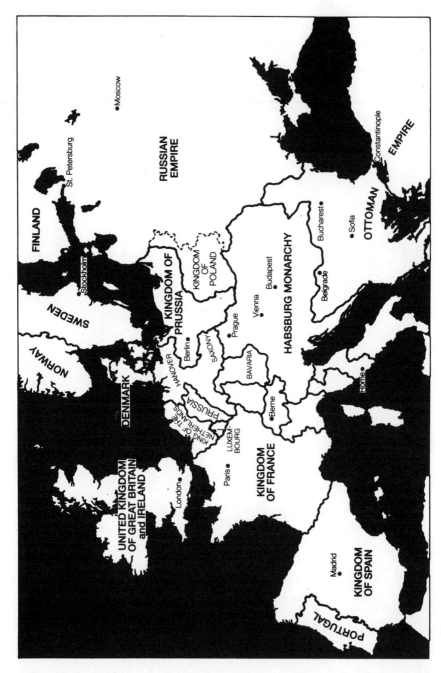

Europe in 1815.

Structuring the State

Chapter One

INTRODUCTION: HOW NATION-STATES
ARE MADE

The concurrence of the German and Italian revolutions
will one day represent one of the most fruitful of
parallels for the philosophy of history.
—Heinrich Treitschke[1]

FOR OVER THE PAST 130 years, Heinrich Treitschke's invitation to scholars to compare the German and Italian national revolutions has gone largely unanswered. Despite the turbulent parallels between nineteenth- and twentieth-century German and Italian political development, the two cases remain an underutilized comparison for the study of state formation, nationalism, and federalism. This study takes up Treitschke's appeal to compare the two great episodes of nineteenth-century European nation-state formation in order to address a puzzle: how are nation-states made, and what determines whether nation-state formation leads to the creation of federal or unitary patterns of governance?

In an age when the issues of state building and federalism have returned to the center stage of politics in discussions of the European Union and nation building more broadly, a comparative analysis of nineteenth-century European nation-state formation offers a fruitful way to investigate questions that are once again concerns for scholars and policymakers: What are the conditions under which a new political entity is created? What determines the institutional form of that entity? What are the conditions under which federalism can be created? In moments of institutional founding, how much impact do political leaders actually have in designing political institutions? Can political leaders who seek federalism simply adopt a constitution that guarantees federalism? Can a federal constitution be violently imposed? Or must it emerge "bottom up" from a collection of symmetrically powerful subunits negotiating themselves into existence?

This study focuses on Europe during the nineteenth century because it is a period that casts new light on these issues. Though the rise of nationalism is normally attributed to the French Revolution, it was in fact during a decisive period between 1830 and 1880 in Europe, North America, and South America that many contemporary nation-states were created through the dual processes of imperial disintegration and national integration. Left standing in Europe were the new modern creations of Greece, Belgium, Italy, Germany, Bulgaria, and Romania.[2] This period that I call the "national moment" transformed the political map of Europe, North America, and South America. The political systems that emerged out of this set of nearly simultaneous experiences of nation-state formation were marked by a wide array of institutional forms that provide a diverse set of empirical cases for contemporary scholars of political development.

In particular, in one area of nation-state structure—the institutionalized territorial distribution of power between national and subnational governments—the new nation-states of the late nineteenth century displayed an institutional diversity that raises the question of how nation-states are formed and how the relationship between national and subnational governments comes to be established. While some newly formed polities such as Germany and Canada became explicitly *federal* political systems, others such as Italy and Belgium became classically *unitary* systems. In federal systems, like Germany and Canada, regional states were absorbed but remained intact as constitutionally sovereign parts in the larger "national" political framework: regional governments had formal access to the national government, discretion over public finance (i.e., taxing and spending), and administrative autonomy. By contrast, in states such as Italy and Belgium, any existing regional governments were erased from the map as sovereign entities and left without formal access to the new national governments, without public finance discretion, and without formal administrative autonomy. While experiencing a similar timing in their formation, the new nation-states of the nineteenth century experienced divergent institutional political arrangements of territorial governance after national unification. That both federal and unitary systems were the products of these institution-building experiments raises a deeper theoretical paradox of federalism's origins that is the central question of this book: How can a state-building political core that seeks to integrate its neighbors be strong enough to form a larger nation-state, but also not be too strong to entirely absorb and erase existing units, thereby creating a unitary nation-state? If the core is too unyielding, will not a unitary system result? If too accommodating, will not a union be impossible to forge in the first place?[3]

In brief, I argue that to explain why federal and unitary nation-states form, we must answer two analytically separate questions: why do nation-states form? Why do nation-states take on unitary or federal structures? The first part of this study answers the first question. The second answers the second question to argue that once a process of national unification is under way, the way out of the paradox of federalism's origins for political leaders with federal aspirations is for the political core to absorb states with high levels of what I call "infrastructural capacity"—the ability to tax, maintain order, regulate society, and generally govern their societies.[4] If a political core absorbs these types of states, then the potentially contentious relationship of a political core and its subunits that makes federations so difficult to construct can be overcome. With highly infrastructural states in place, a process of primarily negotiated nation-state formation is possible in which authority is conceded to the subunits. Why? Only subunits with high levels of infrastructural capacity can deliver the gains to the core and the subunits that were sought with the project of national unification the first place. If, by contrast, a political core—whether militarily strong or weak—begins the process of absorbing states that do not have this infrastructural capacity, then a more difficult relationship between core and subunits emerges. Since absorbed states are perceived as not able to deliver the benefits of national unification, they are viewed simply as an impediment to unification. This makes negotiation less likely, resulting in a path of nation-state formation through *conquest*, and the creation of a unitary political system. In order to explain whether nation-state makers adopt federal or unitary structures of governance, a central ironic lesson of this book emerges: If state makers seek federalism but absorb infrastructurally underdeveloped states, they may find themselves constrained by the domestic governance structures of the very states they incorporate in the project of national unification.

FEDERALISM'S ORIGINS, INSTITUTION BUILDING, AND EUROPEAN NATION-STATE FORMATION

The study of federalism's origins is particularly important for at least two reasons. First, in recent years, federalism has been increasingly viewed as an institutional solution to a broad range of problems. Some scholars such as Barry Weingast have highlighted the positive impact of federalism on the creation and sustaining of free markets.[5] Others, such as Jonathan Rodden and Erik Wibbels, have pointed to the potential benefits and pitfalls of federalism for fiscal performance, the growth of government, and economic performance more broadly.[6] Still others, such as Michael Hechter and Nancy Bermeo, have argued that federal structures, when contrasted with unitary patterns of governance, have a broad set of beneficial effects for accommodating minorities, reducing ethnic conflict, and holding nation-states together.[7] Not only scholars but also policymakers, international institutions, and political leaders increasingly view federalism as a potential solution to a diverse range of problems.[8] Though we know a great deal about federalism's consequences, our understanding of federalism's causes remains relatively underdeveloped. If federalism is such a critical potential institutional device, what are the conditions under which, and processes by which, nation-state makers can actually adopt this institutional form? A literature has begun to develop that explores the *sustainability* of federal political systems. But less attention has focused on the *origins* of federalism.[9] Can a federal constitution be imposed in any institutional, cultural, socioeconomic context? Or must federalism be negotiated from within? What are the pathways by which political leaders can move their polity in the direction of federalism? How, in the process of nation-state formation, does the bundle of federal institutions rather than unitary institutions emerge?

Second, the study of state formation and federalism's origins contributes to our understanding of the political development of Europe itself. Though scholars of European political development have long noted the presence of national institutional diversity across the continent of Europe, little comparative attention has been paid to the important and persistent divide among federal and unitary nation-states in the development of Europe. To explain the origins and persistence of other macro institutional differences, there has developed a wide-ranging scholarship in the tradition of Alexander Gerschenkron and Barrington Moore that identifies how diverse pathways of nation-state formation have given rise to outcomes such as the nature of national patterns of absolutism, regime type, the national organization of capitalism, and the choice of electoral institutions.[10] One area that has oddly remained out of the focus of scholars' attention is the "federal-unitary divide"—the presence of four federal states and thirteen unitary states among the seventeen largest states of contemporary Europe. By first examining two key cases of nineteenth-century Germany and Italy and then in the last chapter placing these cases in the broader context of the seventeen largest cases of western Europe, this study explores the source of this diversity in the structure of European nation-states, generating insights that potentially travel well beyond Europe's borders.

Concepts, Research Questions, and Expectations of Existing Theory

Before undertaking an explanation of nation-state formation and federalism, I need to provide some definitions. By *nation-state*, I refer to the specific set of sovereign territorial units that emerged in Europe, North America, and South America after the French Revolution, that were modeled on the French and British national experiences, and that were neither absolutist states nor multinational imperial orders. They were instead novel "national" amalgams of civic, ethnic, and state modes of organization and identification.[11] The definition of *federalism* is more contested. Some scholars define federalism in cultural or ideological terms.[12] Others have expanded the definition to incorporate as necessary components such concepts as "democracy" or even "political stability."[13] I find it more useful, when engaging in empirically based social scientific analysis, to define "federal" nation-states as those with subnational sovereign governments that possess three *constitutionally embedded* institutional characteristics that tend to cluster together: (1) formal and informal access of subnational governments in the decision-making process of national governments, (2) subnational public finance (taxing and spending) discretion, and (3) administrative autonomy of regional governments within a nation-state.[14] My definition of federalism describes the relationship between a central government and its regional governments in strictly dichotomous terms: Even if subnational goverments exist, only nation-states with *constitutionally protected* subunits qualify as federal. If only one level of government exists or subunits are not constitutionally protected, the entity is a unitary nation-state.[15]

The central research questions of this study are these: Under what conditions does a state-making core incorporate but leave existing subunits intact, creating a federal nation-state? Under what conditions does a state-making political core incorporate but dissolve the authority of regional governments to take on more unitary characteristics? Why, in some instances, can federalism be successfully constructed? Why, in other instances, does federalism fail to take root? Political science and historical scholarship on these questions has been dominated by accounts that focus on one of three main variables: *ideas, culture,* or *power.* Table 1.1 presents a schematic overview of each approach.

Each of the main approaches to the study of federalism offers prima facie convincing explanations of why a nation-state might adopt a "federal" pattern of center-periphery relations. The first approach, usually associated with scholars such as Michael Burgess, argues that the ideas of political leaders and constitutional designers as well as society at large are decisive in shaping the structure of political institutions in a nation-state.[16] The second perspective takes history and culture seriously, focusing on the nature of cultural or ethnic divisions within a society. Though this second perspective usually emphasizes "primordial" differences in ethnicity, the argument can be extended to deep-seated cultural differences between regions or high levels of regional loyalty—even without "ethnic" roots—to argue that federal institutions will emerge in a polity with a regionally fragmented population with deep-seated regional loyalties.[17] Finally, the third perspective, most closely associated with William Riker[18] and, more recently, with a set of works that have formalized the logic of Riker's argument, argue that federalism emerges and can sustain

TABLE 1.1
Overview of Competing Theoretical Expectations

Theory	Causal Mechanism	Predicted Outcome
"Ideational" theories of federalism (e.g., Burgess)	Configuration of ideas in a society	The greater the ideological commitment to decentralist ideas in a society, the more likely federalism
"Cultural-historical" theories of federalism (e.g., Umbach)	Configuration of cultural divisions in a society	The greater the prenational cultural independence of regions, the more likely federalism
"Social contract" theories of federalism (e.g., Riker)	Configuration of political power in a society	The militarily weaker the political center vis-à-vis the political periphery during the process of negotiating national unification, the more likely federalism

itself only as a delicate "bargain" between an equally powerful "center" and "periphery," in which neither the center is strong enough "to overawe" the regions, nor the regions powerful enough to "undermine" national integration.[19]

OVERVIEW OF CASES: THE PUZZLE OF FEDERALISM'S FAILURE IN ITALY AND ITS SUCCESS IN GERMANY

This study takes advantage of what is almost a natural experiment in the development of political institutions in nineteenth-century Europe to test these three hypotheses of nation-state formation and the causes of federalism. In the 1850s and 1860s, two states—Piedmont in Italy and Prussia in Germany—undertook the national unification of the Italian and German states under similar ideological, cultural, and power-structural conditions that ought to have led to similar institutional outcomes. After the failed democratic national revolutions of 1848 in Italy and Germany, the pragmatic political leadership of two militarily powerful states (Piedmont and Prussia) adopted the agenda of nationalism to expand each state's zone of political control in Europe. The similarities between the two cases are striking: First, as this work will make clear, the chief architects of national unification in Italy and Germany in the 1860s—Cavour and Bismarck— undertook their political projects with a similar *ideological* awareness of the dangers of excessive centralization, and in both cases there was a similar ideological commitment among key intellectual and political leaders to the notion of "federalism" as a solution to the history of regional divisions in both contexts, given international misgivings over the potential of creating two powerful and centralized states in the middle of Europe. Second, the deep-seated *cultural-historical* regional forces for and against national unification—rooted in regionally uneven economic gradients in both sets of territories—were similar. Third, in both cases two politically powerful regions sought to secure a position of dominance in the new nation-state after unification. In both cases, the goal of unification was the same: to assure geopolitical significance for the state while maintaining monarchical control.

Yet, despite these three similarities, the two late-developers of western Europe adopted very different patterns of territorial governance for each new nation-state. In Germany after 1866, the Prussian leadership, despite support in key sectors of the military for the conquest of southern Germany, combined their direct annexation of states of Germany's center and north with a path of *negotiated unification* to create a system of federal territorial governance that formally institutionalized the other states as "regions" in the new political entity. The new political construction had three distinct dimensions: (1) a territorial chamber was constituted by representatives chosen by the regional monarchs of the formerly independent constituent states; (2) these member states retained a relatively high level of autonomy in public finance (taxing and spending) that also represented a high degree of policy autonomy; and (3) each of the member states retained control over its own independent administrative apparatus.

By contrast, in Italy, the 1859 Piedmontese leadership, despite widespread support for a federal political order, pursued *unification by conquest* across all of Italy in which Cavour's Piedmont usurped all fiscal, policy, and jurisdictional authority and shifted power away from the seven Italian states to create a unitary Italy, with the Piedmontese parliament, constitution, and king at its core. Unlike Germany, the new Italian state formally erased region from its political map. With regard to the three dimensions above, the outcomes were these: (1) the formerly independent constituent states had no formal seat in a territorial chamber at the national level; (2) these states retained no public finance discretion; and (3) the formerly independent states retained limited administrative autonomy. Despite similar starting conditions in the factors normally thought to cause federalism, national unification resulted in two starkly divergent outcomes in Italy and Germany: a unitary system in Italy and a federal system in Germany.[20]

Italy's centralism and Germany's federalism are often mistakenly viewed, in retrospect, as inevitable features of each country's national political culture.[21] But to assume that the institutional format that actually "won" in each case in the 1860s was the only possible outcome is to miss the important dynamics by which institutions are created. In a sort of retrospective "case-fitting," observers sometimes loosely cite the influence of the "Franco-Napoleonic model" in Italy and the long history of independent regions in Germany to explain why the patterns of territorial governance that emerged in the middle of the nineteenth century were nearly inevitable in each country.[22] Yet such claims of inevitability do not stand up to closer analysis since Germany's and Italy's leading regional states were both independent before unification and were both organized in centralized prefectoral systems modeled after the French system of administration.[23] Moreover, such an account fails to specify the mechanisms of institutional creation. The formation of Germany's federalism and Italy's centralism, when the cases are viewed as a comparative pair, was surprising and highly contingent and in fact sharply challenges much of the conventional wisdom on the origins of federal political systems.[24] In table 1.2 we see an overview of the cases of Italian and German nation-state formation in terms of the three most widely recognized determinants of federal political order as well as in terms of the actual institutional outcomes in Italy and Germany after national unification.

First, as table 1.2 makes clear, if we consider idea-centered explanations (Burgess 1993a; 1993b) that argue that federalism is an institutional outcome in societies where an ideological predisposition for decentralized political organization predominates, our cases raise an empirical anomaly. As recent scholarship on nineteenth-century Germany and Italy has demonstrated, the ideology of federalism thrived in both cases.[25] In the German context, this is perhaps less surprising. As Stefan Oeter has written of nineteenth-century Germany, "For Bismarck and his contemporaries it was utterly self-evident that a union of the German states could only take a federal form."[26] Though most scholars recognize that decentralist ideas were a vibrant part of nineteenth-century German political culture, it is all too often forgotten that, as Binkley has noted of the 1860s in Italy, "the idea of confederation had been present in Italian statecraft for more than a generation, not as an exotic political invention but as a seemingly inevitable alternative to the situation established in 1815."[27] One important historian of nineteenth-century European history has similarly written of post-1815 Italy, "The political discussions and proposed solutions returned time and again to the question of unity or federalism in a manner unknown even in Germany."[28]

TABLE 1.2
Existing Theory and Outcomes: Summary of Italian and German Cases

	Germany	*Italy*
Potential explanation no. 1		
Preunification ideological debate by elites	Mixed support for military conquest by Prussia; support for federal order	Mixed support for a federal order to accommodate different regions exists
Potential explanation no. 2		
Historical-cultural legacy	Strong regional loyalties	Strong regional loyalties
Potential explanation no. 3		
Distribution of political power	Prussia as "power center" with military capacity to conquer and establish a unitary state	Piedmont as "power center" with less military capacity to conquer and establish a unitary state
Institutional outcome		
Territorial chamber in new regime	Federal: territorial chamber represents states	Unitary: former independent states have no formal seat at national level
Public finance in new regime	Federal: member states have public finance autonomy	Unitary: former independent states have no public finance autonomy
Administrative system in new regime	Federal: member states retain control over an independent administrative system	Unitary: former independent states have no formal control over administrative system

Indeed, in the nineteenth century at least three self-consciously federalist intellectual strands existed in Italy: (1) the neo-Guelphs, such as the priest Vicenzo Gioberti, who advocated a confederation of princes under the lead of the pope;[29] (2) liberals such as Cattaneo and Ferrara who argued for the creation of a federal and democratic Italy;[30] and (3) regional autonomists, mostly found among prominent political leaders in Sicily and Italy's south, who advocated a decentralized governance structure that would protect regional autonomy.[31] In the realm of ideas, federalism was a vibrant part of the political culture of Italy's intellectuals, thinkers, and visionaries.

But it was not only constitutional scholars and intellectuals who advocated federalism in Italy. Important political leaders, first and foremost Count Cavour himself, were frequently open advocates of a vague decentralization throughout the 1850s. As prime minister Count Cavour made an important speech in parliament in 1850 that reflected the dominant Piedmontese liberal-conservative consensus of the era by criticizing France's centralized prefectoral model. Even in the early 1860s, Cavour criticized excessive centralization when calling for more regionalist concessions to Italy's south.[32] In his biography of Cavour, Mack Smith writes, "Cavour had always been a theoretical champion of decentralization and local self-government."[33] And, similarly, the "energetic group of men" that dominated the "Right" and Italian politics after Cavour's death until 1876, including Ricasoli, La Marmora, Minghetti, Lanaza, Spaventa, Sella, and Peruzzi, were longtime advocates of the confederative principles of Gioberti and Balbo.[34] Yet by 1865 unforeseen events intervened, and federalism was abandoned in Italy. In short, though an ideological commitment to decentralization may perhaps be a *necessary* background condition for the creation of federal institutions, the failure of federalism in Italy in the 1860s shows that a widespread ideological predisposition for decentralized political organization is clearly not *sufficient* to guarantee the creation of a federal polity.

We confront similar problems when considering cultural-historical arguments asserting that, the greater the prenational historical embeddedness of independent regions and territorial divisions in a society, the more likely federalism will emerge. As table 1.2 also indicates, in Italy and Germany we find two similarly historically divided societies yet two different institutional outcomes. Recent important scholarship by Langewiesche, Umbach, and Confino has convincingly made the case that contemporary German federalism is in part a historical legacy of the Holy Roman Empire, a long history of regional autonomy, and the German Reich of 1871.[35] Though accurate in the German context, such accounts cannot explain why a similarly long history of independent city-states, regions, and provinces did not produce a federal political system in Italy in the 1860s or after 1945. Why did Italian city-states and regions, as the locus of deep allegiance and loyalty since the Middle Ages, not produce the same federal institutional outcome that was generated by German city-states and regions? Moreover, those who emphasize importance of the post-1815 German Confederation as a cause of German federalism overlook the frequent attempts in Italy after 1815 to forge a similarly organized Italian confederation. It is clear that the existence of a German Confederation contributed to the success of federalism after 1866, but why was a confederation so difficult to construct in Italy despite repeated ef-forts? An explanation that accounts for German federalism with reference to the German Confederation must be able to explain, in a comparative framework, why the German Confederation made up of highly effective parliamentary monarchical states worked in Germany, but not in other contexts.[36] Again, we see that the explicit comparison of Italy and Ger-many dissipates the analytical power of conventional explanations.

Finally, with power-centered theories (Riker 1964) we also discover em-pirical difficulties when seeking to explain the success of federalism in Germany and its failure in Italy. Riker, whose work provides the basic as-sumptions of most political science scholarship on federalism, conceptual-izes federalism as a "bargain" between regions. From this perspective, the success of the bargain is a function of the territorial distribution of "mili-tary power" in a society.[37] At the heart of this argument is an assumption that Riker himself identifies: A unifying political center's first preference will always be a unitary system and the only factor that can thwart this goal is the "military incapacity" of the political center.[38] The expectations of this theory are clear and logical: the militarily stronger the political center vis-à-vis the regions, the less likely a federal structure, and con-versely, the militarily weaker the political center vis-à-vis the regions, the more likely a federal or confederal structure.

But in Germany and Italy, we have a set of cases that runs directly counter to these theoretical expectations: Prussia, according to all tradi-tional measures of military power, could have easily conquered southern Germany while Piedmont, according to these same measures, was much weaker vis-à-vis southern Italy. Several years before national unification, Prussia possessed 57 percent of the future German Reich's population, 54 percent of all public expenditures on military by German states, and 54 percent of the future German Reich's territory. By contrast, in the 1850s, Piedmont possessed only 6 percent of the future Italy's population, only 29 percent of Italy's soldiers, and only 22 percent of Italy's territory.[39] Why did the militarily powerful state of Prussia, after defeating Austria and its southern German allies in 1866, establish a federal system of territorial governance, while the less militarily powerful and less dominant state of Piedmont, after defeating Austria in 1859, established a unitary system? Why did a strong center create a federal system and a relatively weak center create a unitary system? In short, the power-centered account, given the territorial distribution of military power in Germany and Italy, would pre-dict precisely the opposite outcomes that we in fact find.

In sum, the three most important explanations of the genesis of federal-ism cannot account for the two most prominent cases of national unifica-tion in nineteenth-century Europe. This puzzle draws our attention to the more general explanatory weakness of each of these theoretical approaches. If the origins of the institutional divergence between Germany and Italy in the 1860s are not to be found exclusively in the configuration of *ideas*, *culture*, or *power* in each setting during national unification, where ought the analyst look?

The Argument: Overcoming the Paradox of Federalism's Origins

The puzzling cases of Germany and Italy and the limits of existing theory present an opportunity to rethink the theoretical paradox of federalism's origins presented at the outset—how can a political core be unyielding enough to forge a national government but be accommodating enough to make federal concessions to the subunits it absorbs? That Prussia was able to establish a federation while Piedmont was not can illuminate which factors and strategies of state formation help nation-state builders overcome the paradox of federalism's origins and which do not.

The argument I develop identifies a different route to overcoming the paradox of federalism's origins during the process of nation-state formation. While I agree with existing accounts that negotiated paths of nation-state formation tend to lead to federations, I offer two amendments to existing theory. First, I argue that the bargaining that gives rise to federations is not related to the military power of the center. Against the expectations of existing theory, limiting the military power of the political core to create symmetrically powerful units to negotiate a federal "contract" between the core and subunits is not the pathway to federalism. In fact, as the Prussian case demonstrates, militarily strong centers can sometimes make concessions that militarily weak centers cannot. Second, I argue that the key issue in the establishment of a federation is not the coercive strength of the center vis-à-vis the subunits, but instead the relative infrastructural capacity of the subunits vis-à-vis their *own* societies. To achieve federalism, credible negotiation partners are necessary, as are effective governance structures to govern *after* nation-state formation. If such actors exist, the paradox of federalism's origins is overcome in the moment of nation-state formation because the subunits deliver the precise governance benefits the political core seeks with unification, and a negotiated path of state formation that leads to federalism is possible. It is true that federations, once established, have the *effect* of balancing military competition among subunits as well as ameliorating ethnic or religious territorial cleavages, but one clear lesson of this book is that the *effects* of federalism cannot explain its *origins*.[40] Instead, the origins of federalism are found in the internal structure of the subunits of a potential federation at the moment of founding.[41]

In the following I present my central argument in greater detail, highlighting the different dimension of state capacity that I identify as the crucial factor in shaping nation-state structure and specifying the different set of mechanisms that gives rise to federal or unitary outcomes. Finally, I present the research design of my study, highlighting how through a series of focused controlled comparisons, we can clarify the conditions under which federalism is possible.

"Infrastructural Power" and the Pathway to Federalism

A central claim of this book is that to understand when federalism is possible we ought not focus on the relative "military power" of the constituent states, as most theory does. Instead, we should focus on what Michael Mann in his important book on state formation, calls "infrastructural power." If *military power* refers to the social organization of physical force, deriving from the necessity of defense and aggression, *infrastructural power* describes state-society relations that determine the capacity of a central state to penetrate its territories and implement decisions logistically.[42] The distinction between these two dimensions of state capacity is crucial. Existing theory posits that once a unifying state decides to unify with its neighbors, federalism emerges as the structure of the new larger nation-state only when the political center lacks the military capacity to "overawe" constituent states, and therefore turns to a federalizing negotiation with constituent states. The account I offer identifies a different precondition of the negotiation necessary to create federalism: highly developed infrastructural power of the subunits. The process of negotiation and bargaining between a "political center" and subunits necessary for the formation of federation *presupposes* subunits that possess high levels of infrastructural power—that is, high levels of (1) state rationalization, (2) state institutionalization, and (3) embeddedness of the state in society.[43] The point that forms the centerpiece of my argument is not that high "infrastructural power" means these states cannot be conquered. Rather, if the subunits of a potential federation are constitutional, parliamentary, and administratively modernized states, they can both serve as credible negotiation partners in a process of nation-state formation and can also govern in a federation afterwards, leading the way to a federal outcome. Not only do parliamentary states serve as more effective negotiation partners, but more importantly, states with highly developed infrastructures can deliver the precise benefits that nation-state builders seek: greater tax revenue, greater access to military manpower, and greater social stability. As a result, the relationship between subunits and core is perceived by the core's political leadership as mutually beneficial, producing benefits that can be captured at multiple levels of government, undoing the paradox of federalism's origins.[44]

If, by contrast, the subunits of a potential federation are patrimonial states in the classic Weberian sense—lacking constitutions, parliaments, and rationalized systems of administration—negotiation usually breaks down and the prospects of self-governance after nation-state formation are limited, leading the way to unitary political institutions.[45] In this latter scenario, without credible negotiation partners, political leaders of the initiator of unification will turn to coercion, conquest, and the direct absorption of existing states. Moreover, when annexed states lack the basic governance capacity vis-à-vis society to carry out basic governance functions, political leaders in the political center are tempted by the prospects of sweeping away existing units, leading the way to greater centralization. As the evidence in this book will demonstrate, absorbed states with low infrastructural capacity prompt the political center's centralization of political power.

In short, we see that when new nation-states are forming and when political leaders seek federalism, it is not the military power of the political center that determines whether negotiation or conquest is adopted as a form of political integration. Instead, the negotiation necessary for federalism is possible only when the negotiation partners of potential federation are credible, institutionalized, and high infrastructural states. Moreover, it is only when subunits have the capacity to govern after nation-state formation, that the paradox of federalism's origins can be overcome.

Comparative Historical Method and Findings: Three Questions, Four Comparisons

This study explicitly draws upon a methodological tradition in comparative historical analysis that is marked by three attributes: a concern with causal analysis, an emphasis on processes over time, and the use of systematic and contextualized comparisons.[46] The study is structured around three empirically overlapping but analytically separate questions that, as Edward Gibson and Tulia Falleti have noted,[47] Riker conflates: First, what gives rise to national or political unification of disparate political entities? Second, what determines the broad institutional form (i.e., federal or unitary) of these new, larger political entities? And, third, what determines the precise *type* of institutional form (e.g., decentralized or centralized federalism) these newly designed political entities take?[48]

Since factors that are arguably the causes of national unification—for example, "external threat" or "the benefits of economic integration"—have been linked to the *type* of institutions adopted by a state (e.g., federalism), the literature on federalism's origins is marred by conceptual conflation.[49] To disentangle these issues, each of the three questions must be answered separately to isolate the causes of national unification, the causes of federalism, and the causes of the type of federalism adopted by a state.[50] By systematically testing hypotheses for each, it is possible to come to a answers that differ from existing analysis.

To answer the three questions that form the centerpiece of this study, I draw upon the empirical cases of nineteenth-century Germany and Italy and then place these cases into the context of the seventeen largest nation-states of western Europe to make four different systematic and controlled comparisons.[51] I answer the *first* question—on the causes of national uni-fication—by using two different comparisons simultaneously, a combina-tion of what John Stuart Mill himself called the "method of difference" and the "method of agreement."[52] The purpose is to test two important hypotheses—one economic and the second political—on the causes of po-litical unification. Following the advice of Skocpol and Somers, I first make explicit use of the method of agreement by searching for a common set of causes across two diverse cases that nevertheless have similar out-comes—the successful national unification of Italy and Germany in the 1860s and 1870s.[53] I argue that despite differences along dimensions that some theorists of national unification might consider decisive in determin-ing if national unification occurs, nineteenth-century Germany and Italy experienced national unification for the same analytical reasons.[54] My ac-count highlights the similar causal dynamics of the two cases despite other potentially decisive differences. But, as many methodological critics have noted, Mill's method of agreement, if used alone, suffers from an artificial truncation on the dependent variable, weakening its analytical power. As a result, my search for the causes of national unification follows the recom-mendation of Skocpol and Sommers and proceeds according to the method of difference by introducing focused contrasts *within* my two cases at the subnational level.[55] My analysis uses the controls of a subna-tional comparison of twenty-five German and Italian prenational states, by contrasting prenational regional states that supported national unifica-tion and regional states that resisted national unification. By testing the same set of hypotheses to explain national unification both *within* the two national cases as well as *across* the two national cases, my conclusions gain a level of confidence that would otherwise be more difficult to achieve. The design allows me to highlight the complex interaction of economic change and the motivations of political leaders that, taken together, gave rise to the "national critical juncture" of national unification in both cases.

The third comparison I undertake repeats Mill's method of difference but with a different set of hypotheses to explore the *second* central question of this study—the causes of federal versus unitary outcomes.[56] Here, I sample on the independent variable, showing how apparently similar contexts—prenational nineteenth-century Germany and Italy—produced divergent institutional outcomes after national unification. By exploring the limits of three dominant theories of federalism's origins with my focused comparison, I demonstrate with both quantitative and qualitative evidence how an alternative *institutional* or "state-centered" cause was decisive in structuring the strategies of German and Italian nation-state-building elites as they forged each new nation-state. As the following chapters will reveal, the "coming together" pathway of federalism was not the outcome of the military power of the subunits vis-à-vis each other, as classical theories of federalism's origins suggest. Rather, I argue that the goals of state builders are constrained above all by an *institutional* inheritance and logic that have little to do with military capacity: the internal structure of the subunits of a new nation-state vis-à-vis their own societies at the very moment of nation-state formation. If the state-seeking core faced subunits with high levels of what "infrastructural capacity"—the ability to regulate society, to tax, to maintain order—then state builders can establish the federations they seek. If not, it is likely that a unitary governance structure will usurp power from the institutionally incapable units no matter how militarily strong or weak the "political center." It is most useful to think of federalism, in this sense, as an outgrowth of a very specific path of nation-state formation in which state building and political development at the subnational level *precede* national unification, leaving in place a set of states that can both negotiate the terms of national unification and effectively govern *after* national unification.

Finally, a fourth comparison is made in the last chapter across seventeen national cases in western Europe to add nuance to my argument regarding the question of whether a "unitary" or "federal" pattern of governance is the outcome of nation-state building. Here, I allow ideology to vary: in some instances political leaders pushed for federalism and in other instances they did not. What happens to my argument in this instance? By extending the argument to the seventeen largest cases of western Europe, we see that the core argument of the book is sustained. But in the end, the findings suggest that two factors taken together are jointly sufficient to explain why states take on federal or unitary structures: the ideology of political founders and the political institutions of the subunits at the moment of polity formation.

Looking Ahead

The remaining six chapters are a comparative historical study of national unification in Italy and Germany, focusing largely on the period 1815–71. In chapters 2–4, I trace the main contours of the national critical juncture in Italy and Germany in which new polities were formed. In chapter 2, I present a quantitative analysis using subnational states of all of the prenational Italian and German states for which data are available. I use an original economic and political dataset on the regional states of Italy and Germany to carry out several statistical tests to identify the main factors that explain why some states pushed for national unification while other states resisted national unification. In chapters 3 and 4, I test the lessons from chapter 2 in an in-depth analysis of the regional bases of national unification in Italy and Germany, using a mixture of primary and secondary evidence. Here, again, we see the importance of interregional dynamics in explaining the emergence of new nation-states in Italy and Germany in the 1860s and 1870s.

In chapters 5 and 6, I turn my attention away from the conditions of national unification to explore issues of institutional design in Italy, examining the question of why federalism succeeded in Germany in 1871 while federalism failed in Italy in the early 1860s. In these two chapters, I first provide original quantitative evidence on differences in the levels of "political development" and "infrastructural capacity" in the Italian and German prenational states in the 1850s, using indicators that allow for a comparative assessment of infrastructural capacity in each case. Second, I trace how political leaders responded to these different prenational institutional settings as they carried out different strategies of national unification, creating two very different but relatively stable political orders by the 1870s. In the conclusion (chap. 7), I extend, test, and refine my argument with an analysis of seventeen national cases, showing how the argument developed works in a wider range of cases. Finally, in this last chapter I discuss the book's broader theoretical contributions for the study of political institutions.

Chapter Two

THE NATIONAL CRITICAL JUNCTURE: AN OVERVIEW OF THE DYNAMICS OF REGIONALISM AND NATIONAL UNIFICATION

> Politically, the centralized state was a new creation called
> forth by the commercial revolution.
> —KARL POLANYI[1]

> Its [the state's] actual engine was the political drive to
> dominate and to master the entire complex of human
> relationships that seemed capable of centralization. This
> is achieved by a unified will that orders and guides, by a
> vision that transcends accustomed patterns of life, that
> grasps things to come and discovers in them the
> blueprint of a future edifice of power.
> —OTTO HINTZE[2]

BETWEEN 1859 and 1871, conservative Prussian and Piedmontese monarchs undertook the bold political project of forging modern German and Italian nation-states out of a fragmented collection of independent and foreign-ruled regional states of Europe. The project of fusing together formerly independent regional states into larger modern nation-states was an elite-negotiated process of political change that gave rise to a diverse range of regionally based political reactions *for* and *against* national unification. It was the intersection of these entrenched and at times opposed regional political forces that gave rise to a national critical juncture in Germany and Italy in the 1860s.[3] To contain these regional forces, the Piedmontese and Prussian leaders, like the leaders of any new polity, invented and institutionalized the basic national political institutions of territorial integration reflected in each new nation-state's constitution.[4] Furthermore, the constitutional or institutional "solutions" adopted in the national founding moments would—despite important interruptions in the middle of the twentieth century—display remarkable persistence over the next century.

This chapter and the next two chapters explore the question: what gave rise to national unification in Italy and Germany? In answering this question, I make three broad points. First, national unification was driven by essentially very similar economic and political dynamics that generated a push to integrate and consolidate new and larger "national" territorial units in the heart of Europe. Second, in providing an explanation of the push for national unification, I also explain why some of the Italian and German states, for example Prussia and Piedmont, pushed for national unification and others, including Bavaria and the Kingdom of Two Sicilies, resisted. Finally, by focusing my analysis on the prenational states in each setting, this chapter and the next two provide a snapshot of the regional forces of "push" and "pull" that shaped the national founding constitutional moment in each setting.

OVERVIEW OF THE GERMAN AND ITALIAN STATES DURING THE NATIONAL CRITICAL JUNCTURE

The regional responses that structured the national critical juncture in both settings were multifaceted and diverse. In response to the parallel Prussian and Piedmontese monarchs' initiating efforts to unify Italy and Germany, the reactions followed three trajectories: some regional state monarchs and political leaders such as the nationalist duke of the miniature state of Saxony-Coburg in Germany or the nationalist Italian political leadership in the Austrian-ruled state of Lombardy-Veneto quickly allied with plans of national unification. Others such as the conservative but militarily weak King George of Hannover and grand duke of Tuscany passively resisted, hoping for Austrian protection from Prussian and Piedmontese expansionism. Still others—most notably the economically backward but politically ambitious Bavarian crown in southern Germany and Neapolitan crown in southern Italy—militarily resisted the Prussian and Piedmontese nationalist plans.

To what extent do these four positions—*initiation*, *support*, *passive resistance*, and *military hostility*—capture the responses of political leaders in Italy and Germany in general in the 1850s and 1860s? Using a methodology I discuss in appendix A, we can code each of the prenational states in terms of the orientation of the political leadership toward national unification in the years immediately preceding unification.[5] As table 2.1 makes clear, the political leadership of the regional states of Italy and Germany responded to national unification in a variety of ways in their last decades

TABLE 2.1
Overview of Italian and German States, 1850–70

German States 1860–70	Political Leadership's Orientation to National Unification	Italian States 1850–60	Political Leadership's Orientation to National Unification
Bavaria	Hostile	Piedmont	Initiator
Oldenbourg	Resistant	Two Sicilies	Hostile
Hannover	Resistant	Tuscany	Resistant
Bremen	Supportive	Modena	Resistant
Baden	Supportive	Parma	Resistant
Weimar-Saxony	Supportive	Lombardy	Supportive
Coburg-Saxony	Supportive	Papal States	Hostile
Württemberg	Resistant		
Kurhessen	Resistant		
Holstein	Resistant		
Hessen Darmstadt	Resistant		
Nassau	Supportive		
Hamburg	Supportive		
Prussia	Initiator		
Saxony	Resistant		
Mecklenburg Schwerin	Resistant		
Mecklenburg Strelitz	Resistant		

of independence. Above all, this diversity of regional responses to national unification highlights the extent to which the classically conceived process of nation-state formation as a one-dimensional conflict between center and periphery can instead be more usefully conceptualized as a multicornered process of internal territorial conflict.[6]

Furthermore, by recognizing this diversity of regional responses to national unification in prenational Germany and Italy, we can explore an often unexamined question regarding the relationship between nationalism, regionalism, and state building: Why did some regional states take the lead and others resist the effort to create nation-states out of the diverse territories of Italy and Germany? This question not only poses an interesting theoretical puzzle but also draws our attention to the main contours of the "national moment"—a critical juncture in which political leaders invent and institutionalize the main national political institutions that hold new nation-states together. But what were the conditions behind the diverse regional and conflicting reactions to national unification that produced this national critical juncture?

The central argument I propose centers around two deeply rooted structural factors that determined the political position taken by regional political leaders vis-à-vis national unification in the 1850s and 1860s. First, the commercialization of economic life before and after 1815 was, as European economic historians have long noted, a regionally uneven process that left the populations of early-commercializing regions in Italy and Germany more predisposed than the populations of late-commercializing regions to support the creation of a national market and national political institutions.[7] In the densely populated western provinces of Prussia, in the city-states of northern Germany, and in the northwestern Italian states of Lombardy and Piedmont, the early and successful commercialization of land and labor under Napoleon's direct rule before 1815 allowed for an important pronational social alliance after 1815 that was a necessary condition for the creation of national political institutions.[8] Yet the regionally embedded commercialization in those German and Italian regions that were closest to France was by no means sufficient to give rise automatically to the unification of Germany and Italy. Rather, the push for national unification took place in Italy and Germany only where and when a second factor was present: In order for national unification to be undertaken, the state leadership of early commercializing regions (i.e., the Prussian state and Piedmontese state) had to have the military, administrative, and fiscal means and the motives of political aggrandizement to co-opt nationalist social mobilization and to expand their zones of political control. In short, the uneven regionally based commercialization of economic life in Germany and Italy before and after 1815 provided the necessary social ingredients for national unification in many regions across Germany and Italy. But it was only in those two regional states—Piedmont and Prussia—where these economic groups could be co-opted by and form a critical political alliance with the leadership of an externally oriented and powerful state that national unification could be *initiated*.

To summarize the rest of my findings: In response to these two regionally based unification *initiators* of Germany and Italy (Prussia and Piedmont), three other broad but identifiable types of responses formed in the independent regional states in Italy and Germany in the 1850s and 1860s. One response came from political leaders of early-commercializing regions that were politically weak, where there was social support for nationalism but insufficient political capacity—military and administrative—to carry out national unification. As a result political leaders were typically *passive supporters* of national unification (e.g., Saxony-Coburg and Lombardy).[9] A second response originated with monarchies and political leaders of similarly politically weak but late-commercializing regions that had neither the political capacity nor the regional social support to carry out unification themselves (e.g., Württemberg and Tuscany).[10] As a result, here one could find leaders who were *resistant* but largely inactive in response to the project of national unification, relying on the counterinitiative of larger European powers. The final response, and the most analytically important location of resistance, emerged from monarchs and political leaders of politically and militarily powerful but late-commercializing regions whose populations were not particularly supportive of unification but where political leaders believed that they had the political or military capacity to resist unification efforts and as a result were actively and self-consciously *hostile* toward national unification (e.g., Bavaria and the Kingdom of Two Sicilies).[11]

The purpose in identifying and explaining these four regionally based responses to national unification is not to argue that they capture all the nuance and diversity within each Italian and German regional state in the moment of national unification. Beneath the surface there were many similarities and differences across the regional states that are not captured by these four categories. Indeed, regional politics in this period were often whimsical and shifting, based on short-term tactical calculation, personality and personal conflicts between leaders.[12] Nevertheless, my aim is to look systematically beyond such factors to clarify how deeper political and social conditions helped give rise to the four broad regional political responses that emerged for and against national unification by the 1850s and 1860s. By doing so, my account makes two contributions: First, I present an alternative to modernization theory and the traditional historiography's juxtaposition of nationalism and localist regionalism as two opposed forces in the process of national integration.[13] In contrast, my account provides evidence that regionalism served, paradoxically, both as the main *impetus* for unification and as the main *constraint* on national unification.[14] Second, by identifying the strikingly similar regional conditions and actors that pushed for and resisted the regionally based projects of national unification in Italy and Germany in the national moment, this chapter identifies the main regional forces of "push" and "pull" out of which the main institutions of the nation-state would be constructed *after* the national moment.

The Origins of the National Critical Juncture: Societal and State Actors in Germany and Italy

The extensive monographic scholarship on the unification of both Germany and Italy has generated an abundance of rich historical research. Two general strands have developed to explain the unification of Germany and Italy. The first, a "society-centered" tradition, focuses on the *social* configurations of preunification Germany and Italy. Karl Polanyi's statement at the beginning of this chapter—"The centralized state was a new creation called forth by the commercial revolution"—can be seen as paradigmatic of this approach. The range of specific societal actors emphasized within this tradition, however, is wide. Some argue that a critical economic group, namely the liberal middle class, especially in the western provinces of Prussia and in Italy's north, as an agent that sought larger national markets and a stable political setting, provided a decisive impetus to national unification.[15] Others have explored the importance of national intellectuals, liberal publicists, and their secret societies and publications.[16] Both arguments, though they identify different agents of unification, emphasize the changing organization and structure of prenational society in Germany and Italy as the key factors that bred national unification.

In contrast to these accounts, a second strand of scholarship offers a "state-centered" mode of analysis that explores the political motivations of state leaders, with more explicit reference to the two initiator regional states of Piedmont and Prussia. Otto Hintze's assertion in the epigraph to this chapter reflects this tradition's main claim: the state is the decisive actor in the drive toward political centralization. Some accounts in this state-centered tradition argue that national unification in both Italy and Germany was above all an instance in which Prussian and Piedmontese political leaders sought to assert themselves as powers on the European stage by expanding their zone of political influence.[17] Another more recent strand of analysis in this same state-centered tradition, which has developed furthest in the German historiography, focuses on the motivations of state officials who sought to create a larger fiscal zone of control in order to remove themselves from debt.[18] All of these arguments, whether centered on society or state, offer important and plausible accounts of why nation-states emerged, the dynamics behind political centralization, and the push to unify Italy and Germany in the nineteenth century. How do we distinguish which account is correct? How do we identify the precise causal weight and relationship of the societal and state variables that each account highlights?

The Determinants of Regional Resistance and
Support for National Unification

To answer these questions, this chapter and the following two chapters are constructed around a research design that focuses on subnational "region" rather than "nation-state." Typically, studies of national unification have explored its causes at the national level of analysis and as a result have confronted both conceptual and methodological pitfalls.[19] First, at a conceptual level, as recent scholarship has made clear, any discussion of "German" or "Italian" political and economic developments before the unification of the member states of each entity is an inadequate abstraction that can sometimes conceal more than it reveals.[20] Within Germany, the structure of land-tenure arrangements and the manufacturing sectors diverged widely from the north to the south.[21] Likewise, in terms of political change, pushes for constitutional reform in the south were unmatched in the north, where autocratic control proceeded unchallenged until much later.[22] Similarly, in Italy, just as the striking difference in agricultural and manufacturing structure between north and south had important consequences, so too did the prenational differences in political regime between Italy's regions.[23] Most importantly, nationally centered accounts that juxtapose national integration and "particularist" regionalism as two opposed forces in the process of national unification ignore, first, that the project of national unification emerged from two regions in particular (Prussia and Piedmont) that sought to extend their influence over other regions in Germany and Italy. And second, as recent historiography has emphasized, regional identity in southern Germany and in southern Italy, though often resistant to national unification, in the end provided an important "integrative" function after national unification.[24]

A second pitfall of working solely at the national level of analysis with only two cases is methodological: there is limited variation on the dependent variable—level of support for national unification—with which to assess the analytical leverage of each of the two modes of explanation.[25] In order to increase the number of observations and to untangle the competing arguments (state centered vs. society centered), my analysis utilizes a subnational comparative method. In this way, I can test the impact of the two arguments on the diverse twenty-four regions of Germany and Italy during the decisive years of the late 1850s and 1860s.

The following undertakes a systematic comparative line of inquiry that asks of each prenational political regional state in Germany and Italy two questions: (1) where and which *societal* groups began and supported the push for territorial change and where and which *societal* groups resisted the move to undo barriers in Germany and Italy in the years immediately

TABLE 2.2
A Summary: The Determinants of Regional Support for, and
Opposition to Political Unification

	Large State Size (state budget above national mean)	Small State Size (state budget below national mean)
High commercialization (GDP per capita above national mean)	1. Initiator E.g., Prussia, Piedmont (political and social support)	2. Supporter E.g., Bremen (social support no political support)
Low commercialization (GDP per capita below national mean	4. Hostile E.g., Bavaria, Kingdom of Two Sicilies (social and political resistance)	3. Resistant E.g., Württemberg Tuscany (no social support no political support)

preceding national unification? This first question provides a point of entry to the issue of what gave rise to the initial push for closer ties between states. But the societal configuration of interests and preferences in a society does not automatically translate into political action. States and their political leaders do not just passively respond to social change but rather have motives and interests of their own.[26] It is thus important to ask a second question: (2) which regional *state* political leaders initiated, supported, or resisted efforts to unify Germany and Italy between the 1830s and 1870s? By exploring both of these questions and using the region as the main unit of analysis, we can untangle the relative weight and impact of each of the two existing lines of inquiry.

What explains the level of support different regional governments displayed toward the project of national unification in the 1850s and 1860s? To address this question, I have developed a model that centers around the structure of each region's state and the organization of each region's society in those two decades: (1) the political strength or size of each regional state, and (2) the level of commercialization or economic modernization of each region.[27] Table 2.2 is a heuristic summary of the expectations of the model with reference to some of the most important regional cases drawn from the larger dataset on Germany and Italy.

First, we can expect unification to be initiated by political leaders and social groups in the most politically powerful regions (i.e., regions with a large state) and in those regions where commercialization occurred relatively early, political support ought to be greatest, and it is there that we can expect unification to be initiated (cell 1 in table 2.2). Second, in

politically powerful regions where commercialization occurred later, political leaders have access to a large state, and as a result it is here where
we can expect to discover the greatest and most hostile resistance to unification plans (cell 3). Third, in states that are small but where commercialization occurred early, social support but ambivalent or passive political support for unification ought to be found (cell 2). And fourth, a
passive resistance to national unification is predicted in small, politically
impotent states where neither social nor political support for unification
can be found (cell 4).

EVIDENCE: THE RELATIVE IMPACT OF SOCIETAL AND STATE FACTORS ON REGIONAL SUPPORT FOR NATIONAL UNIFICATION

The next two chapters—chapters 3 and 4—will present a detailed application of this framework to the German and Italian cases, showing in detail
both the strengths and the limits of my focus on regional political and
economic developments in explaining the dynamics of national unification. But to provide some preliminary evidence of the potency of the two
variables that I have highlighted, we can conduct several statistical tests,
using economic and political data from the twenty-four German and Italian states in the 1850s and 1860s for which systematic and comparable
data are available.[28]

First, in table 2.3, we can see an overview of the twenty-four regional
cases, grouped into the four combinations that make up the four quadrants
of table 2.2: (1) big, poor states, (2) small, poor states, (3) small, rich states,
and (4) big, rich states. The dependent variable, listed in column 1 of table
2.3, is the political orientation of each state's leadership toward national
unification. To code the dependent variable, I borrow from an approach
that has been recently used by scholars of historical political research: I
undertook an extensive and systematic review of a wide sample of the secondary German-language, Italian-language, and English-language literature on the period.[29] Each regional state was coded using an ordinal scale
that assesses how supportive of the project of national unification the political leadership of each region was during the last decade before national
unification (1850–60 in Italy and 1860–70 in Germany). I operationalize
the concept "support for national unification" in terms of how the secondary literature evaluates two dimensions of each regional state's actions: (1)
policies toward the civic organization of a "national society" (Associazione
Nazionale in Italy and Nationalverein in Germany), and (2) public statements, correspondence, and votes in diplomatic meetings of political
leaders of each state regarding national unification. My scale (1–4)

TABLE 2.3
German and Italian Pre-National States, 1850–60

	Political Executive's Orientation towards National Unification	Economic Modernization, 1849–61 (GDP per capita)	State Size, 1850–52 (budget size x 1,000)
1. *Big, Poor States* (above national mean state size, below national mean wealth)			
Bavaria	Hostile	385 RM	64,143 RM
Kingdom of Two Sicilies	Hostile	174 lire	151,000 lire
2. *Small, Poor States* (below national mean state size, below national mean wealth)			
Mecklenburg Schwerin	Resistant	474 RM	9,570 RM
Mecklenburg Strelitz	Resistant	474 RM	2,233 RM
Württemberg	Resistant	489 RM	21,943 RM
Kurhessen	Resistant	496 RM	11,353 RM
Papal States	Hostile	230 lire	41,000 lire
Tuscany	Resistant	239 lire	33,000 lire
Modena	Resistant	236 lire	9,000 lire
Parma	Resistant	236 lire	11,000 lire
Hessen Darmstadt	Resistant	539 RM	11,266 RM
Baden	Supportive	486 RM	18,217 RM
Holstein	Resistant	533 RM	20,387 RM
Hannover	Resistant	464 RM	28,160 RM
Oldenbourg	Resistant	455 RM	4,910 RM
3. *Small, Rich States* (below national mean state size, above national mean wealth)			
Bremen	Supportive	750 RM	3,197 RM
Hamburg	Supportive	800 RM	9,413 RM
Saxony-Coburg	Supportive	553 RM	653 RM
Saxony-Weimar	Supportive	553 RM	4,577 RM
Saxony	Resistant	671 RM	24,880 RM
Nassau	Supportive	604 RM	6,773 RM
4. *Big, Rich States* (above national mean state size, above national mean wealth)			
Prussia	Initiator	565 RM	227,017 RM
Lombardy-Veneto	Supportive	358 lire	89,000 lire
Piedmont	Initiator	401 lire	112,000 lire
National Mean Scores			
Italian states	NA	268 lire	64,000 lire
German states	NA	547 RM	66,956 RM

TABLE 2.4
Impact of State Size on Support for National Unification

Large States (above national average budget size)	Small States (below national average budget size)
Mean = 2.35 (N = 4)	Mean = 2.25 (N = 19)

measures a range of four possible outcomes: hostile, resistant, supportive, and initiator.

The two independent variables—"state size" and "level of regional economic modernization"—are estimated using the limited available regional-level data from the prenational period. "State size" is measured by size of state budgets (total expenditures) of each of the prenational German and Italian regional states for the years 1850–52.[30] To assess "level of regional economic modernization," I estimate regional GDP per capita using a combination of provincial and regional data provided by two of the most recent regional estimates.[31] Since data are available only at the provincial level, I aggregated these data and adjusted for population to estimate the GDP per capita of each of the Italian and German prenational political units.

To assess the impact of state size on the level of support for national unification and to assess if there is an interaction effect between state size and economic modernization, we can compare the mean scores of the dependent variable for large and small states. Using an ordinal scoring of the dependent variable (where 1 = hostile, 2 = resistant, 3 = supportive, 4 = initiator), state size appears to have very little *independent* impact on support for national unification: As table 2.4 shows, small states, on average, have a score of 2.25, while rich states, on average, have a score of 2.35. With average scores that suggest similar orientations toward national unification, it appears at first glance as if the leaders of small and large states both have orientations toward national unification that fall approximately half way between support and resistance.

Yet when level of economic modernization is included in the analysis, as displayed in table 2.5, we see dramatically different results, and the main patterns predicted by the theory are supported: First, regional governments of big, rich states have an average score that ranks them as *initiators* of national unification (average = 3.7). Second, regional governments of small, rich states have an average score that ranks them as *supportive* of national unification (average = 2.8). Third, regional governments of small, poor states have an average score *resistant* of national unification (average = 2.0). And finally, regional governments of big, poor states show

TABLE 2.5
Comparison of Mean and Support for Unification among
Italian and German States

	Large States (above national average budget size)	Small States (below national average budget size)
Rich states	Mean = 3.7	Mean = 2.8
Above average GDP per capita	SD = 0.6	SD = 0.4
	N = 2	N = 6
Poor states	Mean = 1	Mean = 2.0
Below average GDP per capita	SD = 0	SD = 0.4
	N = 2	N = 13

Note: The coding of "rich" vs. "poor" and "large" vs. "small" states is established by each state's ranking vis-à-vis the "national" average in each context. The mean GDP score in Germany is 547 RM and in Italy is 268 Lire. The mean state size score in Germany is 66,956 RM and in Italy is 64,000,000 Lire.

them to be *hostile* to national unification (average = 1.0). Table 2.5 provides some compelling prima facie evidence of the regional bases of national unification.

Next, we can examine how support for national unification differs depending on wealth of a state. In the analysis below, I analyze the Italian and German states separately to examine if similar dynamics are at work in both national sets of cases. In table 2.6, I summarize findings on the impact of state size on a state's support for national unification in both rich and poor German states. After the dependent variable is recoded to a scale of 0–1, the findings confirm the central hypothesis of this chapter: among rich states, increasing state size brings increasing support for national unification, while among poor states, increasing state size brings increased resistance to national unification. Though there are only seventeen cases available for analysis, the findings nevertheless are significant at the .10 level and show that there is an interaction effect between state size and wealth that produces divergent regional responses to the political project of national unification. Among high-GDP states, the smallest state has .6 level of support (scaled 0–1), while the largest state shows a score of .97. By contrast, among low-GDP states, the smallest state has a score of .43 (lower than any of the high-GDP states), and support for national unification drops as state size increases.

Because there are only seven Italian cases (two high-GDP states and five low-GDP states), it makes little sense to conduct regression analysis. Yet the dynamics in the Italian states, as table 2.7 shows, are consistent with the German findings: First, among high-GDP states, the smallest state is

TABLE 2.6
German States: Impact of State Size on Support for National Unification, by GDP

	Coefficient	SE	p-value
High GDP (> national mean) (N = 7)			
State size	0.37	(.17)	0.08
Constant	0.60	0.00	.00
$R^2 = 0.49$			
Low GDP (≤ national mean) (N = 10)			
State size	−1.2	(.56)	.06
Constant	.43	(.06)	.00
$R^2 = 0.57$			

Note: For the German states, the national mean in GDP per capita is 547 RM. For a complete discussion of the coding of the dependent variable (orientation toward national unification), see appendix A.

only supportive of national unification while the largest state is the initiator of national unification. Second, among low-GDP states, the three smallest states are all resistant to national unification and the two larger states are hostile to national unification. In essence, we see here the same dynamics as in Germany, though the limited number of cases generates findings that are not statistically significant.

In sum, we see that similar processes were at work in Germany and Italy in the 1850s and 1860s: (1) the richest and biggest states in each setting, Piedmont and Prussia, initiated national unification efforts; (2) poorer but big states, such as Bavaria and the Kingdom of Two Sicilies, actively and hostilely resisted national unification; (3) rich but smaller states, such as Hamburg, Bremen, and Lombardy, supported the national unification efforts of Prussia and Piedmont; and (4) poorer and small states, such as Tuscany and Württemberg, were passive resistors of national unification, usually supporting the policies of the more powerful antinational regional states of Bavaria and the Kingdom of Two Sicilies.

CONCLUSION: THE MAIN CONTOURS OF THE
NATIONAL CRITICAL JUNCTURE

This chapter has described a set of conditions associated with the emergence of what scholars of national political development have called a "critical juncture"—a moment in the development of a national polity

TABLE 2.7
Overview of the Italian States (scaled, 0–1)

	GDP Per Capita	State Size	Orientation Towards National Unification
High GDP states			
Piedmont	1.00	0.73	1.0
Lombardy	0.81	0.56	0.67
Low GDP states			
Tuscany	0.29	0.17	0.33
Parma	0.27	0.0	0.33
Modena	0.27	0.01	0.33
Papal States	0.25	0.23	0.0
Two Sicilies	0.0	1.00	0.0

in which the basic features of the political system of a nation-state are constructed. The particular critical juncture identified in this chapter is one that Lipset and Rokkan, in their influential work, called the "the national revolution."[32] In the moment of national revolution or, as this chapter has called it, the "national moment" in both Italy and Germany in the 1860s, regional forces pushed for and against the creation of a territorially integrated nation-state. As in all new nation-states, it was out of this regional push and pull that the basic national institutions of center-periphery relations for each nation-state would eventually be created.

The model presented in this chapter, though identifying two potentially important factors in understanding the regional determinants of national unification, cannot tell us *why* politically potent commercialized regions initiated national unification nor why regions that possessed other attributes developed other orientations toward national unification. To explore these issues and to examine how the forces identified in this chapter played themselves out in the German and Italian cases, it is necessary to examine in greater depth the dynamics of regional support for unification in Germany and Italy. It is this task that the following two chapters undertake.

Chapter Three

THE NATIONAL MOMENT IN GERMANY:
THE DYNAMICS OF REGIONALISM AND
NATIONAL UNIFICATION, 1834–1871

IN 1865 the Prussian writer Gustav Fischer looked back to New Year's Eve of 1833, the night before the German Zollverein (Customs Union) was created, as the beginning point of Germany's path to unification.

> The elder generations still remember how joyfully the opening hour of the year 1834 was welcomed by the trading world. Long trains of wagons stood on the high roads, which until then had been blocked off by customs lines. At the stroke of midnight every turnpike was thrown open, and amid cheers the wagons hastened over the boundaries which would henceforth be crossed in perfect freedom. Everyone felt something great had been achieved.[1]

Indeed, the year 1834 can be viewed as having initiated a long-term political project of undoing regional barriers and creating a Prussian-led process of national integration: (1) the Zollverein of 1834 gave Prussian-led Germany a common "national" market; (2) the Norddeutsche Bund gave the emerging entity more concrete political expression in 1866 when Bismarck forced an alliance of nineteen states, creating a political union at the outbreak of war with the German Confederation; and (3) the German Reich of 1871 served as the point of culmination in which the first German nation-state was formed.[2] At the most basic level, these three steps represented a series of territorial pacts between regional political leaders that established an expanding common national framework for the functioning of a new political, economic, and cultural entity in some of the German-speaking territories of Europe.

This chapter explores how commercializing changes in Europe before and after 1815 reconfigured societal and political interests across the German states to generate support for national unification in the most commercialized and most politically potent German states. If the last chapter presented the outlines of how regionalism shaped the national critical juncture in general, then this chapter explores, in a more detailed fashion, how the regional forces for and against national unification played themselves out in the specific context of the German states between 1834 and

1870. This detailed view allows me to identify the regional forces of "push" and "pull," out of which the basic national institutions of center-periphery relations would eventually be constructed.

This chapter first explores how different groups in different regions reacted to economic change after 1815. Here we see how the social "ingredients" for territorial change congealed in the most commercialized regions of Germany and how the least commercialized regions of Germany provided the main locus of resistance to national unification. But it is only by then tracing, in parallel fashion, the interests of regional state and political leaders in these same regions through this same time period that we can begin to see the complete story: it was in the sometimes strained *interplay* of societal interests and state interests in the politically powerful commercialized region of Prussia that the push for territorial unification emerged, and it was in the politically powerful but *slowly* commercializing region of Bavaria that resistance to this political project was greatest.

The following account focuses on the two critical steps of national unification: (1) the creation of a national market in Germany in 1834, and (2) the creation of a political framework for Germany between 1866 and 1871. Though these dates encapsulate a long time period in which the independent regional German states experienced a wide range of constitutional and economic changes, which arguably might have undermined regional orientations toward national unification, this chapter emphasizes the extent to which persistent social and political forces had already begun to consolidate after 1815 to make certain regions consistently more pronational than other regions in both social orientation and political action.

A View From Below: Social Change in Germany's Regions

As a rough indicator of how supportive regions were of the national unification process, we can begin with a look at the percentage of the population of each region that held membership in the most vocal and politically important civic organization of the era—the National Union (Nationalverein)—that advocated the unification of Germany after the 1859 unification of Italy. In 1861, the year in which the organization had its highest membership, the 16,243 members of the organization were spread out across the German states (over 50 percent in Prussia) in the most economically modernized regions and provinces of Germany. Figure 3.1 makes clear that those regions that experienced the greatest degree of economic modernization were also the regions that supported greater national unification ($r = 0.52$).[3] The region with the highest percentage of its population with membership in the Nationalverein was the Prussian province of

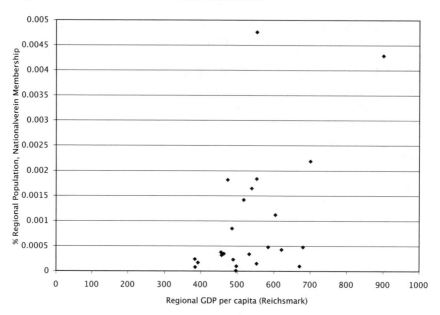

FIGURE 3.1. German Regional Economic Modernization and Support for National Unification, 1861

Westphalia; The region with the lowest percentage of the population with membership in the Nationalverein was Bavaria.

But what was the source of this pattern of variation, and how did it make itself felt politically between 1834 and 1871? It is the argument of this chapter that the regional differentiation in the organization and structure of manufacturing and agriculture—above all between a rapidly modernizing and commercializing northwestern Germany and a largely economically traditional and static southern Germany—produced two remarkably predictable regional political responses to the project of national unification.[4] Some economic groups, usually though not always found in the most commercialized regions of northern and western Germany, sought to rescue themselves from the high international protectionism after 1815 by clamoring for the elimination of internal tariffs to "carve" out a national zone of free trade among the German states. Likewise, in those same regions, we tend to find a well-developed ideological linking of the ideas of "progress" and "national integration." Also, here local regional identity was less likely to be viewed as incompatible with a larger national identity. By contrast, other groups, found largely in the less commercialized regions of southern Germany, where small-scale precommercial manufacturing and agriculture was predominant, sought the continuation of internal trade barriers that protected what were perceived to be less competitive industries.[5] Here, also, one often found a more well-developed "localist" attachment to the *Heimat* that was not always compatible with an effective national identity.[6] It is important to note, as Sidney Pollard has, that economic change did not always correspond to political borders.[7] Yet still, the emergence of a deep but shifting societal cleavage between the rapidly commercializing northwest and the less rapidly commercializing south is the critical feature of German economic life in understanding the regional bases of national unification in both 1834 and between 1866 and 1871.[8]

First Stage of National Unification: The German Customs Union, 1834

In the *first* stage of German unification (the creation of a national market in 1834), "Immediate business interests were in many cases the only basis for a pro- or anti-Zollverein attitude."[9] These conflicting business interests—those that supported and those that resisted a national market—must, however, be understood within the context of the unevenly developed regions described in the previous chapter. Indeed, the supporters of a custom union were usually found in the densely populated manufacturing regions of the modernizing and wealthy western provinces of Prussia (e.g., Westphalia, the Rhineland) among economic groups who saw the benefits of a new larger, integrated and unrestricted market across the divide between East and West Prussia and the western provinces.[10] As table 3.1 makes clear with the earliest available data, in the parts of the Rhineland Province (Cologne and Aachen) as well as in parts of the Westphalen Province (Arnsberg and Düsseldorf), according to estimates from 1849, per capita income was, as in Saxony, approximately 120 percent of the German national average and was higher than anywhere in Germany with the exception of the cities of Berlin, Hamburg, and Bremen.[11]

Why, however, were the western Prussian Rhineland provinces rather than, say equally economically advanced Saxony, such an important locus of social support for the creation of a national market? Indeed, this question is important because Saxony consistently stands out as an outlier in the data presented in chapter 2, as a regional state with a high GDP per capita, yet a political leadership that was resistant to national unification. First, in Rhineland cities such as Cologne, Aachen, and Crefeld, a set of commercializing political reforms were undertaken between 1789 and 1811 before such reforms were implemented anywhere else in Germany, including in Saxony. With the elimination of guilds in the 1790s, the creation of chambers of commerce in 1801, and the loosening of restrictions on the establishment of new businesses, direct French rule provided the Rhineland an institutional legacy that left it at the forefront of the German commercial revolution, even ahead of Saxony, where traditional

TABLE 3.1
Per Capita GDP, German Regions, 1849

State	GDP per capita (RM)	State	GDP per capita
Posen	384.3	Schleswig-Holstein	532.8
Bavaria	385	Darmstadt	539.2
Hohenzollern	392.8	Saxony-Weimar	552.5
Oldenburg	455.8	Saxony-Coburg	552.5
Pommern	457.7	Thüringen states	552.5
Hannover	463.7	Prussian Saxony	584.2
Mecklenburg	473.6	Nassau	603.9
Baden	485.7	Rheinland	620.8
Württemberg	489.2	Saxony	670.6
Kassel	496.4	Brandenburg (Berlin)	679.8
Silesia	497.6	Hamburg	800.0
Westfalen	517.2	Bremen	750.0

economic regulations persisted until 1840.[12] Similarly, under the direct rule of France, the Rhineland represented the earliest and most complete commercialization of agriculture in Germany, making it arguably in 1815 the most economically developed region in Germany.[13] While economic development remained restricted by guild systems and other legal restrictions on the formation of new businesses in other German states until a much later date, the French-occupied territories of the Rhineland experienced an economic and societal transformation.[14] Though Napoleon had had influence and ruled other parts of Germany indirectly, it was the Rhineland's cultural and geographical proximity to France that made it especially amenable to French administrators' reform plans.[15] The consequences of these reforms were felt immediately: In the city of Crefeld, for example, the number of silk firms doubled; seven new cotton-spinning firms were founded; the average size of the firms increased rapidly; capital investments doubled; and manufacturing replaced river trade as the prime source of economic growth. Though Germany in the 1830s and 1840s was still, using Hoffmann's framework, in the "pretakeoff" phase of development, a process of transformative commercialization was under way in the Rhineland.[16]

A second and related factor that made Prussia's peripheral manufacturers in the Rhineland more important for the creation of a national market than even manufacturers in Saxony or Silesia and more supportive than the highly productive Prussian agricultural interests was the Rhineland manufacturers' early and important reliance on German markets. As recent theories of protectionism would predict, those economic interests and firms, such as those found in the Prussian Rhineland, most reliant on interregional markets (in contrast to international markets or local markets) were the greatest advocates for the reduction of tariffs and the increase of ties between the states.[17] First, in comparison to highly developed regions such as Saxony, Rhineland manufacturers relied more heavily on German markets and thus more vigorously sought a common political framework for trade. Even though by 1831 Saxon manufacturers and manufacturers in other states were organized in merchant associations to call for the joining of a Prussian customs union, Saxon manufacturers sold a larger portion of their products on foreign markets than did Prussian manufacturers.[18] Likewise, in contrast to Prussian agricultural interests that also sold their products disproportionately on foreign markets, Prussian manufacturers stood as the most nationally partisan economic group.[19] Evidence from 1823 shows that even at this early date, with high internal trade restrictions, Prussian manufacturers were more reliant on the markets of other German states than German agricultural interests. Of all exports from Prussia to the other German states, 66 percent were manufactured goods, while only 19 percent of exports were foodstuffs.[20] In short, the economic conditions of the western provinces of Prussia provided a set of circumstances in which the push for the creation of a national market made economic sense.

These unique economic conditions in the Rhineland gave rise to new liberal class of business leaders in the 1820s and 1830s: David Hansemann, the leader in a range of important business ventures, including the railroad company that would link East Prussia with the Rhineland, was an active member of trade councils, was involved in city politics in Aachen, and would by 1848 turn to national politics. Similar important business leaders from the Rhineland who also advocated a reformed and united Germany in the 1830s—Ludolf Camphausen and Hermann von Beckerath— also pushed for liberal and national reforms. Such business leaders have attracted much attention from scholars because they were paradigmatic of a new capitalist class that the French occupation had left intact at the top of the Rhineland social hierarchy.[21] It is precisely this business elite that pushed for the creation of a national market after 1815. But beyond dropping tariffs, why did these business leaders of the Rhineland support further political-territorial reform? The embryonic Prussian manufacturing sectors of the Rhineland, Upper Silesia, the Ruhr Valley, and the Saarland that would eventually propel Germany into the industrial era were in 1815 politically and economically marginalized. In political terms, the conservative coalition of king, landed aristocracy, and bureaucracy that dominated

the Prussian government displayed great antipathy toward industrial development up until the 1840s.[22] The emergence of a manufacturing class
that sought to undo trade barriers and all other traditional constraints on
economic activity began the split in the East Prussian aristocracy into its
reactionary and moderate camps. In economic terms, beginning after
1815, the short-term rise in international protectionism posed a serious
economic challenge to the nascent manufacturing interests in the German
states. These economic groups had always been bound economically by
restricted access to their own "national" market. But now, they also suffered under the new burden of rising protectionism abroad.

As a result of this intersection of domestic and international forces in the
western provinces of Prussia, calls for territorial reform took on a sharply
political edge after 1815. In 1818, for example, an association of seventy
manufacturers from the Rhineland sent a petition to King Friedrich Wilhelm of Prussia. In the petition, the signatories complained of the postwar
economic situation and identified the roots of the economic problems
facing them. They stated, "Ever since we left the rule of the French Empire
to join the German fatherland, our once flourishing businesses have begun
to falter. As a result of external tariffs in Europe our products are cut out of
all the markets of Europe's nation-states." In response to this international
context, the petition proposed a solution to the Prussian king: "We ask
your majesty to consider lifting all internal customs for states belonging
to the German Confederation."[23] The petition concludes by noting, "All
European states have now recognized the negative consequences of maintaining internal tariffs within their own borders. Even Spain has eliminated such tariffs, leaving Germany as the only country on the continent
that still maintains such a system."[24] As the German customs union between Prussia and Hessen of 1818 was extended to incorporate most of
Germany by 1834, the Aachen Chamber of Commerce began its first annual report by extending its "most grateful recognition" to the Prussian
government for the Zollverein. The report continues on to say that the
chamber "recognizes the great benefits which already have appeared in all
of Germany and especially in its industrially rich homeland."[25] Likewise,
the leader of the Cologne Chamber of Commerce, Merkens, wrote in
1828, "Prussia, with its striving for a customs union seeks to unify Germany into a great whole." He went on to write that the efforts of smaller
German states to form smaller customs union threatened to split Germany
into two pieces, which he regarded as "obviously a great evil"[26]

If the prospect of a common "German" market did not threaten and in
fact was supported by a thriving and growing commercialized manufacturing sector in Prussia's west, what was the basis of southern Germany's
resistance to Prussian plans of a united national market? While scholars
are correct to emphasize the cultural and religious differences between,

for example, Bavaria and Prussia, it is also clear that economic motivation played a critical part in southern German resistance. In Bavaria, Kurhessen, and Württemberg, where Napoleon's influence had been indirect, feudalism was not eliminated, nor were guild systems formally abolished until after 1815. Likewise, even after 1815, in stark contrast to the Rhineland, "commercializing" political reforms were not undertaken as vigorously as in the Rhineland, and as a consequence the economy remained dominated to a larger degree by traditional systems of small-scale farming and guild-based manufacturing.[27] Though much of this would be transformed by century's end, Jürgen Kocka and others have noted the slower pace of economic reform at the beginning of the century in Bavaria, Baden, and Württemberg.[28] In this still predominately traditional economy, there was nothing to be gained and much to lose in a Prussian-led customs union.[29] In a state such as Kurhessen, for example, where 60 percent of the population was still employed in the traditional agricultural sector after 1815, fear of the flood of Prussian products onto south German markets was great.[30] Whereas guilds had been abolished in the Rhineland by the French in the 1790s, in Bavaria and Württemberg guilds were not eliminated until late 1820s. Despite further commercializing reforms undertaken by the Interior Ministry in Bavaria and Wilhelm I in Württemberg in the 1820s, there persisted great resistance to "factory developments in the west" that were perceived to be "ugly, unaesthetic, and unpleasing to the eye."[31] The antagonism to commercializing changes were evidenced by the rapid increase in the guild petitions submitted to the Bavarian diet in 1827–28 seeking protection.[32] Partly in response to such petitions, the new interior minister, Ludwig von Oettingen-Wallerstein, for example, issued ordinances in the 1830s to protect "works finished in small, family run workshops" and that restricted the establishment of new factories unless older factories closed their doors. His protective ordinances were effective: in 1840 there were actually eight fewer licensed factories in Bavaria than eight years earlier.[33] In contrast to the commercializing reforms in western provinces of Prussia that had been initiated by the French, precommercial institutions and practices remained intact in Bavaria.

Indeed, the resistance and nervousness in southern Germany are confirmed by data from three years after the Zollverein: the creation of a common national market generated twice as many exports from "north" to "south" as in the other direction. The bargain was one that disproportionately benefited Prussian economic interests. Additionally, as table 3.2 shows, the inflow of high-end manufacturing goods from the "north" to the "south" was five times higher than from southern Germany to northern Germany.

These data suggest why the international setting of protectionism linked "territorial change" and "progress" in the minds of manufacturers

TABLE 3.2
Structure and Amount of Trade between "Northern" and
"Southern" Germany, 1837

	Trade "North" to "South"	Trade "South" to "North"
Food stuffs	8.6%	33%
Raw materials	4.3%	36%
Manufactured goods	77.6%	22%
Total trade value	100% (23,636,300 thaler)	100% (9,573,800 thaler)

Note: The data are from the Customs Union Central Office, "Nachweisung von Waaren Übergang im Jahre 1837 aus Bayern, Württemberg und Baden nach den übrigen Teilen des Zollvereins" and "Nachweisung vom Waaren übergang im Jahre 1837 nach Bayern, Württemberg und Baden aus den überigen Teilen des Zollvereins," Staatsbibliothek München, Munich. This source was originally discovered and cited for the first time by Rolfe Dumke, "Anglo-deutscher Handel und Freuhindustrialisierung in Deutschland, 1822–1865," *Geschichte und Gesellschaft* 5 (1979): 175–200.

in Germany's north in the 1820s and 1830s and why resistance was found in the less rapidly commercializing regions of Germany.

Second Stage of National Unification: Political Unification, 1866–71

But even after entering the *second* more explicitly political stage of German unification—the push for political unification between 1866 and 1877—this regional tension between modernizing Prussian manufacturers and what German historians have called south German "particularists" persisted.[34] Beginning even in 1848, the increasingly large-scale manufacturers of cities and regions in western Prussia and their locally based chambers of commerce pushed for even closer ties among the German states. In addition to a common market, these increasingly organized economic interests also had a new set of demands that would only be satisfied with greater political centralization: a single German monetary zone, a single German commerical legal code, and the final elimination of any tolls between German states. The chamber of commerce of Cologne, for example, declared in 1865 the creation of a single system of money issuance "to be the most pressing need of German industry." Likewise, they demanded "the grand creation of a common German law of commerce."[35] In Düsseldorf, the city chamber of commerce called "for a uniform system of patent legislation for all of Germany to meet a general need."[36] And, finally, in West Prussia the Frankfurt an der Oder Chamber of Commerce wrote that "the creation of a common system of coinage, weights, and measures is a warranted demand of modern times."[37] In Prussia, the push for increased ties between the German states continued to be greatest. Indeed, it is no accident that pockets within Prussia's wealthiest and economically booming regions in the 1860s—for example, Arnsberg in Westphalia, with 124 percent of the average German regional GDP per capita—also tended to have the highest percentage of its population with membership in the Nationalverein.[38]

But even in other smaller commercialized states calls for closer ties between states grew. In rapidly commercializing northern and central German states such as Thüringen and Hannover the push by an increasingly organized middle class and its civic organizations sought a transformation of Germany. In Hamburg, the publicist Wilhelm Marr expressed the underlying logic of why economic groups in small commercialized states supported closer ties under Prussian leadership in his essay entitled "Selbständigkeit und Hoheitsrecht der freien Stadt Hamburg Sind ein Anachronismus geworden" (The independence of Hamburg has become an anachronism).

> If the idea of a "north Elbian republic" did not unfortunately belong to the realm of utopia, if Hamburg could acquire a hinter-land, we would be the most zealous defenders of our independence of our sovereign right. But the times of the Genoas and Venices are over. The railroad, the telegraph, the needle gun, and the rifle cannon make them impossible.[39]

But in the 1866–71 period such enthusiasm was, with some significant exceptions, not found among the populations of the southern states of Bavaria or Württemberg or some of the Hessen states. In fact, it was here that the greatest resistance to the national project was to be found. In addition to cultural and religious factors, the southern German regional societal resistance to economic and political unification of southern Germany was rooted in two features of their traditional regional economic structure: (1) the dominance of the preindustrial small-scale crafts sector, and (2) the dominance of small-scale agriculture. In figure 3.2, we see that, in terms of agricultural and manufacturing scale, the southern German states were dominated by traditional economic structure to a greater degree than in the rest of Germany.[40]

Why was this traditional economic structure in southern Germany and Saxony, dominated by small-scale farms and small preindustrial craftsmen, the source of resistance to national unification? First, as Best discovers in his study of petitions at the 1848 Frankfurt Assembly, small-scale craftsmen were the critical socioeconomic group *resistant* to the creation of a national market.[41] Likewise, according to Nipperdey, craftsmen employed in the preindustrial small-craft sector viewed "freedom of trade and indus-

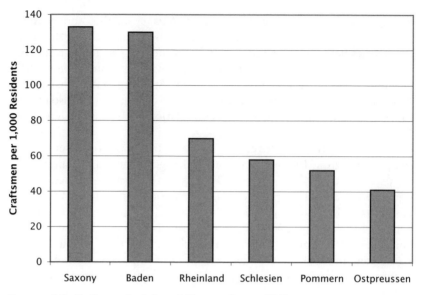

FigURE 3.2. Craftsmen in Selected German States, 1861

try . . . as the true enemy, a total threat to their present and future existence."[42] Just as the modernizing economic interests in the western provinces of Prussia saw an expanded political unit as progress, in the minds of the economic interests embedded in traditional small-scale economic structures of southern Germany, resistance to national unification was based on a fear of national integration. Just as the central locus of societal support for unification was in the western provinces of Prussia, the countervailing source of resistance throughout the period was in Bavaria. Most leading figures in Bavarian state politics before 1866 were explicitly pro-Austrian and anti-Prussian.[43] The reasons were varied, and leading political figures in Bavaria at the time were representative of various strands in Bavarian society: Some such as Oettingen-Wallerstein, though nationalists, were federalists who wanted to preserve Bavarian autonomy; others such as Thurn and Taxis were strictly conservative and pro-Hapsburg; still others such as Schrenk, usually administrators, were interested in preserving the administrative autonomy of the Bavarian bureaucracy. A wide spectrum of Bavarian politics was committed to preserving Bavaria's autonomous place in Europe.[44] But economic motivations were forefront in the minds of Bavarian parliamentarians.

Of course it has to be noted that during the 1860s, especially after the military defeat of 1866, support for national unification did develop in the southern states. Similarly, a distinctive industrialization began to emerge. Indeed it was precisely in the sectors and geographical areas of southern

Germany either where economic change occurred or that were reliant on Prussian markets where proponents of national unification could be found. Such internal variation within Germany's south could be seen in the three historical regions of Bavaria, for example, where distinctive economic structures and sociocultural tendencies gave rise to varying political orientations toward a Prussian-led union. The incorporation of the Protestant industrial districts of Franconia and Swabia by Old Bavaria after 1806 created "islands in an otherwise agrarian-craft economy"[45] that exported goods to Prussia. Additionally, these two predominately Protestant regions had average per capita income levels on par with the German national average (375 RM in Swabia and 505 RM in Mid-Franconia) that were up to 60 percent higher than in Catholic Lower Bavaria (304 RM), where per capita income was only 60 percent of the national average.[46] Likewise, these wealthier regions became electoral strongholds for national liberalism and social democracy. By contrast, in "Old Bavaria" (the catholic southern regions of Lower Bavaria), the Bavarian patriotic tradition lived on with the electoral dominance of the Bavarian Patriot Party throughout the nineteenth century.[47] In short, though support for national unification was to be found in Bavaria, it was precisely in the most commercialized regions, as my account posits.

These competing currents of Bavarian nationalism, federalism, and German nationalism made themselves felt in the Bavarian *Landtag* during the 1860s. An analysis of the *Landtag* debates, for example, of October 1867 in which plans for an increasingly centralized German Zollverein were debated makes clear that two strands of thought—one of resistance to Prussia and the other of support for a united Germany—still existed in Bavaria even after the defeat of July 1866. The political opposition that rejected closer ties to Prussia was led by Joseph Edmund Jörg, the leader of the Bavarian Patriot Party, whose support of Bavarian independence continued to find widespread support in the largely agrarian regions of Old Bavaria. In a heated debate on October 18, 1867, for example, Jörg proclaimed, "It is without a doubt that the acceptance of this treaty will mean submission to the economic dictatorship of Prussia."[48] But by 1867, a new economic class in Bavaria had emerged that took precisely the opposite view. Three days after Jörg's fiery statement, the representative Teuftel proclaimed, "I know some of you think that the Zollverein at its basis is part of a larger [Prussian] political plan, but my dear gentleman, this is not true! It arose out of pure economic necessity!"[49] And a newly organized association of business interests appeared in front of the *Landtag* sitting on October 23, 1867, to call for support for closer economic ties with Prussia. Though the advocates of closer ties to the Zollverein won out, in the next elections a backlash occurred in which the most pro-Bavarian and conservative parties were elected to be Bavaria's representatives in the new

Zollverein parliament. By 1867, forces had begun to shift, yet resistance was still strongest in Germany's economically traditional southern states.[50]

To summarize briefly the main regional contours of support and resistance to national unification between 1834 and 1871, despite the changes wrought by industrialization in this period, it was *consistently* in some of the earliest commercializing, economically booming regions of Germany that the push for national unification was strongest. Conversely, in the regions dominated by traditional economic structures, resistance to a Prussian-led national unification, for a variety of reasons, dominated the orientations of societal leaders. What is also evident from this analysis is that it was in the most commercialized regions of Germany that an economic interest in a national market was coupled with a growing ideological commitment to the idea of a nation-state, while fear of such developments was the basis of resistance in southern Germany. In both 1834 and 1866–71, the regional bases of support and resistance to national unification were critical factors that shaped the subsequent fate of the German nation-state. Yet such an account is entirely incomplete when trying to identify the forces for national unification: it was the Prussian state, and not society, that was the main agent of national unification. Likewise, it was the southern German governments, not southern German society, that first resisted and then negotiated the eventual unification of Germany. It is for these reasons that the next section focuses on developments from the perspective of the "state" across Germany's diverse territories.

A VIEW FROM ABOVE: THE TRANSFORMATION OF STATE INTERESTS

Several puzzles arise from the preceding analysis. First, if commercialized regions throughout Germany had the most to gain from a unified market and a centralized institutional setting, why didn't Hamburg and Bremen initiate unification efforts? Second, why did Bavaria, as a largely uncommercialized region, display greater resistance to national unification than a similarly slowly commercializing region such as Baden or Württemberg? It is in response to such questions that we must turn our attention to the autonomous impact of the state in the process of German unification. Indeed, the story thus far has been one solely of social structure and economic interests. Such a mode of explanation cannot capture the rich regional variation in orientations toward national unification. Nor can it explain why the regional governments of some states initiated unification while others were outright hostile to unification. Throughout the forty years of German unification—beginning with the 1834 Zollverein, proceeding to the 1866 Norddeutsche Bund, and even to the creation of the 1871 German Reich—state constraints, capacities, and interests were absolutely critical in shaping why and how state leaders in different regions responded in different ways to the notion of a single German nation-state.

This section makes the case that only in the commercialized states that were also *politically powerful* (i.e., Prussia) was initiating the creation of a nation-state possible. As small and politically weak states, Bremen and Hamburg, though commercialized and with the economic *motivation* for national unification, did not have the administrative, military, or political *capacity* to lead an effort to create a national market. Similarly, to understand why the politically powerful Bavaria, rather than other slowly commercializing states such as Württemberg, proved to be the most recalcitrant and hostile to the process of national unification, it is critical to understand that Bavaria, as Germany's second largest state with Germany's second largest military, viewed itself as Prussia's arch-competitor. Without social support for a national market, however, Bavaria was doomed to playing a secondary though important role throughout the process of German unification. The small commercialized states of northern Germany had economic reasons to support a common national market but did not have the political "means" to initiate a national project of unification; the larger, less commercialized states of southern Germany such as Bavaria may have had the political means to defend their autonomy, if not to extend it, but did not have the dynamic social base that pushed a common national market or a common single German nation-state. In short, only Prussia had the means and the motives to initiate the creation of a German nation-state, while only Bavaria had the means and the motives to resist it.

The Role of the State: The Customs Union and Unification, 1834–66

The first step of my argument explores the creation of the Zollverein in 1834. It is true that many of the states of Germany sought a larger customs union after the failure to establish one at the Congress of Vienna in 1814–15. Indeed, in the 1820s, two competing organizations among non-Prussian states sought to establish a common German market. But the Prussian Ministry of Finance successfully came to dominate pan-German tariff policy. Utilizing "tariff war" tactics, through a combination of administrative agility and sheer economic weight, Prussia was able successfully to convince other states to join its union. The Prussian state was simply more effective and powerful than any competitor. If resistance had emerged from anywhere, it would have come from Bavaria, the second biggest state in Germany with the second largest military. But here commercialization proceeded slowly and the demand for the creation of an expanded political unit was weak at best. Among the states being challenged by a process of commercialization, Prussia was the most politically powerful and hence the most likely to lead the process of national integration.

But what were the motivations of Prussian leaders? To understand the dynamics of why the Zollverein was created, it is critical to observe that after 1815 a set of three constraints created for all the autocratic states of Germany, but especially for Prussia, a political dilemma: how to generate enough revenues to support efforts to modernize state institutions without granting parliaments "taxing" rights. It was in the resolution of this dilemma that the Zollverein was created. In Europe after 1815, the first constraint facing the leaders of Prussia and the German states was rooted in the premodern organization of German systems of public finance: The small and larger German states allowed (1) limited parliamentary budgetary rights, (2) no universal obligation of citizens to pay direct taxes, and (3) a heavy reliance on income from public lands.[51] While the parliaments of the German states had limited budgetary rights into the nineteenth century, the British Parliament first gained budgetary rights vis-à-vis the Crown in 1215 (reinforced in 1689). Similarly, the traditional public finance instrument of public lands as a main source of revenue had been entirely eliminated by the nineteenth century in both Great Britain and France, while again, as a result of a great unwillingness to rely on tax revenue to raise public money, the German states utilized public lands as a critical source of income for their provincial expenditures.[52]

Why did these premodern tendencies in German public finance persist into the beginning of the nineteenth century? According to Richard Tilly, the source of the unwillingness to rely on tax revenue to raise public money was, in the case of Prussia (in an argument that could extend to all the German states of the period), "a means of maintaining the Crown's independence of constitutional fiscal controls."[53] In the autocratic and undemocratic provincial states of Germany, but again especially in Prussia, the expansion of tax revenues as a source of public revenue would have entailed the even greater expansion of political rights to parliaments and citizens. As a result, provincial monarchs sought alternative "nontax" revenues to avoid the burden of parliamentary approval.[54] In fact, when viewed in cross-national perspective (see table 3.3), the German states' resistance to tax revenues and reliance on nontax revenues as a source of state income is quite clear.

Well into the nineteenth century, all German states faced a serious, politically induced financial constraint: they were less willing to rely on parliamentary institutions, and as a result the German monarchical states relied almost entirely on public lands to raise money.

In the face of this challenge, the German states, including again above all Prussia, as a politically powerful state, increasingly faced a second important constraint. The post-1815 setting imposed an unprecedented set of financial burdens on the newly reconstituted states of Germany. The end of the Napoleonic wars had left all the German states with high levels

TABLE 3.3

Revenue Sources in the German States, France, and Great Britain, 1813–50

	Thirty-five German States (national average)	France	Great Britain
Income from public lands and property	41.8%	0%	0%
Direct taxes	21.5%	43.2%	37%
Tariffs	15.4%	12.7%	17.7%
Other Indirect taxes	16.5%	19%	41.3%
Other revenues (registration fees, postage etc.)	0%	25.1%	4%
Total	*100%*	*100%*	*100%*

Note: Data on France are based on 1813 figures as reported by Schremmer, "Taxation and Public Finance," 377; data on Great Britain are based on 1815 figures as reported by Schremmer, 338–39; 1815 tariff values on Great Britain from B. R. Mitchell, *International Historical Statistics: Europe, 1750–1993* (London: Macmillan, 1998), 827; data on German states from Karl Borchard, Staatsverbrauch und Öffentliche investitionen in Deutschland, 1780–1850 (Göttingen: Dissertation, Wirtschafts und Sozialwissenschaftlichen Fakultät, 1968), 41–51. Since data on all thirty-five German states from this same time period are not available, I have used data from the earliest date available (1850). That data from this much later period show that the German states lagged so far behind Great Britain and France in a much earlier period only confirms my findings. In 1850, according to economic historians, the German states had already undergone a massive "modernization" of public finances (Borchard, 51).

of debt that created a massive fiscal burden on the new states. In 1825, in thirty-three of the thirty-five German states for which the data are available, debts were greater than annual income (see table 3.4). The range of this debt-revenue ratio varied among the states, but a simple bivariate correlation shows that smaller states tended to have large debt burdens ($r = -.22$) with the important exception of Prussia, which had among the highest debt burdens of all the German states as it sought to incorporate new territory and develop its military.[55]

In addition to high levels of war-caused debts, the new states were also burdened with the administration costs of incorporating new territories and the building of the administrative and military structures of modern states. A look at the expenditures of the several German states for which data are available and comparable for this period after 1815 shows that the single largest areas of expenditures for German states were defense and military expenditures (table 3.5). Nowhere was this more the case than in Prussia.

TABLE 3.4
Ratio of Public Debt to State Revenues of Thirty-five German States, 1825

State	Debt-to-Revenue Ratio	State	Debt-to-Revenue Ratio
Prussia	3.20	Mecklenburg Strelitz	1.75
Bavaria	2.65	Reuss Schleiz	1.63
Baden	2.05	Schwarzburg Rudolfstadt	1.04
Württemberg	2.43	Anhalt Dessau	1.13
Saxony	2.42	Schwarzburg Sonderhausen	1.53
Hannover	2.61	Waldeck Pyrmont	3.00
Schleswig Holstein	2.05	Anhalt Bernburg	1.24
Hessen	2.24	Lauenburg	1.28
Kurhessen	0.58	Saxony Coburg	3.00
Mecklenburg Schwerin	3.66	Anhalt Köthen	3.75
Nassau	2.13	Reuss Greiz	1.43
Oldenburg	0.24	Schaumberg Lippe	1.85
Braunschweig	3.20	Hessen Homburg	2.42
Saxony Weimar	2.92	Hamburg	8.86
Saxony Meiningen	3.57	Bremen	5.51
Saxony Altenburg	3.18	Lübeck	12.64
Saxony Gotha	4.01	Frankfurt	7.30
Lippe Detmold	1.22		

For states less willing to use parliamentary-approved tax revenue to generate public income and with aims of "great power" status, there appeared to be one possible outlet: tariff revenue generated by customs charges on products imported into a state's borders. For nation-states such as Great Britain and France tariff revenue served as a critical source of income. But unlike Great Britain and France, all of the German states, including Prussia, faced a *third* constraint: the German states were too small to support the administrative structure necessary for an effective tariff administration. In a protectionist Europe, where tariff revenue was becoming an increasingly important source of public income to support the state-building processes of modernization, the German states were simply too small to participate. What evidence is there for this claim? If we analyze the public finance data provided by Borchard,[56] we discover that smaller states (in terms of area) were not capable of generating a proportional share of

TABLE 3.5
Structure of State Expenditures of Selected German States, 1820

	Bavaria	Baden	Prussia
Debt	23.8%	13.9%	21.5%
Administration	13%	10.9%	6.4%
Defense	26.6%	21.9%	43.4%
Legal/Justice	6.5%	10.8%	8%
Kronrente	8.8%	16.2%	4.9%
Pensions	4.6%	12.5%	5.1%
Roads, Waterways etc.	3.9%	8.1%	4.7%
Other	12.8%	5.7%	6%
Total	100%	100%	100%

Source: For data on Bavaria, see Borchard, "Staatsverbrauch," 123; for data on Baden, see Borchard, 145; for data on Prussia, see Borchard, 169.

tariff revenue. In table 3.6, we see that there is generally a negative relationship between tariff as a share of state income and size of state for the four states for which data are available and comparable, before the Zollverein in 1834.

Though Prussia may have been better off than the smaller German states, this "economy of scale" issue was forefront in the minds of Prussian bureaucrats when they compared themselves to Great Britain, France, and the United States. And importantly, it was only Prussia that had the state capacity to expand its zone of influence. Indeed, it was a Prussian Ministry of Finance civil servant, Ludwig Kühne, who published an influential report in 1836 that examined the economics of tariff administration and concluded that because of the administrative costs required to patrol borders and to prevent smuggling, "there is a minimum size below which it is impossible to introduce a customs union."[57] Other analysts followed Kühne's lead and analyzed the ratio of "border length" to "area of state" to measure administrative costs to similarly conclude that a tariff system was only possible for states with an area of one hundred square *Meilen* (approximately 5,600 square kilometers) or more; this was only possible for ten of the thirty-five German states.[58] For officials in the Ministry of Finance, an expanded territorial unit was the path of least resistance to public finance stability.

With limited tax revenues, increasing costs, and limited access to tariff revenues, Prussia faced a very serious fiscal crisis in the first half of the nineteenth century. In his account of the Zollverein, Dumke reviews the

TABLE 3.6
Tariff as Share of State Income and State Size for Four German States, 1815

	Area (in "Meilen")	Tariff as Share of State Income
Prussia	5,103.95	14.5
Bavaria	1,279.3	8.1
Württemberg	354.3	6.2
Baden	278.4	9.4

Source: Data are drawn from Dumke, *German Economic Unification*, 54–55.

constraints facing the German states and notes, "If this picture correctly characterizes the predicament of most second and third rank German states in the first half of the nineteenth century, one must wonder how and why did they remain viable organizational forms in the face of such a precarious existence. One has the feeling that the whole German political structure of that time was unstable and would dramatically shift upon the slightest shock."[59]

Indeed, this was the case. It is for this reason that Prussian state sought to incorporate more territory into its larger customs union and why other states immediately embraced these overtures.[60] Nearly all the most resistant states, including Bavaria, had been incorporated by 1834 through a series of special "concessions" to the Bavarian state government. While Hannover remained independent until much later, all the states that joined had a rapid growth in their tariff revenues. In table 3.7, the growth in share of tariff revenues as a percentage of total state revenues from the 1820s to after 1834 is quite striking.

What is even more striking is that as a result of the special concessions, Prussia's revenue base did not increase at all, as Ministry of Finance officials had originally hoped, and in fact declined, according to most estimates.[61] Why would the Prussian government willingly incur such public financial losses? In an 1833 essay on Prussian trade policy, the contemporary historian Leopold Ranke confirms the account that I have presented so far. Ranke states succinctly that the aim of the Prussian government's customs union policy during the 1820s had a twofold benefit in providing the resources for state aggrandizement: "to remove internal boundaries as well as to create a respectable position vis-à-vis the rest of the world."[62] In order to achieve this aim of expanded state control (always in competition with Austria), the Prussian government was willing to tolerate financial losses in order to induce the local princes in other states to give up their own tariffs to a Prussian central government. How precisely was this done?

TABLE 3.7
Growth in Reliance on Tariffs as Source of State Revenues,
Before and After Zollverein

	1820–30	1840–49
Bavaria	7.1%	15.8%
Baden	8.4%	16.1%
Württemberg	7.4%	14.6%
Hessen-Darmstadt	1.6%	10.5%

Source: For data on Bavaria (1825 and 1849) see Borchard, "Staatsverbrauch"; for data on Baden (1830 and 1840) and on Württemberg (1830 and 1842) see Meminger as cited in Dumke, *German Economic Unification*, 54; for data on Hessen-Darmstadt (1820 and 1840) see Hahn, *Wirtschaftliche Integration*, 317–18.

Put in brief, the Prussian Ministry of Finance, under Finance Minister Motz, developed a revenue transfer system that gave the governments of other German states a disproportionate amount of the expanded fiscal resources of the German customs union in return for gaining free access to these markets; the transfer scheme, as developed by the 1834 Zollverein, as a result, however, left the Prussian government financially worse off than before the creation of the customs union.

The irony was perhaps lost on Prussian officials. Throughout the period they remained committed to the notion that in order assert themselves on the European stage and to extricate themselves from what was perceived to be an autocrat's state-building dilemma, they had to increase revenues without granting parliamentary taxing rights. As the most highly trained and modernized bureaucracy among the German states, the Prussian Finance Ministry in 1834 came upon the novel "national" solution: by expanding the territorial zone of the Prussian customs union, the Prussian government hoped to begin to establish itself as a "great power" on the European stage. In this first stage of national unification, Prussian state officials were the main agents of national unification.

Turning finally, to the *second* stage of German unification (1866–71), we see again the role of the state. But rather than public finance motivations, in this period of war it was state survival that was forefront in the minds of Germany's monarchs. To understand the political determinants of a state's position on the question of national unification from 1866 to 1871, we can look at the particularly revealing German Confederation Bundestag's decisive vote on June 11, 1866, on the eve of the outbreak of war between Austria and Prussia. At this special sitting of the Bundestag, as the prospect of war approached, the Austrian monarch's representative proposed a resolution condemning Prussia's occupation of Holstein.

TABLE 3.8
State Vote on Austrian-Sponsored Bundestag Condemnation of
Prussia, June 11, 1866

Vote against Condemnation	Vote for Condemnation	Abstention
Hamburg	Bavaria	Schaumberg Lippe
Bremen	Saxony	Baden
Lübeck	Württemburg	Reuss juengere Linie
Schwarzburg-Rudolfstadt	Hannover	
Schwarzburg-Sonderhausen	Kurhessen	
Anhalt Dessau	Hessen-Darmstadt	
Oldenburg	Nassau	
Mecklenburg Strelitz	Reuss Aeltere Linie	
Mecklenburg Schwerin	Saxon-Meinungen	
Lippe	Frankfurt	
Braunschweig	Lichtenstein	
Waldeck	Austria	
Luxemburg-Limburg		

Source: Ernst Rudolf Huber, ed., *Dokumente zur Deutschen Verfassungsgeschichte*, vol. 2 (Stuttgart: W. Kohlhammer Verlag, 1964), 541.

All of the German state monarchs were present at the vote, which represented the single instance in which they could formally express their position vis-à-vis the Prussian-Austrian conflict, thus representing an ideal case in which to examine support for or resistance to Prussia's plans for national unification. Put simply, a vote against the Austrian resolution was a vote *for* Prussia's "nation-state" *kleindeutsch* plans for a Germany without Austria. By contrast, a vote for Austria's resolution or an abstention was a vote *against* Prussia and a vote for the continuation of the loose prenational German confederation.[63]

The Austrian proposals passed the unusual voting system of the Bundestag (in which smaller states' votes were pooled into voting blocs) narrowly by a margin of nine to five, and Prussia's actions in Holstein were condemned, leading, as all actors involved had expected, to the dissolution of the German Confederation. More interesting than the pooled vote, for our purposes, is the vote of each individual state, as shown in table 3.8.

Why did some states take Prussia's side and other states take Austria's in this decisive vote? To understand why some German states supported the creation of a Prussian-led nation-state and others resisted, siding with

TABLE 3.9
State Votes on Formal Condemnation of Prussia, June 11, 1866, by State Size

	Votes in Support of Prussia	Vote against Prussia
Large states (above German mean in state population)	0 (0%)	7 (63.6%)
Small states (below German mean in state population)	13 (100%)	4 (36.4%)
Total (N=24)	13 (100%)	11 (100%)

Note: My own calculations. Data on population of German states are from Borchard, "Staatsverbrauch," 91–93.

Austria and Bavaria, the results of this decisive German Bund vote represent a critical test. Though the number of cases involved and data limitations prevent a rigorous statistical test of this question, we can still try to identify any underlying patterns in how states voted to disentangle the question of why some states supported Prussia while other states supported Austria. After excluding Austria itself from the analysis, in table 3.9 we see how the political "power" of a state, measured first in terms of population size vis-à-vis other German states and second in terms of state military expenditures vis-à-vis other German states, affected the likelihood that a state would support Prussia or Austria in this decisive vote.

We see that a "power-balancing" thesis seems to be largely confirmed: monarchs of small states tended to vote with Prussia and larger states voted against Prussia. These data support the claim that has formed a centerpiece of this chapter: we see that while Prussia, as Germany's largest state, *initiated* unification, it was the *large* but less commercialized states (i.e., Bavaria, Württemberg) that most actively resisted unification and the *small* commercialized and less commercialized states in between that found themselves reluctantly siding with either Germany's largest power, Prussia, or its second largest power, Bavaria.

But beyond this quantitative evidence, qualitative evidence also reveals why it was in Prussia that the push for national unification began and why it was in Bavaria that the greatest resistance to national unification outside of Austria was to be found. In Prussia, the political push for closer ties between the German states in the 1860s was initiated by the Prussian state in response to two challenges. The first part of the post-1848 challenge for the Bismarck-led Prussian state—the growing popularity of liberal na-

tionalism in Prussia—came to a head with the Prussian constitutional conflict of 1859–66 in which liberals demanded greater parliamentary control
over the military.[64] The upsurge in the popularity of liberals, in the form
of the newly founded Nationalverein and Fortschrittspartei (Progressive
Party), was utterly evident with the elections of 1858 and 1861 as the
liberals won majorities in the Prussian state parliament.[65] The liberal leaders such as Leopold von Hoverbeck, Theodor Mommsen, and Hermann
Schulze-Delitzsch were liberals *and* nationalists and opposed the persistence of the autocratic conservative "particularist" Prussian regime. By
calling for parliamentary control over the budget, "The liberals wanted to
persuade the crown to terminate its old alliance with the Junkers and enter
into an alliance with themselves."[66] Furthermore, the liberals saw national
unification as a means of reducing the military obligations of, and thereby
liberalizing, the Prussian state.[67] Of course the Prussian reactionary aristocratic Right, like reactionary conservatives throughout Germany, resisted
liberal calls for constitutional and national reforms. When Bismarck was
offered the position of prime minister on September 22 1862, he began to
carry out what can be called a "national solution" to the growing domestic
tensions that a modernizing society had unleashed on the Prussian state.
To preserve the crown's authority within Prussia and to increase its power
in Europe, Bismarck adopted a new national strategy that combined domestic and foreign policy goals. In reaction to the obvious signs of weakness displayed by Austria in its recent wars in Italy, Bismarck over the
course of the next four years turned on its head the antinational orientation of the Prussian government. In its place, in a series of ongoing negotiations with the Prussian parliament, the Prussian king, and the monarchs
of the other German states, Bismarck sought to benefit strategically by
instrumentally blocking Austrian reforms to the German Confederation
and then proposing his own "reforms" to it.[68] Second, as that failed, Bismarck presented an alternative Prussian-centered "national" vision of Germany that would detach Austria from the rest of Germany. With Austria
excluded, Prussia would have Germany's largest population, largest geographical area, and highest levels of expenditures on military. The aim for
Bismarck was threefold: First, he aimed to co-opt one of the central planks
of the liberal nationalists. Second, he promised monarchical control of the
new nation-state that was intended to appeal to the Junker conservatism.
Third, he would guarantee Prussian hegemony of German Europe.[69] In
short, as the Prussian state managed the tensions of a changing international setting and changing Prussian society, the path of nation-state formation made increased sense.

In reaction to this course of events, small and midsized states, such as
Coburg, Hamburg, and the states of Thüringen, found themselves forced
to ally with Prussia. By contrast, the four most politically powerful states

in Germany after Prussia and Austria—Bavaria, Württemberg, Baden, and Saxony—all allied with Prussia's Hapsburg competitor; indeed, none of the midsized states joined Prussia. But, after 1866 a new period of "realism" confronted political leaders even in Baden and Württemberg: The king of Baden even sought admission to Bismarck's North German Confederation in the wake of Prussia's victory against Austria in the summer and fall of 1866; the centralizing reforms of the Zollverein were approved largely without discussion in 1867 even in Baden and the Hessen states.[70] Only Bavaria and Württemberg, among the strongest states in Germany, remained hostile to the Prussian plans of a nation-state.[71] While some of this resistance can be associated with the uneven economic developments between Prussia and southern Germany, a decisive factor that can explain why Bavaria in particular resisted Prussia was its size, the development of its administrative and military structures, and of course its political status in Germany even after 1866. Taken together, these factors explain why the Bavarian crown would want to preserve and protect the autonomy of the well-developed and powerful state of Bavaria.[72]

Evidence for this can be seen in the Bavarian parliamentary debates of 1867 and 1871. With the formation of the Prussian-led North German Confederation in 1866–67, Bavarian parliamentarians feared Bismarck's southern objectives. In debates in the 1867 Bavarian parliament on centralizing reforms of the Zollverein, the Bavarian particularist Jörg called for the Bavarian rejection of the proposed plans by proclaiming that the acceptance of the reforms would all lead to an eventual absorption in the Prussian-led North German Confederation that would undermine state and bureaucratic autonomy of Bavaria. In a speech in front of the Bavarian parliament, Jörg told his colleagues to examine the North German Constitutions, "If you look at articles 3 and 4 of the constitution, you will ask, what will stay in our house? Post, telegraph, railway, social legislation, and civil law—these areas that we have worked so hard for and spent so much money on in Bavaria [will pass on a centralized authority]." Not only was it a question of state autonomy, it was more profoundly a question of state survival. Jörg also insisted that any joining of Bavaria to the rest of Germany might undermine the very existence of Bavaria. He proclaimed, "This decision is a question of whether Bavaria will still count and have any weight on Europe's map."[73] Though a regionalist politician could make this claim in the large state of Bavaria, no political leader in the miniature states of, say, Saxony-Coburg or even Hamburg would make such arguments.

Indeed, it was only in the state of Bavaria, in 1867 and in 1871, that regional political leaders could realistically resist Prussian overtures. In both 1867 and 1871, the Bavarian crown and the required two-thirds of the Bavarian parliament accepted Prussia's Zollverein reforms and offer of

admission into a German Reich only when these questions of state autonomy and survival were addressed.[74] The king's representative in the parliament, future chancellor Hohenlohe, convinced his colleagues to support
closer ties to Prussia by insisting, first in 1867, that an "alliance" with
Prussia would still guarantee some important areas of state autonomy: the
Bavarian crown would still be sovereign in Bavaria and the Bavarian crown
would control its own military.[75] Similarly, Hohenlohe argued in 1870–
71, on the eve of war with France, that joining Prussia was now necessary
for the survival of Bavaria. In the memoirs of his son, Hohenlohe is quoted
as provocatively presenting Bavaria's dilemma after 1866: With the dissolution of the German Bund in 1866, Bavaria was faced with two choices—
either a forced "union" with France or a voluntary "merger" with Prussia.[76]

CONCLUSION

By the eve of German unification in 1867 and then in 1870–71, economic
and political conditions had solidified to make Prussia the largest rapidly
commercializing state in Germany, the most likely initiator of national
unification, and Bavaria, as the largest slowly commercializing state, its
most likely opponent. But with the threat of war with France, even Bavaria
joined the larger territorial, fiscal, administrative, and military unit of the
German Reich. Economic changes in commercialized regions of Germany
initially spawned the push for German unification after 1834. But it was
the interests—above all fiscal and military—of the regional governments
of the German states that sealed the unification of Germany in both 1834
and between 1866 and 1871. Though the Bavarian government and the
other resistant states did eventually join the Prussian-led nation-state, it
was the persistent push and pull between independent monarchs over the
course of the nineteenth century that created the main contours of the
national critical juncture in Germany.

Chapter Four

THE NATIONAL MOMENT IN ITALY:

THE DYNAMICS OF REGIONALISM AND

NATIONAL UNIFICATION, 1815–1860

BETWEEN 1859 and 1861, Piedmontese political leaders achieved the national unification of Italy abruptly and unexpectedly.[1] In contrast to the piecemeal Prussian-led unification of Germany, the Piedmontese-imposed unification of Italy was an affair of high political drama, charismatic personalities, and well-orchestrated political maneuverings. In the effort to come to analytical grips with this drama, a group of important scholars of nineteenth-century Italian history has recently argued that Italian national unification was not the carefully planned project of Piedmontese state-builders inspired by nationalist social mobilization across Italy's north that the classic scholarship once posited.[2] Though Cavour, Mazzini, and Garibaldi—the holy trinity of Italian national unity—are still recognized as decisive actors in the events of the late 1850s, some scholarship has become skeptical of both the "nationalist" social support these actors enjoyed and of the political coherence of the Piedmontese state-builders' goals.

Indeed, the "myth" of the Risorgimento—that the north, inspired by mass sentiment, undertook a nationalist project to unify the divided nation—has come under attack. It has become increasingly clear, first, that the social mobilization that imploded the seven ancien régime Italian states leading to national unification was neither rooted entirely in "the north" nor even always explicitly nationalist in motivation. Rather, the grievances varied from one Italian state to the next, often had roots in center-periphery troubles within each state, and were directed, especially in the case of Sicily, against "foreign" rule, with the aim of establishing greater autonomy, not necessarily *national* unification. The second part of the "myth" that has come under attack is the notion that Piedmontese state-builders had a well-developed plan to carry out a project of state formation. It is now also usually quite accurately claimed by historians that Cavour and the Piedmontese crown largely stumbled into Italy's south with the short-term goal of containing political instability and instead found themselves having annexed the southern half of the peninsula, unintentionally winning the "prize" of a united Italy.[3]

It is true, as this revisionist historiography has shown, that neither a disembodied nationalism nor a self-conscious Piedmontese plan provided *all* of the social and political ingredients for successful national unification. Yet it is a main contention of this chapter that a "revolution by accident" theory of Italian unification is essentially limited. Despite the role played by contingency and chance, the successful national unification of Italy was more than a fortuitous aggregation of a series of unintended consequences. Rather, the unification of Italy, like the nearly simultaneous unification of Germany, represented the demise of a prenational form of imperial or confederative political organization in Europe and the rise of a new, more centralized national form of political organization. If we want to understand why nation-states emerged out of loose confederations of states and wide-flung empires throughout Europe in the last third of the nineteenth century, it makes sense to search for the precise political and economic conditions that gave rise to the project of national unification.

This chapter identifies and explains the regional forces *for* and *against* national unification in Italy in the late 1850s. I explore the following questions: Why did Italy come to be unified when it did? Why did a single nation-state replace the loose set of pre-1861 Italian states? And why was Piedmont, rather than the myriad of other Italian states, the main regional actor that undertook the project of national unification? By answering these questions, my analysis seeks, first, to identify the main regional contours of the "national" moment" in the development of the Italian nation-state by identifying how different regional governments responded in different ways to national unification. Second, this chapter sets the stage for the puzzle of why, if the regional forces for and against national unification were so similar in Germany and Italy *during* the national moment, such divergent political institutions emerged *after* the national moment.

SOCIETAL AND STATE ACTORS IN THE ITALIAN RISORGIMENTO

In the societally centered literature, earliest accounts followed Gramsci's lead to emphasize the impact of Italy's weak "bourgeoisie," who were said to seek a larger national market and thereby supported Piedmontese efforts to create a single territorial unit during the post-1815 period to the detriment of southern economic life and Italian political life in general.[4] Other accounts in this same tradition have presented a more flattering portrait of Piedmontese liberals as modernizing agents of national unification and have disparaged the weak "bourgeoisie" of southern Italy and of Sicily in particular as the cause of regional resistance to national unification.[5] Still another school of thought in the same society-centered tradition has sought to move beyond the ideologically loaded terminology of "bourgeoisie" to emphasize a more subtle social amalgam of middle-class and aristocratic intelligentsia.[6] For these scholars, this "amalgam" was itself a product of economic modernization in Italy's north and was constituted by diverse range of figures, from Mazzini and Cattaneo to Cavour and Ricasoli: these intellectual leaders and their secret societies and nationalist organizations, journals, and magazines helped assure the "myth" of Italy and provided the critical nationalist ingredient that pushed public opinion toward the creation of Italy.

In contrast to these societally centered accounts, other scholars have focused on the "power politics" of Italy's Risorgimento and have treated Italy's unification as an instance of state building by examining the Piedmontese political leaders such as Cavour and Garibaldi who sought to extend Piedmont's influence throughout Italy and thereby assure Piedmont's position in Europe.[7] Other accounts in that same tradition focus on Lombard desires to evict the Austrian empire from Italian soil.[8] And still others focus on the problems of administrative modernization faced by all the Italian states after 1815. From this latter perspective emerges the insight that the greatest challenge facing the restoration states of Italy was what I have termed in the last chapter the autocrat's state-building dilemma of creating centralized administrative structures, sufficient public finance revenue, and access to a military via universal conscription, all without granting parliamentary rights of representation. In her important scholarship on the Risorgimento, Lucy Riall has argued that it was the Piedmontese crown's ability to solve this dilemma after 1848 by a creating a parliament that drove it toward a strategy of national unification by the late 1850s.[9]

While all of these accounts correctly identify some of the critical actors who pushed for Italian unification, the multiple explanations have left analysts with a wealth of potential causes that are difficult to untangle. In light of the lessons drawn from the discussion of German unification, the following two sections borrow from the insights of each of these approaches and show how societal and state actors interacted to make one region—Piedmont—the initiator of national unification; while other regions, such as the Kingdom of Two Sicilies and the Papal States, resisted unification; and still other state governments imploded in the face of national unification, leaving aristocratic leaders in states such as Tuscany, Parma, Modena, and even Lombardy following less decisive paths of passively supporting or quietly resisting the Piedmontese state-building efforts.[10] The following two sections look at the early stirrings of a commercial society in north central Italy, to argue that as in Germany, the creation of a new commercial class in Italy's richest regions (notably Lombardy and

Piedmont) generated a push for political reform and territorial change. Partly in response to pressure from such groups, but also acting as *autonomous* political force in its own right to modernize its own bankrupt system of public finances, extend its influence, and to co-opt liberal pressures for change, the Piedmontese crown and state had the means and the motives to initiate national unification. By offering an expanded national market that eliminated internal customs duties, an expanded national system of public finance that rescued Piedmont from its own fiscal crisis, a nationalist rhetoric that co-opted the idiom of a radical liberal-national revolution, and a national king to gain the commitment of the traditional antirepublican aristocracy in Piedmont, the Piedmontese state's leadership had the political resources to unify Italy. Just as Prussia was the only German state both facing a "commercialized" society and possessing the political means to extend its influence, so too was Piedmont the only Italian state with both the *motives* and the *means* to create an Italian nation-state. Conversely, it was only the Kingdom of Two Sicilies that had the motives and political means to actively resist the Piedmontese-led unification project.

A View From Below: Social Change in Italy's Regions

The most organized challenge to the seven restored ancien régime states of Italy and the greatest social push for national unification in Italy before and after 1848 originated largely in Italy's northern regions.[11] Not only Mazzini's Associazione Nazionale but also both the Lombard liberals and the "realist" Società Nazionale Italiana (SNI) began their activities in Lombardy and Piedmont under the leadership of an intellectual strata rooted in a transforming north central Italian society. Likewise, among all the Italian states, the SNI's regional membership base—as a percentage of regional population—was highest in the central Italian state of Tuscany.[12] The correlation between region and social support for national unification is easy to identify. More challenging are these questions: Why was the nationalist movement most vibrant and organized in Italy's north? And, why despite some disorganized though highly important peasant revolts and aristocratic tensions with the Neapolitan crown in southern Italy in 1820 and 1848, did southern Italy appear to lack the critical social base that generated the impetus for national unification?

To understand why Italy's northern and central regions became, like the Prussian Rhineland in Germany, the locus of regional social support for national unification, several factors immediately suggest themselves: degree of regional social organization and level of economic development.[13] First, as Robert Putnam has found in his important study of post-Risorgimento Italy, social organization tended to be more developed in northern Italy,

TABLE 4.1
Regional GDP Per Capita, Italian Regions, 1861 (in 1911 lira)

Northwest	391	South	171
Piedmont	416	Abruzzi	178
Liguria	288	Campania	203
Lombardy	401	Apulia	174
Northeast Central	229	Basilicata	153
Veneto	245	Calabria	168
Emilia	236	Sicily	149
Tuscany	239	Sardinia	199
Marches	239	Italy	227
Umbria	177		
Latium	308		

Note: Regional GDP per capita data are calculated and reported by Alfredo Giuseppe Esposto, "Estimating Regional Per Capita Income: Italy, 1861–1914," *Journal of European Economic History* 26 (1997): 589. According to my own analysis with fifteen geographical regions of Italy in 1861, regional GDP per capita is a reasonably valid measure of economic modernization insofar as it very strongly correlates with other potential measures of economic modernization for which data are available, including regional literacy rates ($r = .91$). Data source for regional literacy rates is Zamagni, *Economic History of Italy*, 13–14. It should be noted that the regions reported in this table do not correspond to the seven regional states of post-1815 Italy.

which might explain why social support for national unification might have been strongest in north central Italy. Since there were more organizations in general per capita in north central Italy, it makes sense that specifically *nationalist* organizations would also be more active.[14] Additionally, we see that, as table 4.1 shows, using GDP per capita as a measure of economic modernization, there were large regional differences in the Risorgimento period that correspond, at least in broad strokes, to the areas in which nationalist activity, according to most scholars, was strongest.

But despite this apparent correlation between level of economic development, level of social organization, and support for national unification, it is the central contention of this section that behind both of these persistent and often-cited features of life in regional Italy lies a third and more decisive factor that generated regionally based support for national unification after 1815 and that may additionally explain the higher levels of "social capital" and higher levels of economic output in northern Italy than in southern Italy. Though the origins of economic inequality in Italy have generated a long tradition of scholarship, one important and often-overlooked source of the divergence between north-center and south in Italy was—as in Germany—the geographically uneven legacy of Napoleon's rule between 1798 and 1815. Whereas France directly ruled Italy's northern and central regions of Lombardy, Piedmont, Tuscany, and Emilia after Napoleon's invasion in 1798, Napoleon adopted a strategy of indirect rule in southern Italy and never even had pretensions of political authority on the British-controlled island of Sicily. As with Napoleon's regionally uneven rule in Germany, these two patterns had important consequences in Italy: In northern and central Italy, Napoleon's rule provided a shock to the still relatively traditional economic structure by introducing a set of successful commercializing reforms that utterly transformed north central Italian society.[15] As in the Prussian Rhineland, the legal and societal framework in which the north central Italian aristocrats lived after 1798 was transformed, patterns of agricultural ownership were undone, and economic output increased rapidly. In southern Italy, by contrast, indirect and ineffective rule under Napoleon's brother Joseph Bonaparte hampered the radical efforts at commercialization, As a consequence, traditional economic structures remained largely intact after 1815 despite the passage of new antifeudal laws.[16] These two self-contained patterns of administrative rule within Italy had important economic, social, and political consequences.[17]

In Italy's north central regions such as in Lombardy and Piedmont, French administrators created commercialized agricultural relations through two concrete institutional and legal changes that, first, made land a commodity that could be bought and sold, and, second, created a social base of landholders who would respond to market pressures and be willing to invest and to pursue a profit.[18] First, in north central Italy feudalism was effectively abolished between 1797 and 1799. In Piedmont, for example, all noble titles in Piedmont were eliminated, families owning feudal titles and deeds were required to hand them to the French authorities, property was seized, and primogeniture rights were eliminated.[19] Similarly, in Emilia, in the fertile Po Valley, all juridical bonds were eliminated and all forms of property were rendered alienable.[20] Though the aristocracy returned to a position of economic dominance throughout north central Italy after 1802, direct French state intervention effectively transformed land into a commodity that could be purchased and sold by private owners.

Second, again in contrast to developments in southern Italy, French administrators induced the new landholders in north central Italy to engage in market-oriented agricultural practices by eliminating tax privileges and abolishing legal protection against the collection of debt from aristocrats. As a result, land passed from the hands of landowners who viewed property as a source of prestige to landowners who viewed it as a source of potential profit, which promoted the willingness to invest in increasingly productive means of agriculture. In northern and central Italy, by 1815, aristocrats were forced to participate in the market to survive and a middle class began slowly to emerge. On the important agricultural plain of Bologna, for example, the growing abundance of middle-class buyers and land speculators transformed noble lands from 78 percent of total land in 1789, to 66 percent in 1804, to 51 percent in 1855.[21] The Italian historian Renato Zangheri described the new "bourgeois" property owners around Bologna as bringing to the area "a new spirit of enterprise unknown to lordly landownership."[22] This critical influx of new landholders, the elimination of legal protection for aristocrats, and the stable institutional setting guaranteed by French direct rule transformed the way in which land was viewed in central Italy, even among aristocrats. Similarly, in Piedmont, though aristocratic families remained the predominant landholders in the sixty-eight communes of the plains of Vercelli and Cuneo in Piedmont, the elimination of privileges pushed landholders from traditional land-tenure practices toward profit-seeking, commercial-minded agrarian business practices.[23] As Cardoza writes, "Despite the wealth, power and prestige the great aristocratic families continued to enjoy under the Napoleonic regime, their positions now rested upon new circumstances that were antithetical to the old institutional status of the nobility."[24]

These two broad conditions—the effective elimination of feudalism and the creation of a social base that would respond to market pressures—had economic and political consequences. These changes in agrarian social relations contributed to northern and central Italy's above-average agricultural productivity: As table 4.2 makes clear, in 1857, three years before national unification, Piedmont, Lombardy, and Tuscany all were above the national average in agricultural production per hectare, while the Papal States and the Kingdom of Two Sicilies still lagged far below the national average.

Additionally, this transformation of agrarian relations set the stage for the industrialization of northwestern Italy in the middle of the nineteenth century. It was the commercialization of agriculture that, according to Hobsbawm, "melt[ed] that great frozen ice-cap above the fertile soil of economic growth."[25] Indeed, as Rosario Romeo and Alexander Gerschenkron have also both found in the Italian context, the commercialization of land in the early part of the nineteenth century created the basis for a rapid increase in agricultural output between 1861 and 1880, which in turn facilitated subsequent industrial investment and output, mostly, it must be noted, in the same early commercializing regions of Italy's north.[26]

TABLE 4.2
Agricultural Productivity, Italian Regional States, 1857

Regional State	Value of Agricultural Production, per Hectare (lire)
Lombardy (without Veneto)	238
Parma-Modena	174
Piedmont	169
Tuscany	117
Kingdom of Two Sicilies	81
Papal States	68
Italy, average (including Veneto region)	104

Source: Data from Zamagni, Economic History of Italy, 14.

But beyond the economic consequences, as in the Prussian Rhineland, how did these steps of commercial transformation and increased agricultural productivity give rise to support for national unification? The successful commercialization of land and labor created a vibrant set of social relations and gave rise to the critical "nationalist" social alliance: a well-developed commercialized aristocracy and a professional and educated, manufacturing-based middle class in northern and central Italy that would challenge the restoration regimes after 1815 and that would push for the creation of a united Italian nation-state. The reasons, in this sense, were both economic and ideological: The combination of the early commercialization of land and labor, a long export-oriented tradition, and the resurgence of protectionism abroad and in Italy after 1815 all gave rise to the search for national markets. As table 4.3 makes clear, economic exchange among the Italian states after the reinstatement of the ancien régime states in 1815 was restricted not only by different currency systems, weight and measurement systems, and underdeveloped transportation systems, but also by high tariff levels that restricted the export and import of goods between states.

Additionally, in the minds of the well-developed and post-1815 flourishing manufacturing and agricultural interests, economic development and "national" progress became linked.[27] The critical point is that in Italy's north—an early commercializing set of regions—the "free trade" platform came to provide a meeting point for a new coalition of liberal agrarian and commercial interests.[28] Nowhere was this decisive "nationalist" social coalition stronger than in the states of Tuscany, Piedmont, and Lombardy. It is partly for this reason that the population of these three states that together constituted approximately only 35 percent of the Italian popula-

TABLE 4.3
Tariff Levels, Italian States, 1846

Tuscany	34%
Naples Province (Kingdom of Two Sicilies)	28%
Piedmont	21%
Parma	18%
Modena	16%
Lombardy	15%
Papal States	15%

Note: The tariff levels are based on my own calculations of total tariff revenue as a percentage of total state revenue. Data source: *Archivio economico dell'unificazione italiana*, various issues (1959–63).

tion shared a disproportionate 50 percent of the national membership in the *Società Nazionale Italiana* (SNI).[29] Indeed, in addition to this quantitative evidence on these three states, it is useful to focus on three paradigmatic examples of the commercialized aristocracy and liberal-minded, manufacturing-based middle class that themselves were a product of these economic changes and contributed to the Risorgimento: Count Ricasoli in Tuscany, Count Cavour in Piedmont, and Carlo Cattaneo in Lombardy.

First, in Tuscany, contemporary accounts frequently described how the new commercial-minded aristocratic landholders—such as the Ricasoli family—turned to "modern" techniques to increase productivity and profits.[30] These commercial-minded aristocrats, often educated abroad, were motivated by the decline in profits but also found inspiration in the "liberal" British agricultural reforms. In response, the *mezzadria* system, for the first time, came under attack in Tuscany by the landlords themselves, such as the Ricasolis.[31] Count Bettino Ricasoli, who would play a decisive role in the politics of the Risorgimento, frequently expressed his admiration for English agricultural reforms. Known as the "Puritan of Brolio," Ricasoli viewed his family's long-standing holdings, and Tuscan subsistence-level agriculture in general, as backwards and in need of desperate reform of scientific management and reorganization to increase production and profits. He viewed himself as a modern "missionary" whose task it was to "make an assault . . . against the prejudices of the peasants."[32] The economic and societal consequences of commercialized aristocratic and middle-class business leaders began to be felt throughout Tuscany: As early as the 1830s, the leading Tuscan agricultural and manufacturing sectors, now *both* highly reliant on exports, complained to the grand duke of Tuscany of the problems of protectionism. In a revealing report to the British government in 1837, John Bowring reported that Tuscan straw hat and straw tress merchants, among the leading manufacturing producers in Tuscany at the time, exported 24,000 dozens annually and were increasingly frustrated by rising tariffs.[33] Likewise, important agricultural producers of wine, potash, and juniper berries also wrote to the Tuscan grand duke, calling for the elimination of tariffs.[34] As a consequence of successful commercialization and protectionism between Italian states and abroad, the social ingredients for a "nationalist" alliance between agricultural and manufacturing interests were congealing.

In Piedmont, likewise, Count Cavour himself, a follower of Jeremy Bentham and the eventual prime minister of the Savoy kingdom, was representative of larger Piedmont-wide commercial-aristocratic effort to reform agriculture by promoting improved methods of farming and stock-raising by disseminating the latest scientific information. Cavour, who, as myth has it, learned English by waking up every morning at four to study Adam Smith, claimed to be "not an absolute partisan of the English agricultural system."[35] Yet Cavour was an advocate of a modernized agricultural system and represented the wing of the Piedmontese aristocracy along with Cesare Alfieri that established organizations such as the Associazione Agraria Subalpina, constituted by a group of "prominent nobles and bourgeois notables" that aimed at transforming agriculture in Piedmont.[36] It is also critical to note, as other scholars have observed, that in Piedmont during this post-1815 period, the phenomenon of property-owning peasantry had developed the furthest among Italy's regions as a result of the Napoleonic commercializing reforms. In light of both of the attack on the *mezzadria* and the growth of a new property-owning peasantry, commercial agriculture developed quite far in Piedmont. A new social base for economic and political modernization—represented by Cavour—was emerging that would in 1848 challenge the Piedmontese restoration regime and *after* 1848 would increasingly call for national unification.[37] It was precisely the fusion of economic frustration imposed by the divided Italian peninsula and an ideological commitment to national progress that set the stage for the growth of the nationalist alliance in Piedmont. Of course, as in Prussia, some conservative elements of the Piedmontese aristocracy actually resisted efforts at national unification. Yet in Piedmont a younger generation of commercialized, business-minded aristocrats like Cavour supported free trade, sought the expansion of national markets, and viewed national unification as the best way to achieve these goals.[38]

Kent Greenfield has provided the most thorough discussion of similar changes in Lombardy, where Napoleon's reforms had also similarly been rapid, complete, and effective.[39] In the face of the same commercializing reforms that transformed Tuscan and Piedmontese agriculture, the desire for profits—conditioned by French reforms—and admiration of the British system led to the final commercialization of agriculture under the direction of a moderate aristocracy that continued to dominate economic life. Reforms in Lombardy became the subject of liberal publicists of the period, such as Carlo Cattaneo, who saw in Lombardy a model for the rest of Italy. Both agricultural and manufacturing interests experienced economic growth, and both were reliant on exports to other Italian states. Here, an productive agricultural sector that included silk production, rice, grains, and dairy farming increasingly replaced the ramshackle estates of the pre-1800 period. Interestingly, a large portion of this booming agricultural sector was exported to other Italian states. Despite the high tariff walls, the majority of dairy exports, for example, were exported to the Papal States, Naples, and Parma, totaling exports worth twenty million francs annually in 1836.[40] Similarly, preindustrial manufacturing production, especially in the production of silk, was also growing in importance, reliant on international and domestic markets. It is out of these two communities that the most active pushes for the creation of a national market were found. It was, according to Greenfield's account, "the conservative proprietary class who gave the tone to Lombard society."[41] But it was liberal publicists such as Cattaneo who articulated a "nationalist" and "democratic" vision for a united Italy. In fact, as Greenfield has discovered, publicists such as Cattaneo helped form journals such as the *Annali Universali di Statistica*, which praised in 1834 the German Zollverein as a model for Italy's path to national unity.[42] When news of the creation of a "national market" starting January 1, 1834, reached Italy, the publishers of the Lombard journal *Annali* proclaimed, "Heaven send that like dispositions may be proposed and adopted for the states of Italy!"[43] Similarly, by 1844 Cesare Balbo's best-selling book *Speranze d'Italia* summarized all of these ideas with his call for the creation of an Italian "league." The same sentiments also inspired the influential Milan Chamber of Commerce, which issued reports, like those issued by city chambers of commerce in the Rhineland, that called for the elimination of internal tariffs, closer trading ties between Italy's independent regions, and the creation of a single national market.[44]

Indeed, in all three states of Tuscany, Lombardy, and Piedmont, the push for a single national market had its roots not among the *borghesia* that crude theories of modernization might predict. Instead, it was, as Romanelli and Lyttelton have also found,[45] the modern "missionaries" of the liberal-minded aristocracy and manufacturing middle classes that found their commercial interests frustrated by protectionism at home and abroad. Likewise, with this newly commercialized society facing the reinstatement of "restoration" Austrian regimes in Tuscany and Lombardy and the Savoy regime in Piedmont, economic and societal leaders fused their economic frustration with a "democratic" vision of a heroic Italian national entity independent of "foreign" domination.

If commercializing reforms in Italy's north generated a nationalist co-alition of regional social *support* for national unification, why was south-ern Italy missing this critical nationalist social alliance? What left the so-cial structure of Sicily, the Papal States, and the Bourbon mainland, like Bavaria in Germany, less organized as the impetus for national unifica-tion? Just as level of economic development and degree of "social capital" are incomplete explanations of support for national unification in north-ern Italy, so too must one look elsewhere—namely to the timing and extent of commercialization—to understand the weakness of the nation-alist movement in the southern parts of Italy after 1848. Unlike in north-ern Italy, in southern Italy, the late and incomplete commercialization of land and labor left the nationalist social coalition of agrarian and manu-facturing interests divided. First, if northern agricultural and small-scale manufacturing interests of Lombardy and Piedmont *both* supported, and were as a result able to form a critical *social alliance* to mobilize on behalf of the creation of, a "nationally" integrated market, the structure of trade among the Italian states divided social support between agrarian and manufacturing interests in southern Italy and thereby prevented the for-mation of an effective pronational social alliance. The high tariffs be-tween Italian states outlined in table 4.3, viewed as a barrier among the highly productive agrarian interests and increasingly productive manu-facturing interests of Lombardy, Piedmont, and even Tuscany, were per-ceived not as a restriction but rather as protection by a slowly developing manufacturing sector across large segments of southern Italy. For exam-ple, as Judith Chubb has found, tariffs between the Italian states pro-tected a growing textile industry that had begun to emerge in cities like Palermo and Naples.[46] Similarly, as De Rosa has found, a modern metal-lurgical industry grew up in Naples protected behind the high tariff walls of the Bourbon regime.[47] As a consequence of their "late" emergence vis-à-vis the north, these commercial interests were *defenders* of the Bourbon regime and were critical of liberal or nationalist efforts to promote free trade among the Italian states. When, for example, the Palermo govern-ment, in bold and new free-market gesture, granted Messina on Sicily the status of a free port in 1848, the Neapolitan Chamber of Commerce responded rapidly, calling on the Bourbon crown for the abolishment of such "free trade" special treatment.[48] In contrast to the early commercial-izing chambers of commerce in northern Italy, the Neapolitan Chamber of Commerce did not call for *more* free-trade ports but rather threatened that merchants in manufacturing sectors would dismiss their employees unless the port at Messina were closed.[49]

Although the late-developing manufacturing sectors were closely allied with the Bourbon crown's protectionism, some southern and Sicilian agrarian interests—having experienced the *formal* abolishment of feudalism in 1808 and 1812 respectively—often petitioned the Bourbon king, calling for freer trade and the lifting of tariffs. It is true that out of this agrarian lobby some liberal leaders such as De Augustinis, Dragonetti, Scialoja, and Durini emerged as strong advocates for freer "nationally" integrated trade and as critics of the Bourbon regime. But the impulse was divided between manufacturers and agrarian interests. As John Davis has summarized the social cleavage within the Kingdom of Two Sicilies after 1848: manufacturers, in general, supported the restoration regime, while agrarian interests in general supported national changes.[50] In short, no coherent "nationalist" social coalition could emerge.

Why, however, was the pro-free-market agrarian lobby not a sufficiently strong advocate of national unification? According to Zamagni's figures, southern economic agricultural producers were both less productive and less reliant on domestic trade and exports than were their northern Italian counterparts, making them less supportive of national integration.[51] With lower output per hectare, some agricultural interests of course benefited from and supported continued tariffs.[52] But even with the better-developed, free-trade-oriented Neapolitan agrarian lobby that called in 1840, for example, for free trade, the focus was on freer *international* trade with Great Britain, not freer *national* trade with other Italian states.[53] One example of the impact of a reliance on international trade rather than domestic trade can be seen with the island of Sicily's agricultural producers, whose agriculture had shifted under the post-1815 Bourbon rule away from wheat production to the cultivation of "luxury" crops such as wine grapes, vegetables, and fruits.[54] For these agricultural regions, trade to Great Britain was ten times as important as to the regions of Italy's north.[55] As a consequence, as theories of protectionism would predict, little focus on freer "national trade" emerged even among the free-trade agrarian lobby. But even including trade with other regions and foreign countries, the southern regional states were less reliant on exports than northern Italian states. Table 4.4 shows the importance of exports for each regional state's economy, including manufacturing and agricultural products.

Taken together, both the structure of trade and lower levels of productivity inherited from the delayed commercialization left the labor-intensive and unproductive agricultural and manufacturing interests of southern Italy divided on the question of national unification. In fact, these fears, it appears in retrospect, were justified: When national unification did arrive in 1860, the high protective tariffs of the Bourbon regime were replaced by the much lower Piedmontese nationwide tariff system that most

TABLE 4.4

Exports Per Capita, Italian States, 1858 (in millions of lire)

State	Exports Per Capita
Kingdom of Piedmont	59.25
Parma-Modena	48.89
Tuscany	41.58
Lombardy-Veneto	31.43
Papal States	19.69
Kingdom of Two Sicilies	15.11

Note: My own calculations based on data provided by Zamagni, *Economic History of Italy*, 14–15.

economic historians argue contributed to the persistent underdevelopment of Italy's south.[56]

But why—and to what extent—was commercialization delayed in southern Italy? First, on the island of Sicily, the British, rather than Napoleon, ruled in the first fifteen years of the nineteenth century. Whereas feudalism was abolished even on the south Italian mainland in 1808, the process of eliminating feudalism followed a much more hesitant path on Sicily. In 1812 feudalism was for the first time "legally" eliminated, but because debt protection remained in place until 1824 and because the systems of entails and primogeniture were officially intact until 1815, commercialization was much less meaningful and occurred later than in Italy's north.[57] Even once complete, the agrarian reforms were still largely ineffective. Some of the problems were rooted in the weakness of the Bourbon state in Sicily after 1815, and others were simply rooted in a resistant society. Without sufficient administrators on the island of Sicily, the Neapolitan crown left the implementation of agrarian commercialization reforms in the hands of local councils who themselves were usually the traditional feudal landowners. Additionally, into the 1820s, there were vast "common lands" where one person owned the lands, another the trees, a third the right to cut down the trees, and fourth the pasture for his animals.[58] Similarly the elimination of guilds in the early 1820s on Sicily foundered for lack of governmental oversight; the guilds remained intact as secretive, quasi-criminal organizations that tightly controlled trades and remained under the influence of old family networks. With only minimally changed agricultural practices, the old families still in possession of most property, and a weak middle class that largely imitated the practices of the antimodern aristocracy, it makes sense, as Mack Smith argues, that "the latifundi went on being called 'fiefs,' the landowners 'feudatories,' and the peasantry 'villains' right down to the twentieth century."[59] To expect competitive and productive agricultural practices to emerge in this setting was, to the dismay of the Bourbon crown, unrealistic.

In addition, on the south Italian mainland, though commercialization spread slightly more effectively and rapidly than on Sicily, the Italian-language and English-language historiography makes clear that it took place still later and less effectively than in north central Italy.[60] As a consequence, in contrast to the extensive and successful pre-1800 reforms undertaken in Piedmont, Lombardy, and Tuscany, such reforms did not find their equivalent on the south Italian mainland until at least 1808. Even then, the commercializing land reforms of Joseph Bonaparte undertaken between 1808 and 1815 confronted barriers to implementation that made them largely ineffectual, and left south Italian society without a coherent "commercialized aristocracy" or middle class as well developed as in north central Italy.[61]

What evidence is there for this claim? First, efforts to deconcentrate the ramshackle latifundia and common lands that covered most of the south Italian mainland, though meeting some success, were confronted with societal and political challenges. One example of the political barriers to commercialization can be seen with the Feudal Commission, established by Joseph Bonaparte but led by Giuseppe Zurlo and charged with implementing agrarian reforms. In contrast to the equivalent state agency in northern Italy, the South Italian Feudal Commission did not even have an official land register with which to identify property, property ownership, and estimated values of property on the south Italian mainland.[62] In addition to such basic logistic problems, in contrast to north central Italy, two further societal obstacles in the Kingdom of Two Sicilies were the dominating position of ecclesiastical properties and the actual size of the feudal estates in southern Italy. While in the central Italian province of Romagna, church-owned property dropped from 42 percent of total agricultural land in 1783 to 11 percent in 1812, efforts in the Kingdom of Two Sicilies at privatizing agricultural land were faced with the fact that at the end of the eighteenth century nearly 70 percent of land was owned by the formidable Catholic Church.[63] Second, the smaller-scale system of *mezzadria* estates that dominated agricultural life in north central Italy were easier to dismantle than the massive latifundia of the south Italian mainland.[64] And despite all efforts at breaking the vast landholdings apart, land census data from the period reveals that these large estates remained intact until after World War II.[65]

In sum, while in the early-commercializing north central Italy a social alliance formed between agrarian and nascent manufacturing interests to support a national unification, in southern Italy and on the island of Sicily, the failure of commercializing reforms before 1815 left a divided society vis-à-vis the question of national unification: while some agrarian interests temporarily allied themselves with Cavour's free-trade agenda by the 1850s, small-scale manufacturing interests feared the creation of a national market, as did landowners still wedded to a precommercial agricultural structure. It is out of these conservative social classes that Bourbon sympathizers emerged and persisted even after the implosion of the regime in 1860–61. But beyond these pure economic reasons, the stalled commercialization of economic life in southern Italy failed to create the critical "modernized" social base that actively perceived national unification as the route to progress. As a result, it was only in Italy's north center that active, coherent, and explicit support for national unification was found.

A View from Above: The Transformation of State Interests in Italy

The effort to unify Italy not only was inspired by the social transformation that accompanied the commercialization of agriculture in northern Italy. If social transformation were a sufficient basis of national unification, the political leaders of the transforming societies of Tuscany and Lombardy—two rapidly commercializing societies—should have actively pursued national unification. That only Piedmont, the politically most powerful and "modernized" state, was the main political agent for national unification after 1848 draws our attention to the fact that not only social change but also a specific set of political factors are necessary to bring about the push for national unification. What precisely were these political factors that made Piedmont rather than Lombardy, Modena, Parma, or Tuscany the main political agent of national unification? And why was the Kingdom of Two Sicilies the greatest source of regional resistance to national unification?

First, quantitative evidence provides some initial clues that among the commercialized states of Italy's north, it was *only* Piedmont that had the *state capacity* to carry out the unification of Italy. Conversely, if we look at the two slowly commercializing regional of Italy's south, it was only the Kingdom of Two Sicilies that, as the largest state (in terms of population and population), had the capacity to attempt to resist national unification. Table 4.5 presents an assessment of the Italian states according to a crude measure of state size, the number of civil servants employed by each state, in order to provide a first step in understanding why Piedmont—of all commercialized states—initiated unification and why the Kingdom of Two Sicilies resisted unification.

TABLE 4.5
Size of Preunification Italian State Bureaucracies, 1859

State	Total Number of Civil Servants
Kingdom of Two Sicilies	24,970
Lombardy	11,399
Piedmont	10,950
Papal States	7,565
Tuscany	4,517
Modena	1,908
Parma	1,477

Source: Alberto Caracciolo, *Stato e società civile* (Turin: Einaudi Editore, 1960), 119.

As table 4.5 makes clear, the fight over unification in 1859–61 was be-tween two of the three largest Italian states, one—Piedmont—an "early" commercializing state and the other—the Kingdom of Two Sicilies—a "late" commercializing" state. It is in this sense that by incorporating the concept of political capacity, we can begin to look at the unification not only as a tale of "class conflict" or ideological triumph, but also as an instance of state formation.

But if commercialized regions generated social support for national uni-fication and political capacity was necessary to initiate unification, why did Piedmont and not Lombardy—also apparently a "large state"—initiate national unification? Do the data in table 4.5 challenge the hypothesis of state capacity emphasized throughout this chapter? In fact, it is here that a discussion of state capacity must move beyond the measure of state capac-ity—number of civil servants—presented in table 4.5. If we utilize a more expansive concept of state capacity that incorporates the notion that politi-cal capacity includes the political ability to transform society, then we see that the concept of state capacity remains important insofar as Piedmont was the only early commercializing region with the political capacity to transform the polities and societies of other Italian states by initiating unification.[66]

What evidence is there for this claim? First, Piedmont, unlike all other Italian states, including Lombardy, entered the Risorgimento not under direct or even indirect foreign rule. Not only did Piedmont as a conse-quence become the sole object of loyalty among nationalists searching for a political symbol of their struggle for national independence and auton-omy, but also the Piedmont crown had the administrative capacity of a centralized regional state and independent military to carry out unification. Especially after 1848, administrative reforms and expansion of state functions in Piedmont created a state with a budget that doubled between 1824 and 1859, greater public investment, a reorganized state administration, and an autonomous military that sought to prove its relevance on the European stage by participating in the Crimean War of 1859. By contrast, the administrative structures of Lombardy, though well developed, were simply part of the larger Austrian Empire, ruled from Vienna. Without a central administration, the northeastern Italian regions of Veneto and Lombardy were provinces in the vast imperial structure in which local rule was carried out by a governor in Milan who was the Austrian emperor's brother, Archduke Maximilian. The administration of taxation, education, accounting, and policing and military duties was carried out by local officials but always under the auspices of "home offices" in Vienna.[67] Without an autonomous centralized state structure, the political elites of Lombardy were either co-opted by Austrian rule or simply incapable of seeking national unification. Similarly, in small north central states such as Tuscany, Parma, Modena, and even the Papal States, all efforts to either lead or resist Italian unification were thwarted as a result of political incapacity. Indeed, the Tuscan military was described by contemporary observers in this period as consisting of twelve battalions of infantry, three squadrons of cavalry, and one or two pieces of artillery— "Nobody imagined they could have duties more serious than the embellishment of festivals."[68] Similarly, in the small state of Modena, in 1830, the duke of Modena sought to expand his state outwards to unify at least the northern parts of Italy. The efforts of the duke of this small regional state, with a population of less than half a million and with a miniature state budget, not surprisingly failed. Similarly, the proposals from Tuscany and the Papal States in 1847 for the creation of a German-like league of Italian states foundered when King Charles Albert of Piedmont unilaterally refused to participate. It was only when the state of Piedmont undertook unification in 1859 and afterwards that national unification had a realistic chance of success.

In addition to possessing the means of national unification, the Piedmontese crown, after 1848, had its own motives for national unification. First, its expanding budget, its administrative modernization, and the development of an effective military all left Piedmont in the late 1850s in a state of fiscal crisis. With the aim of being a power on the European stage, the Piedmontese crown was increasingly constrained by its own public finance limits. In table 4.6 we see that the Piedmontese crown, like the Prussian crown in Germany, was the leading debtor among the Italian states.

What was source of Piedmont's rapidly growing debt? Because it was the leading power in Italy, the ambitious crown's expenditures increased

TABLE 4.6
Public Debt Per Capita, Italian States, 1860

State	Debt Per Capita (lire)
Piedmont	248.8
Kingdom of Two Sicilies	76.9
Tuscany	73.2
Lombardy	47.3
Modena	47.2
Parma	29.4
Papal States	11.3

Note: My own calculations. Debt data reported by Shepard B. Clough, *The Economic History of Modern Italy* (New York: Columbia University Press, 1964), 43. Population data reported by Zamagni, *Economic History of Italy*, 14.

extremely rapidly when compared to the monarchies of the other Italian states.[69] Additionally, as table 4.7 makes clear, an ever-growing share of public debt was required to fund the costs of the growing Piedmontese military. Not only were military expenditures increasing each year, but military expenditures were increasing as a share of the ever-expanding state budget, totaling 55 percent in 1859, the year before national unification.

Why did this crisis in public finance lead to national unification? The expenditures on military and the rising debt only reinforced the view so dominant in this era, as Sheperd Clough has described it, "that national wealth could most readily be obtained by territorial acquisition."[70] From the perspective of officials within the Ministry of Finance, it was clear that one route to fiscal solvency was by expanding the tax base of Piedmont through territorial expansion. According to historians of Piedmont political development, this realization became increasingly predominant within the lower house of the parliament as well as in the Finance Ministry itself by the late 1850s, as the costs of war with Austria became overwhelming.

Though such considerations were important in creating a prenational coalition within the highest levels of state power in Piedmont in the late 1850s, more decisive was Cavour's concern, as prime minister, for maintaining his centrist's coalition's control over the Piedmontese parliament. It is in this sense that the Piedmontese king and Cavour jointly embraced the national agenda after 1859, like Bismarck and the Prussian king in the mid-1860s, as a tactical response to a changing Piedmontese society. One of the important lessons from the previous section on commercializing

TABLE 4.7
Makeup of Public Expenditures of Piedmontese State, 1830–59

	Total Expenditures	General Burdens	National Defense	Public Debt	Public Education	Other
1830	70,606	27%	41%	13%	1%	18%
1835	74,314	25%	43%	15%	1%	16%
1840	76,705	26%	44%	14%	1%	15%
1845	80,503	29%	40%	13%	1%	17%
1850	162,776	40%	25%	16%	1%	18%
1855	158,549	11%	36%	27%	1%	25%
1859	262,395	13%	55%	18%	1%	13%
1860	445,851	10%	62%	15%	1%	12%

Source: The original data can be found in G. Felloni, "La Spese Effettive e Il Bilancio degli Stati Sabaudi dal 1825 al 1860," in *Archivio Economico dell'Unificazione Italiana*, ser. 1, vol. 9 (1959): 5.

reforms is that throughout northern Italy, a transformed and modernizing society challenged the traditional political structures of restoration Italy. Part of this challenge included calls for free trade, democratic reforms, and above all national unification. Like Bismarck in Prussia, Cavour in Piedmont, however, was constrained by conservative and ecclesiastical elements who were resistant to change. To isolate the most conservative elements of the aristocracy, Cavour created in the early 1850s a self-defined "centrist" coalition out of the liberal-minded aristocracy and middle class in the Piedmontese parliament. In the mid-1850s, it was this famous *connubio* (marriage) that would defeat the conservative clerical forces. To achieve his goals of modernization, Cavour melded aristocratic loyalty to the Piedmontese crown with the liberal-democratic goal of national unification. After electoral successes of the conservative-clerical party led by Thaon di Revel in the mid-1850s, Cavour discovered the "national" solution that would assure the dominance of his centrist coalition. It is with this domestic goal and the goal of upsetting the balance of power on the European stage that the expansion of Piedmont into other parts of Italy was conceived by Cavour in 1859.[71] Of course, as the next chapter will make clear, the proximate impetus that actually resulted in troops being sent to southern Italy to begin the process of annexation was less intentional: to maintain control over unfolding events in the fall of 1860 to prevent the intervention of northern radicals in support of revolution in Sicily. But nevertheless, the political conditions—within the Finance Ministry, within the court of Victor Emmanuel, and within the halls of the Piedmontese parliament—had made the situation ripe, finally, for the Piedmontese pursuit of national unification.

But how were to understand the resistance of the Kingdom of Two Sicilies? And what form did this resistance actually take? The Kingdom of Two Sicilies, led by the young King Francis after 1859, was a massive, sprawling state with a military of nearly one hundred thousand, a bureaucracy more than twice as large as the next largest Italian state, and a population three times as large as the next largest Italian state.[72] Yet, without mobilized social support for national unification and without the administrative effectiveness to even rule Sicily, the prospect of the Kingdom of Two Sicilies *initiating* national unification of Italy has barely been conceived as a useful historical counterfactual. But if we want to understand the contours of regional political *resistance* to national unification, it is important to note that into the summer of 1860, it was the Neapolitan crown, its military, and its massive civil service system that stood as the greatest barrier to national unification. That the regime imploded by the fall of 1860, and that the king eventually fled to Bavaria, does not change the fact that until the late 1870s, the continuing source of resistance to the Piedmontese-imposed national unification came from the territories formerly ruled by the Bourbon crown and came from what Piedmontese officials insisted were the Bourbon "loyalists" who continued to present problems of governability for the Piedmontese state.[73] If Piedmont and Prussia provide analogous example of initiating regional states, then the Kingdom of Two Sicilies, like Bavaria in Germany, served as the main hostile counterweight to national unification, giving shape to the national critical juncture in the development of the Italian nation-state.

CONCLUSION

Despite the role of personality and chance in national unification of Italy, it is still possible to identify, in broad strokes, why unification happened when it happened, and why some regional states initiated national unification and others did not. First, the successful commercialization of agriculture created a pronational social coalition out of liberal-minded aristocrats and a new middle class, especially in Italy's northern regions. But it was only in the state in northern Italy without direct foreign occupation and rule—Piedmont—that the process of unification could be initiated. Though Cavour himself, Italy's nationalist hero, had neither visited southern Italy nor had any political interests in Italy south of Tuscany, by the late 1850s, the "national" solution to a set of domestic and international political developments proved to be increasingly appealing. While commercialized Lombard nationalists remained frustrated under the rule of the Austrian Empire without the means for national unification, the underdeveloped Kingdom of Two Sicilies had the geographical size but did not have the social base to support a project of national unification. In fact, only the Piedmontese state, which was supported by a loyal regional aristocracy, had the *means, motives,* and *opportunity* to unify Italy. It was, as Sidney Tarrow has argued, the successful combination of two factors that allowed national unification to proceed: *state-seeking nationalism* (on behalf of newly commercialized middle and aristocratic classes of Italy's north) and *state-led nationalism* (on behalf of the Piedmontese crown and administrative state).[74] Taken together, these two conditions gave rise to the "national moment" in which the new nation-state was to be designed. But the persistence of regional tensions between north and south, between Bourbon "loyalists" and the Piedmontese state-builders, would exert influence on how the new nation-state would be actually be constructed.

Chapter Five

FROM STRONG REGIONAL LOYALTIES TO A UNITARY SYSTEM: NATIONAL UNIFICATION BY CONQUEST AND THE CASE OF ITALY

> There seems no doubt that fusion [between north and
> south] would make Sicily the Ireland of Italy and this,
> instead of making our nationality more compact and
> secure, would be a real and perennial source of weakness
> from which an enemy could profit.
> —FRANCESCO FERRARA, 1860[1]

As THE LAST three chapters have made clear, the deeply embedded regional forces for and against national unification were quite similar in Italy and Germany in the 1860s. Additionally, before unification an ideological commitment to a federal solution to the problem of Italy's regional diversity among key Piedmontese political leaders made federalism appear to be a viable institutional alternative for the new Italy. And finally, as a relatively weak military power vis-à-vis the rest of Italy, Piedmontese officials faced stiff though disorganized regional resistance, especially from Italy's southern provinces, until the 1870s.

These cultural, ideological, and power-structural preconditions ought to have led, according to most theories of federalism, to the successful creation of what William Riker calls a federal "bargain" among the regional states of Italy.[2] But, despite the presence of these conditions, events by 1859 took a centralizing turn. Between 1859 and 1865, Piedmontese political leaders adopted a highly centralized political system in which (1) the formerly independent regional states had no formal representation in the new national government, (2) the independent regional states had no public finance discretion (i.e., no taxing and spending discretion), and (3) the independent regional states lost all administrative autonomy. Neither the visions of Italy's *federalisti* intellectuals such as Carlo Cattaneo and Francesco Ferrara nor the decentralizing plans of Piedmontese Ministry of Interior officials such as Marco Minghetti and Luigi Farini were enough to prevent Italy's regions from been literally erased from the political map as formal political units.

The Argument: Unification by Conquest
and Its Institutional Legacies

To explain this case of a "failed" effort to create a federal political system, despite the presence of the three factors normally cited to explain federalism, this chapter argues that a fourth dynamic prevented the successful creation of a federal system. The main argument is that the central problem confronting Piedmontese state-builders was the *infrastructural incapacity* in Italy's annexed regions. After centuries of foreign rule in Italy, and an incomplete experience of political modernization in Italy's prenational independent regional states, Piedmontese officials confronted the problems not only of regional resistance but also of regional institutional weakness, especially in the Kingdom of Two Sicilies—a regional state that constituted 36 percent of Italy's territory and 37 percent of its population in 1859. But it was not only in the extreme case of the Kingdom of Two Sicilies that Piedmont annexed a state without the capacity to do the work of modern governance. To varying degrees, the other five states (Tuscany, Papal States, Modena, Parma, and Lombardy-Veneto) that Piedmont inherited in 1859–60 were also marred by a history of incomplete rationalization of authority after 1815 (i.e., no constitutions), no parliamentary structures, and, to varying degrees, poorly developed administrative institutions.[3] Available evidence suggests that as a result of this incomplete state building *before* national unification, the states Piedmont inherited possessed limited institutional capacity to do the basic work of modern governance: (1) maintain civil order, (2) tax resources effectively, (3) conscript manpower, and (4) implement policy goals.[4]

But how did these preexisting regional institutional conditions of low political development and low infrastructural capacity translate themselves into a unitary state for Italy? Here we must focus on the important role played by Piedmontese officials and the post-1859 interim leaders of the Italian states outside of Piedmont as both sets of actors sought to orchestrate the unification of the seven Italian states in this context of uneven levels of infrastructural capacity across the Italian peninsula. Since the governing center-right coalition within the Piedmontese political leadership inherited what it largely regarded as ineffective regional political structures and actors that could not serve as effective monarchical negotiation partners in the process of national unification, Piedmontese officials found themselves adopting a centralizing pattern of political authority during the critical years of 1859–65, often violently so, despite their own "liberal" ideological commitment to decentralization.[5] Additionally, because of the absence of local institutional resources to manage local problems and the resulting revolutionary atmosphere of the Italian Risorgimento, interim leaders of regions outside of Piedmont, for example, in Emilia, Romagna, and Tuscany, rushed to adopt Piedmontese legislation and pushed in 1859 for rapid annexation by Piedmont to avoid papal or Austrian intervention that might fill the power vacuum left behind by the weak states of the restoration period. Like Prussia in its project of national unification, Piedmont feared foreign intervention. But unlike Prussia, Piedmont was without regional governments in place and without the time to construct them. As a result, the easiest and quickest route to national unification for Piedmont was the adoption of a centralizing strategy—or what I call "unification by conquest." By responding to pressures from within and outside of Piedmont to carry out unification rapidly, the Piedmontese leadership itself unwittingly undermined the infrastructural capacity of the potential subnational regional governments by destroying the political entities that might have served as autonomous subnational regional governments in a federal but united Italy. It was thus the *unification by conquest* path of nation-state formation itself that doomed subsequent efforts to create a federal polity in Italy in the 1860s, 1870s, and 1880s.[6]

This chapter will present two types of evidence to support my argument. First, I will present original institutional-level data that show, when compared to the states that Prussia inherited after its national unification in 1866 and 1871, Piedmont absorbed regional states in 1859–61 that were plagued by deep problems of infrastructural capacity. Second, this chapter will focus on how Piedmontese state-building elites and interim leaders outside of Piedmont themselves interpreted and responded to the gap in institutional level of development between Piedmont and the rest of Italy. Here, I will focus on the perceptions and actions of Piedmontese and non-Piedmontese leaders as they carried out the three tasks of nation-state formation in the years between 1859 and 1865: (1) ending the war of unification, (2) forging the union, and (3) making the new rules of the new political entity. This chapter contends that these three tasks of national unification are generic features of the process of nation-state formation in the creation of any new polity, though the distinctive form they take varies according to national experience. In the Italian case, it was both the institutional weakness outside of Piedmont and the resulting "centralizing" Piedmontese response to each of these "tasks" of national unification that further debilitated regional governments in Italy after national unification. Though the three stages of unification or "tasks" of unification that I have identified were not always in the minds of the political actors themselves, the Piedmontese pattern of national unification—"unification by conquest"—had an important impact on the final institutional outcome that emerged *after* national unification. At each of the three stages of national unification, Piedmontese officials were confronted with the perceived and real problem of institutional incapacity in Italy's regions. As a result, also at each stage, Piedmontese officials were tempted by and turned to an explicitly "unitary" rather than "federal" solution to the challenges of national unification.

In this sense, as my analysis will make clear, the response of Piedmontese officials as they faced each new task of nation-state formation contained what path dependence theorists have called a "self-reinforcing" or "positive feedback" dynamic—a logic that gives a set of events a causal weight of its own as an initial move in a particular direction encourages further movement along that same path.[7] In the context of Italian unification, the centralizing responses to each of the three tasks of national unification increased the likelihood, over the course of the six years of institutional creation (1859–65), that Piedmontese officials would adopt a unitary political system. In short, it was not Piedmont's military strength, as Riker's classic argument might expect, that led to the creation of a unitary system. Rather, it was precisely Piedmont's partly self-inflicted inability to devolve authority to Italy's weak regional governments that forced Piedmontese leaders to adopt a unitary political system for Italy.

INHERITANCE OF INFRASTRUCTURAL INCAPACITY IN ITALY'S REGIONS: OVERVIEW OF THE PRENATIONAL ITALIAN REGIONAL STATES

Though Napoleon is often credited with having thoroughly modernized Italy's political structures in his brief rule of the peninsula, the project of political modernization was in fact uneven and incomplete. With the return of the seven independent restoration regimes in 1815, the political development of the Italian states stalled along three dimensions: First, any existing parliamentary structures were undone; second, monarchs ruled once again—unconstrained by constitutions—according to the absolutist principle of divine right; and third, administrative structures, though formally differentiated and modernized, became once again informally subject to the whim of personalistic and unchecked monarchs.[8] The causes of the incomplete political development of Italy's regional governments—and the regression to pre-1800 conditions *after* 1815—are themselves the subject of a wide-ranging research agenda.[9] But for our purposes what is critical is that along three dimensions the Italian regional states that Piedmont inherited in 1860 were *less* politically developed than their German counterparts that Prussia inherited in 1866 and 1870: (1) the development of constitutional rule, (2) the existence of parliamentary structures, and (3) the development of administrative structures. This incomplete political development in the absolutist Italian kingdoms had a very immediate consequence: The Italian states suffered from poorly developed institutional capacity to do the work of modern governments: tax, conscript manpower, maintain civil order, and carry out political projects of social and economic reform.[10]

As recent scholarship on the restoration period in Italy has taught us, there were important variations across time and among the seven states themselves.[11] For example, the period following 1815 was the most reactionary: Victor Emanuel I in Piedmont briefly abandoned all of the Napoleonic parliamentary, constitutional, and administrative reforms, as did Duke Francesco IV in Modena, and Pope Leone XII after 1823 in the Papal States. But, simultaneously, the regimes of the grand duke in Tuscany, the Medici in Naples, and the Austrians in Lombardy-Veneto pursued policies of greater moderation. Here, and eventually in the Papal States and Piedmont as well, political leaders adopted a political structure of consultative monarchy in which local councils served a quasi-representative function, with the aim of forestalling the demand for a parliament.[12] Likewise, though not granting a parliament, the Medici in the Kingdom of Two Sicilies viewed administrative centralization, or what was called administrative "modernization," as a route to preserving absolutist control of the distant regions of their kingdom.

Nevertheless, despite any gradual reform efforts, in all of the Italian states *before* 1848—including Piedmont—parliaments had been eliminated, constitutions were nonexistent, and administrative structures, though in place, were hardly autonomous and independent. Until 1848, none of the Italian states, with the exceptions of Piedmont and the Kingdom of Two Sicilies, had yet undergone the hallmark of administration modernization: formal differentiation. All government functions were still fused under each monarch's *consiglio di stato*.[13] As a result, though centralized, administrative structures were viewed as means of assuring monarchical divine-right control over the state territory, were frequently subject to personnel purges, and were explicitly not autonomous from the personalistic concerns of state monarchs.[14]

Though the variations before 1848 were important, even more important in shaping post-1860 developments were the constitutional, parliamentary, and administrative structures of the Italian regional states *after* 1848. Table 5.1 presents a summary of each of the Italian cases in terms of the three dimensions of political development that I have identified as well each state's cumulative political development score for the period between 1850 and 1859.

It is true that the tumultuous revolutions of 1848 had left all the Italian states—with the exception of Lombardy-Veneto—with constitutions and parliaments, usually modeled on the French constitution of 1830. Nevertheless, as table 5.1 shows, by 1852, all but one of these constitutions and parliaments had again been revoked and suspended, and absolutist regimes had been reinstated, leaving Piedmont as the single Italian regional

TABLE 5.1
Political Development of Italian State Structures, 1852–59

	Piedmont	Two Sicilies	Modena	Parma	Tuscany	Lombardy	Papal States
1. *Rationalization of authority* (i.e., working constitution)	2	0	0	0	0	0	0
2. *Parliamentary tradition* (i.e., parliament with access to budget process)	2	0	0	0	0	0	0
3. *Development of administration* (i.e., differentiation and concentration of bureaucracy)	2	1	1	2	2	2	1
Cumulative political development score	6	1	1	2	2	2	1

Note: The cases were coded using an ordinal coding system: 0 = not existent, 1 = existent but weak, 2 = existent and effective. While it is relatively easy to code each of the states for the existence or nonexistence of constitutions and parliaments, the coding for administrative development is less straightforward. My focus, as becomes clear in the narrative description in the text, is on the *concentration* and *specialization* of tax administration structure, which are taken to be indicators of administrative development more generally.

state with a functioning parliament and constitution until national unification in 1860. Scholars of the restoration period argue, additionally, that in the post-1848 period it was the weakness of parliamentary and constitutional structures that hindered the growth of the third dimension of state development—the administrative development of state structures.

But, as table 5.1 makes clear, in contrast to the record of Italian prenational regional states along the parliamentary and constitutional dimensions of political development, none of the restoration Italian states were as weak in terms of the development of administrative structures. Indeed, after 1848, all of the Italian regional states, including the absolutist Bourbon state, sought to re-create some of the main elements of the "modern" administrative prefectoral systems that Napoleon had imposed earlier in the century. First, after 1848, all the restoration states multiplied the number of ministries, creating differentiated administrative structures, usually subdividing the state's functions, as Piedmont had since 1814, into separate ministries of (1) foreign affairs, (2) finance, (3) domestic affairs, and (4) war and navy.[15] Likewise, after 1848, all of the restoration state ministries were run by bureaucrats with some level of bureaucratic autonomy. Additionally, in the 1830s and 1840s, each of the Italian states followed the European-wide trend of establishing official state statistical offices to collect economic, demographic, and social statistics, a development that both reflected and reinforced the state's ability to govern.[16] And finally, all of the states' administrations were organized as centralized *intendant* or *prefectoral* systems in which the regional monarch had direct administrative access to the "periphery" of his state.[17]

But despite these relatively "modernizing" administrative developments, even after 1848 the Italian regional states lagged far behind their German counterparts in terms of the *concentration* and *specialization* of administrative structures. One important and revealing area of comparison is tax administration, a defining area of the structure of modern states.[18] First, in terms of administrative *concentration*, though there were seven states on the Italian peninsula until 1860, there were nine different zones of tax administration: Neither the monarch of the Kingdom of Two Sicilies nor the political leadership of the Papal States had a monopoly across their entire territory over public revenue. Instead, in the Kingdom of Two Sicilies, an entirely independent tax administration set and collected taxes on the island of Sicily. Similarly, in the northern part of the Papal States—in Emilia, Marches, and Umbria—an independent tax administration, guided by different laws and different regulations, oversaw tax administration.[19] This lack of institutional concentration—especially in the important area of tax collection—was viewed with trepidation by Piedmontese Finance Ministry officials in the early 1860s, who frequently reported back to Cavour on the "deplorable" condition of the weak and fragmented tax administration in regions outside of Piedmont.[20]

Second, in terms of administrative *specialization*, the tax administrative structures—to use the same example—diverged from each other (and the German states) in their complexity of organization. Though after 1848 all of the Italian states finally had separate tax administrative structures, they differed both in the number of employees and in the number of agencies within the tax administration ministry. The most specialized tax administrative structure was in Piedmont, which in 1859 had twenty-one separate agencies and seven thousand employees. The least specialized tax administrative structure was in the admittedly much smaller state of Modena, with only ten agencies and one thousand employees.[21] In short, we see that if political modernization means the development of parliamentary institutions, constitutions, and the concentration and specialization of administrative structures, then the Italian states were marked by two important characteristics: (1) low levels of development across all of the states outside of Piedmont and (2) a large gap between Piedmont and the rest of the Italian states.

What were the consequences of these structures for the capacity of each of the Italian states to do the basic work of government—taxation, con-

TABLE 5.2
Infrastructural Capacity of Italian Regional States, 1850–60

	Extractive Capacity: (state revenue per capita, in lire)	Coercive Capacity (conscription rate: military personnel as % of male population)	Regulatory Capacity (enrollment rate of primary school age children)
Piedmont	32.2	2.3%	93%
Two Sicilies	14.2	2.0%	18%
Papal States	14.7	0.7%	25%–35%
Tuscany	19.2	2.0%	32%
Modena	17.9	1.6%	36%
Parma	22	1.2%	36%
Lombardy-Veneto	NA	NA	90%
Ratio of piedmont to average of remaining states	1.83 : 1	1.53 : 1	2.3 : 1

Source: Public revenue data from Izzo, La finanza pubblica, 123; military personnel and population data from Singer and Small, National Materials Capabilities Data; enrollment data from Zamagni, Economic History of Italy, 14–15.

scription, implementing social and policy reform, and maintaining civil stability? Scholars of the state have long agreed on the causal nexus between political development, conceived in the terms I have outlined, and the "infrastructural capacity" of state structures.[22] As a result, it is not surprising that narrative accounts as well as the limited data that are available suggest that the Italian regional states—with the exception of Piedmont—suffered from a deep infrastructural incapacity when compared in absolute terms to the German regional states in the same period. Additionally, and perhaps even more importantly for the purposes of this study, the *relative* gap between Piedmont and the states it inherited was much greater than the relative gap between Prussia and the states it inherited several years later. In table 5.2 we can see an overview of each of the Italian states—using an original dataset that utilizes three measures that capture three distinctive dimensions of state capacity: extractive capacity, coercive capacity, and regulatory capacity.[23]

By using the measure of "state revenue per capita" we can assess the ability of each of the Italian states to extract revenue from its population.[24] By using the measure of "military personnel as a percentage of male population," we can assess the conscription capacity or coercive capacity of each state.[25] Finally, by using the measure "enrollment rate of elementary-age children," we can assess the capacity of the state to penetrate and transform society through education, one of the key arenas of societal transformation for state leaders in the nineteenth century.[26] Taken together, as table 5.2 shows, these indicators allow us to compare the infrastructural capacity of each of the Italian states in the decade before national unification. The data reveal a large gap between Piedmont and the rest of the Italian states; Piedmont on average had twice as much state capacity as the remaining five states, a gap that is much larger than among the German states, as the next chapter will show.[27]

First, in terms of the *extractive capacity*, table 5.2 shows that Piedmont's public revenue per capita was highest in the year before national unification, while the Kingdom of Two Sicilies' was lowest. While Piedmont's public finance administration possessed the capacity to extract a revenue at levels only slightly below other European nation-states in the period, the Papal States, the Kingdom of Two Sicilies, and other states lagged further behind.[28] In large part, the variations across the states in terms of extractive capacity reflect the fact that different state structures generated different burdens and structures of revenue collection.[29] These data also confirm the secondary literature that so frequently discusses the problems of tax protests and rural revolts in the southern parts of Italy.[30]

Second, the *conscription rates* of all of the Italian states—which averaged only 1.6 percent of total male population in 1859 (the year before national unification)—reflect the difficulties, especially in the Kingdom of Two Sicilies and Papal States, in constructing a reliable military. Here, the data again suggest a state infrastructurally weaker than in Germany (where, as the next chapter will show, the national average conscription rate was over 2.5 percent). The secondary literature also confirms that in times of political crisis or civic uprising, as in 1848 and 1860, the Papal States and Kingdom of Two Sicilies called upon "international" forces— usually, the Austrians—to support their regimes. By calling in foreign forces, the regional states of Italy both displayed their inherent institutional incapacity to carry out one of the basic functions of a state—to maintain political stability—and further weakened their own state capacity by calling in external actors to substitute for an effective domestic military vis-à-vis their own population.

Finally, in terms of the capacity to actually implement policy or to *regulate* social life—an area that scholars of the restoration period have only begun to explore—the Italian states, especially in Italy's south, exhibited relative weakness. As scholars of European state-building have long noted, the novel penetration by the state into new realms including public health provision, public education, and social welfare after 1815 reflected the growing visibility of states and the growing capacity and willingness of state elites to regulate social life in their territories. No mission, as James Sheehan has argued in the German context, was so important for nineteenth-century state-building elites as the mission of educating its citizenry.[31] The data in table 5.2 on enrollment rates in primary schools reflect the fact that this ability to regulate social life was furthest developed in Piedmont and Lombardy-Veneto (93 percent and 90 percent enrollment rates respectively), while in the remaining states, such as the Papal States and the Kingdom of Two Sicilies, the state educated less than 30 percent of children of primary school age. Not only reflecting different levels of economic development, these figures more directly reflect institutional developments in Italy: While Piedmont, Lombardy, and Tuscany each had a Ministry of Public Instruction in the 1850s, Modena, the Papal States, and Parma did not.[32] Interestingly, the Kingdom of Two Sicilies did in fact have a Ministry of Public Instruction, but the number of public school teachers employed as a percentage of the population was in fact lower in the Kingdom of Two Sicilies than in any other Italian state.[33] Most importantly, there was a general perception that in Naples, for example, as one historian of education has put it, "The system of elementary education did not need reform; it needed to be created."[34] We see, once again, both a real and perceived gap in the ability of Italian states to carry out one of the basic functions of modern government. In sum, the Italian regional states were constrained by uneven experiences of state building that left state structures and personnel, especially in Italy's south, with low levels of institutional capacity to collect taxes, conscript manpower, maintain civil stability, and to administer basic programs of economic and social policy. Although during the 1850s, Bourbon efforts were made to provide a more solid political basis for the Neapolitan state, the combined effect of institutional weakness and the *perception* of institutional weakness by Piedmontese officials reporting back to Piedmont in the years of 1859–60 gave rise to a "centralizing" temptation among political leaders in Piedmont.

It is in this sense that as a result of infrastructural incapacity in Italy's annexed regions the three tasks of national unification—ending the war of unification, forging a new union, and making new rules for the nation-state—followed a decidedly *centralizing* path in Italy between 1859 and 1865. The following three sections will show how the Piedmontese response to each of these three tasks of nation-state formation was shaped by the persistence of infrastructural incapacity in Italy's annexed regions, giving rise to a centralizing dynamic in which the political actors, political norms, and formal rules that would have given rise to federalism were nonexistent. As a consequence, the centralist temptation was simply too weighty for Piedmontese officials to resist.

First Task of Nation-State Formation: Ending the War of Unification

Recent scholarship has taught us that how a war is ended has critical institutional consequences.[35] It is the main contention of this section that the ending a civil or war of national unification has important consequences for how power is eventually distributed geographically in a new nation-state by institutionalizing or eliminating important political actors: If in a war of unification the political center undertakes an *unconditional conquest* of the periphery, it is more likely regional political actors will be eliminated and that a unitary political structure will follow. If, by contrast, the political center combines coercion with a negotiated or diplomatic settlement with the periphery, it is more likely that regional political leaders will be institutionalized and a federal political system will follow. Though Piedmontese state-builders may not have been aware of it themselves, it is for this reason that the *first* analytically decisive choice they made on their way to national unification—and where they began their divergence away from Prussian state-builders who faced nearly the identical task six years later—was with the question of how to end the wars of unification of 1859–60.

For the Piedmontese, like the Prussians facing the Austrians and south Germans in 1866, two options were considered: (1) an unconditional conquest in which the victors would set the terms of conquest without consultation with the defeated, and existing elites and institutions would be dismantled across the entire future nation-state, or (2) a negotiated conquest in which the victors would set the terms of conquest in consultation with the defeated, and existing elites and institutions would be left intact. In 1859, it looked as if Piedmont might adopt a state-building strategy of accommodation similar to Prussia's in 1866—annexation of some states in the north and center but leaving intact and independent the states of the south. Despite Cavour's ideological preference for negotiation among constituent states as well as international pressure to pursue a negotiated peace with the south, key events intervened that were prompted by the particular institutional landscape of the Italian peninsula. As a result, Piedmontese leaders by 1860 were tempted by centralization across the entire peninsula. As chapter 6 will demonstrate, Prussia's annexation of northern and some central states was coupled with accommodations to the states of southern Germany. By contrast, Piedmont pursued a complete annexation in *both* halves of Italy—first in Italy's northern and central states in 1859–60 and second in southern Italy in the summer and fall of 1860. Like Bismarck, Cavour sought the quickest and easiest route to national unification. Unlike the Prussian minister president, however, because Cavour was carrying out his project of national unification with a set of states lacking similar levels of infrastructural capacity, he adopted a war-ending strategy of unconditional conquest that was unintentionally the first step on the path to a unitary state for Italy.

Indeed, before the wars of unification began 1859, Count Cavour's and King Victor Emmanuel II's territorial aims were moderate. Not only did Cavour's Piedmont spend less money in the 1850s on military than did the Bourbon Kingdom of Two Sicilies, but Cavour's military was decidedly smaller than that of the Bourbon crown's.[36] Beginning as early as May 1858, Cavour had assured both his own king and the French emperor, for example, that the Kingdom of Two Sicilies was well beyond Piedmontese ambitions.[37] After secretly meeting with Napoleon III at the French spa of Plombieres on July 23, 1858, to seek French support for his plans, Cavour proudly summarized the agreement struck in a memorandum to the Piedmontese king.

> After a long discussion, we agreed on the following principles: the valley of the Po, the Romagna and the Legations would constitute the Kingdom of Upper Italy, under the rule of the House of Savoy. Rome and its immediate surroundings would be left to the Pope. The rest of the Papal states together with Tuscany would form the Kingdom of Central Italy . The borders of the Kingdom of Naples would be left unchanged; and the four Italian states would form a confederation on the pattern of the German Confederation.[38]

As a result, in the beginning of the critical year of 1859, only the issue of the Austrian occupation of northern Italy appeared at center stage in the drama of European politics. In response to increasing tension between Austria and France in January 1859 that had sent stock markets into free fall across Europe, Cavour—as head of the only entirely independent Italian state—finalized a "defensive alliance" with France that would assure France's assistance in case of a "defensive" war with Austria.[39] But behind the rhetoric of a "defensive alliance," Cavour also hoped in 1859 to lead Piedmont into war with Austria with his limited immediate territorial aim of annexing the northern part of Italy to create an "Upper Italian Kingdom," similar to Prussia's aims in 1866 in northern Germany.[40] Cavour hoped to evict the Austrian rulers of Lombardy to assure Piedmontese hegemony in northern Italy, leaving central Italy and southern Italy independent.[41] To provoke such a war, Cavour sought a casus belli that would allow the Piedmontese to evict Austria from Italy's north, establishing Piedmontese control of the north. With the active help of the French, Piedmont was successful; as a result of the peace struck at Villafranca in July 1859 between Austria and France, Napoleon exchanged continued Austrian domination of Venice for Lombardy, which it in turned passed along to Piedmont.[42]

But, given the argument about infrastructural capacity, why in 1859 did Piedmont adopt a strategy of conquest to annex the states in central Italy, relatively well developed and institutionalized states and not originally in Piedmont's agreements with the French? In fact, despite Piedmont's efforts at negotiated settlements with key states such as Tuscany, the internal structure of these states made a "negotiated" process of unification unfeasible, making unification by conquest necessary. At first, French resistance to Piedmontese plans of annexation prompted a search for a negotiated solution. In the state of Tuscany for example, Cavour developed a twofold strategy that would be used as a model of incorporation in other states: First, after 1858 Cavour strategically fomented nationalist resistance with the aid of La Farina and the National Society.[43] Second, Cavour sent an envoy to the state, seeking diplomatic relations with the head of state. As early as 1857, Cavour's envoy, Carlo Boncompagni, was instructed to convince Tuscany's Grand Duke Leopold to adopt policies supportive of national unification. Again on March 14, 1859, Boncompagni more concretely proposed to Leopold an alliance with Piedmont to evict Austria from the peninsula and an assurance of the continued autonomy of Tuscany and its ruler.[44] But the grand duke and his close circle of advisers resisted, despite growing unrest among Radicals and Democrats inside Tuscany who were increasingly organized along national lines by La Farina.[45] Finally, with the prospect of war with Austria nearing in April 1859, Cavour insisted that Boncompagni make one last effort at an alliance with Piedmont on April 25, 1859.[46] But again, the proposal was rejected. With the outbreak of war, the grand duke's regime imploded, and the grand duke fled.

The Tuscan grand duke's misdiagnosis of his own population's resistance to his regime as well as his unwillingness to negotiate can be attributed to his absolutist rule. Indeed, as theories of international cooperation and conflict have demonstrated, nonparliamentary states are less likely to come to peaceful settlements and forge alliances.[47] But even more important for the development of the future Italian nation-state, the fragile structure of the absolutist state of Tuscany meant that the grand duke's flight from the city of Florence in the last days of April 1859 left behind an institutional vacuum that could only be filled by local elites such as Ricasoli, Ridolfi, and Salvagnoli. With the grand duke's rapid departure, Boncompagni reported to Cavour that he immediately feared the prospect of "revolution" and "anarchy."[48] Moreover, he reported to Cavour the potential need for a "military government in order to provide for war and to prevent disorder."[49] In response, Cavour asked Boncompagni himself to form an interim government in Tuscany.[50] In a pattern unthinkable in the German states but that would repeat itself in Italy over the course of 1859–60, the diplomatic envoy *himself* became a state builder for Piedmont; without state negotiation partners to forge union, Piedmontese officials themselves took on the role of state builders. The resulting interim Tuscan government was dominated by figures sympathetic to Piedmont such as Ricasoli, who feared the return of the grand duke or Austrian or French intervention. As a result, the interim government called for immediate annexation by Piedmont. The same dynamic of failed efforts at diplomatic negotiation followed by absolutist implosion occurred in the other central Italian states of Modena, Parma, and even the northern provinces of the Papal States.[51]

Though the Villafranca Peace Treaty of July 11, 1859, restored the grand duke as well as the rulers of Modena and Parma, the Villafranca accord was essentially a failure because the dynamic of unification by conquest was already under way. In the summer and fall of 1859, new assemblies in Modena, Parma, Tuscany as well as the legations of the Papal States voted for direct annexation to Piedmont, setting the stage for accession to Piedmont in spring 1860.[52] In short, the absolutist states even in Italy's central regions assured that any diplomatic efforts that were attempted failed, prompting intervention by Piedmont and the elimination of the monarchical leaders who might have negotiated an end to the wars of unification.

What about the Kingdom of Two Sicilies? Though "unification by conquest" would soon be adopted as the strategy of annexation in the south, it is important to note that the annexation of the north and central states in early 1860 did not automatically mean unification by conquest would be necessary in the Kingdom of Two Sicilies.[53] In fact, Piedmont's relations to the south remained diplomatic even after Piedmont had begun the process of directly absorbing the states of the north. The strikingly limited territorial interest in southern Italy, like Bismarck's territorial aims vis-à-vis southern Germany in 1866, reflected both the configuration of international power in Europe and Cavour's instinctive political pragmatism. First, beginning in 1858, all Cavour's agreements with France assured a nervous Napoleon that Piedmont would respect the existing borders of the Kingdom of Two Sicilies. Since France's interest in Italian affairs was limited to the expulsion of Austria out of Italy's north, any moves to assert Piedmontese hegemony beyond the agreed upon borders of an "Upper Italian Kingdom" would, from the perspective of Napoleon III, upset the balance of powers in Europe. Likewise, England officially supported France; Austria, Russia, and Prussia advocated any possible solution that would save the regime in Naples.[54]

Second, Cavour, the main architect of Piedmontese policy, was a pragmatist who had never himself even been to southern Italy. His aim, which he achieved finally with the plebiscite of March 11, 1860, was the union of central and northern Italy under the leadership of Piedmont. Constrained, like Bismarck was in Germany, by the international structure of power, Cavour at first sought a formal *diplomatic alliance* with the Bourbon leadership of Naples that by definition assured the continued independent existence of the southern Italian state. Cavour imagined a future Italy that was acceptable to the French and in which Piedmont controlled Italy's north and the Bourbon crown controlled Italy's south. To Cavour, a German-like confederation might eventually move in the direction of national unification. But Cavour was acutely aware of French concerns and as a result envisioned this unification as only taking place through a gradual and careful process of negotiation. In August 1860 future prime minister Crispi derisively called this the "artichoke" policy, in which unification would be achieved by peeling off each of the resistant regions, one by one, rather than by "courting disaster by staking the whole process of unification on a single throw."[55]

To support his cautious vision of a negotiated settlement between the Kingdom of Two Sicilies and Piedmont, in May 1859 Cavour—following the model he established in Tuscany—sent his diplomatic envoy, Count Salmour, with a proposal from the Piedmontese king Victor Emannuel to the new twenty-two-year-old Bourbon king of Naples, Francis II. Cavour wrote Count Salmour with King Victor Emanuel's message:

> His Royal Highness has chosen to send Your Lordship on a special mission to the court of Naples for the purposes of expressing to King Francis II His Majesty's condolences on the death of his illustrious father. . . . Your Lordship's appointment, however, must not be considered merely the act of an affectionate relative; it has also a highly serious political purpose, which is to unite the two courts in thought and deed . . .[we can ask the new king if] he would join forces with Piedmont, declare war on Austria, and send part of his army to the Po and Adige to fight for Italy alongside the king of Sardinia and the emperor of France. . . . Your Lordship must demonstrate to the king, in the interests of his dynasty, the advantages of this alliance.[56]

Cavour, like Bismarck in Germany, made all efforts to conduct a diplomatic and negotiated relationship with Italy's Southern Kingdom even after events had begun to spin out of control in Sicily in April 1860. In the spring of that year, the possibility of pursuing a negotiated end to the war of unification with Austria by making a diplomatic settlement with Italy's Southern Kingdom was still extremely likely. As late as April 1860, King Victor Emanuel himself wrote to his "dear cousin of Naples" about his vision of a divided but "independent" Italy.

> Italy can be divided into two powerful states of the North and the South which, if they adopt the same national policy, may uphold the great idea of our times—National Independence. But in order to realize this conception,

it is I think necessary that your Majesty abandon the course you have held hitherto; the principle of dualism, if it is well established and honestly pursued can still be accepted by Italians. But if you allow some months to pass without attendance to my friendly suggestion, your Majesty will perhaps experience the bitterness of the terrible words—too late.[57]

Yet, everything seemed to change after April 1860. Cavour's caution was undermined by circumstances beyond his control that were rooted in the infrastructural incapacity of the Kingdom of Two Sicilies. First, a peasant revolt in Palermo, Sicily, on April 6, 1860, unleashed a revolution that, like the Sicilian revolutions of 1820, 1837, and 1848–49 against the foreign Bourbon king, was rooted in tensions that had been simmering between the Bourbon king and Sicilian locals since at least 1815.[58] Second, on May 11, 1860, Garibaldi, the charismatic general, without approval from the Piedmontese crown, took advantage of the political chaos to lead an attack of his "Thousand" on Sicily.[59] Cavour's first reaction to the peasant revolt in Palermo and Garibaldi's attack on Sicily was at best ambivalent. He wrote to his French ambassador, "I regret Garibaldi's expedition as much as [the French foreign minister Thouvenel] does, and I am doing and will do all that I can to see that it does not lead to new complications. I did not prevent Garibaldi from carrying out his plan because that would have required force."[60] A lack of political control had bred a new opportunism. After Garibaldi defeated his Neapolitan opponents at Calatafimi on May 15, Cavour, in a dramatic turnaround from his earlier positions, was confronted with the given fact of Garibaldi's success and called for the immediate annexation of Sicily to the kingdom of Italy. Garibaldi's ultimate aim, inspired by his nationalist and democratic zeal, however, was to move off of the island of Sicily to conquer Naples and eventually even Rome. Garibaldi's revolutionary plans of pushing onwards to conquer or "liberate" southern Italy profoundly challenged Cavour's increasingly unsustainable vision of a cautious negotiated unification between monarchs.

The moment of decision finally came on June 25, 1860, when Neapolitan king Francis II, under French influence and fearing an attack from Garibaldi, finally accepted Piedmont's offer in May 1860 of an alliance. Cavour now faced a decision and came under pressure from all sides—on the one hand, Neapolitan exiles told Cavour not to trust the Neapolitan king; on the other hand, the Piedmontese king and his own instinct tended toward an alliance with the Neapolitan king. He reflected, "If we consent to the alliance, we are lost. If we reject it what will Europe say?"[61] With ambiguous approval from the king and Cavour, Garibaldi did in fact move on successfully to conquer Naples, forcing King Francis II to flee to Bavaria—of all places—on September 6, 1860.[62] To undermine Garibaldi's growing popularity, Cavour in a controversial move dispatched troops to the Papal States, assuring Piedmontese control over the unfolding events. The unplanned conquest that ended the war of unification was complete, and within a month, Cavour was seeking the approval of the Piedmontese parliament for an "unconditional annexation" of all the southern provinces.

What precisely constituted this unconditional conquest could already be seen with the unconditional annexation of Sicily earlier in the year: First, all officials who had supported the Bourbon restoration of 1849 were to be replaced.[63] On the island of Sicily, for example, all twenty-four governors were replaced. Second, the Piedmontese constitution was extended to Sicily (August 3), along with the Piedmontese monetary system (August 17), copyright laws (August 18), system of communal administration (August 26), military code (August 28), and public security law of 1859 (August 30).[64] Most important of all was the role played by the Piedmontese military that sought to guarantee peace and stability in Italy's south. To maintain order in the southern parts of Italy even after unification, Piedmont placed one hundred thousand troops on the southern Italian mainland, as an occupying "police" force in response to requests from Piedmontese officials in the south. Finally, in addition to maintaining civil stability, the organization of other state functions including taxation, education, and the collection of official "state statistics" were shifted from other states to Turin, Piedmont.[65] It was with these acts that the *first* task of state building—ending the expansionary war of unification—had taken its surprising and defining turn.[66] Mack Smith summarizes the shift in Cavour's policy and attitude toward Italy's south during this whole period: "At first [Cavour] had not hoped for anything at all . . . but he gradually allowed himself to be converted, and ended up with the peremptory demand for unqualified surrender by the South."[67]

What changed? What placed Piedmont on the path of *unification through conquest* rather than the *unification through negotiation* that Cavour had planned? Of course one explanation that immediately suggests itself and that ought not be underestimated is the personality of Garibaldi himself. It was his unsolicited contributions to Italian unification that forced Cavour's hand and led to Piedmont's reluctant embrace of Italy's south in the summer of 1860. But in the effort to produce a more generalizable explanation that sheds insight into the causes of federalism, we can move one step back and ask: what conditions produced Garibaldi? Why was Garibaldi able to garner such support and why, as the discussion of Germany in the next chapter will reveal, did an equivalent actor not emerge in Germany? Was it a question of mere chance? Or were there conditions associated with the Italian experience of unification that made the choice of unconditional conquest the most logical means of unification?

Italy's experience of unification, when viewed in comparative perspective, does show that the dominant approaches to the study of federalism cannot account for the first stage of Italy's state building: the ideological or cultural preferences of the actors have little causal weight—Cavour wanted a negotiated unification yet found himself sending troops to southern Italy by the end of 1860. Ideological preferences were undermined by circumstance. Likewise, Riker's hypothesis that military strength assures unconditional conquest makes little sense in the Italian case. First, the most important political leaders in Piedmont did not support, until the very last stages of unification, the unconditional conquest of southern Italy. Second, by all estimations from the period, Garibaldi's "Thousand," and even the Piedmontese military, was clearly outmatched by the Kingdom of Sicily in terms of population, geographic size, and military manpower.[68] Yet despite their ideological predisposition and despite their comparative military weakness, by the summer of 1860 a set of circumstances that were different in Italy than in Germany intervened to make the unconditional conquest of the Kingdom of Two Sicilies the most logical end to the war of unification.

The most critical difference between Italy and Germany in this first stage of state building is to be found in two legacies of the broader *infrastructural incapacity* of Italy's southern regions: an ideological legacy and an administrative legacy. First, as in other peripheral or postcolonial societies, the history of foreign rule and occupation in Italy weakened state institutions—for example, foreign powers were called in to quell any open revolts—thereby creating a self-perception of marginality or backwardness among Italian intellectual elites.[69] The consequence of this politically submissive, invidious, and instrumentalized position vis-à-vis the major powers of Europe was, as in other postcolonial settings, the emergence of coherent and effective revolutionary ideology to justify and explain Italian unification.[70] The influential Mazzinian vision of an Italian unification "from below" was inspired by the persistence of foreign rule in Italy. Whereas 1815 marked the end of France's direct foreign occupation of parts of Germany, in Italy, the perception that foreign powers controlled the Italian states persisted until unification. In Mazzini's view, foreign rule was an instance of national humiliation; Cavour's effort to win French approval for a negotiated unification was "anti-Italian" and would simply make the new united Italy into a "French Dependency" when the goal of unification was independence from foreign powers. In 1859 Mazzini released a statement that outlined his vision to his Party of Action.

> The unity and liberty of an oppressed and dismembered people cannot be attained as a concession or gift of others but must be conquered by the effort and sacrifice of those who desire unity and liberty . . .our party believes that

without unity there is no country; that without national sovereignty there is no nation; and that without liberty, true liberty for all, there can be no real national independence.[71]

The Mazzinian revolutionary vision of unification was not without consequence. In 1849–50 Mazzini had twice tried to convince his close ally Garibaldi to lead a campaign on Sicily. Once again, in the summer of 1859, as Mazzini's agents fomented discontent in Sicily that would by May lead to revolution, Mazzini himself wrote to Garibaldi and encouraged an attack on the island. By 1860, Mazzini's pressure had convinced Garibaldi, and in retrospect, Mazzini wrote, "I prevailed on Garibaldi to act for the king without the king's permission."[72] Also important was the willingness of Sicilian "autonomists" to support Piedmont's annexation as a way of getting rid of the despised Bourbon crown.[73] In this sense, the four most proximate causes of unification by conquest—the personality of Garibaldi, the degree of support he received throughout Italy, the nature of his military attack on Sicily, and the willingness of Sicilian nationalists to support the Piedmontese conquest of the foreign Bourbon crown—were all a direct outcome of the weakness of Italy's governments and Italy's quasi-colonial status in Europe. The uncomfortable impact of the revolutionary ideology of unification on Cavour's state-building strategy was decisive in the months in which Cavour switched from his strategy of negotiation to his strategy of conquest. Cavour had utilized the fear of revolution as a useful political device throughout his career, but by July 1860, according to most accounts, Cavour co-opted the revolutionaries by conquering the south; it was perceived that there was no alternative. For example, he borrowed from Mazzini's longtime plan and undertook the radical's project of invading Umbria and Marches. In this sense, the foreign occupation of Italy was both cause and consequence of the weakness of the Italian prenational state institutions. Simultaneously, it was precisely this history of foreign occupation that generated a revolutionary ideology of unification that both justified the conquest of southern Italy and forced Cavour to adopt a strategy of conquest to expropriate the revolutionary tendency of Mazzini and Garibaldi in order to maintain control over the developments of unification.

Second, however, at a more practical level, the unification conquest was perceived as a *necessity* by administrative actors both within Piedmont and in the newly annexed territories as a result of the very practical legacy of political weakness, uncertainty, and disorganization left behind by the rule of the restoration kingdoms. In northern Italy—in Tuscany, the northern provinces of the Papal States, and in the city-states of Modena and Parma—Austrian defeat left weak "nationalist" interim governments in place that saw Piedmont as the main vehicle of assuring foreign exclusion from the Italian peninsula and of maintaining stability. Also, in southern parts of Italy—in the Papal States and the Kingdom of Two Sicilies, in the early days of unification a similar dilemma emerged. According to Riall, on the island of Sicily, "Almost nobody, as far as the evidence reveals, thought at all about the immense practical difficulties of filling the political and social vacuum left by the collapse of Bourbon government."[74] Indeed, since the dilemma of governance was most stark on the island of Sicily, it is a particularly useful source of insight into similar though perhaps less severe problems throughout non-Piedmont Italy.

On Sicily, the financial and administrative weakness and unpopularity of the Bourbon regime led to its collapse in May 1860, which made Garibaldi's accession to power in Sicily a surprisingly effortless process. But the political chaos that was an inheritance of the Bourbon regime—that was rooted in weak administrative and police forces—also confronted Garibaldi in the summer of 1860, which made an unconditional conquest by the Piedmontese military itself increasingly necessary. Before unification, the Bourbon regime did not have enough administrators, police officials, and bureaucrats to effectively govern its own territory. In the summer of 1860, violence increased rapidly, and Garibaldi began to receive requests from governors in rural areas of Sicily for Piedmontese troops.[75] The possibility of allowing existing political structures and elites to administer Sicily and the rest of the Kingdom of Two Sicilies was limited both by the revolutionary atmosphere of the period and by the simple administrative breakdown. The crime, social conflict, banditry, and political chaos of the post-Bourbon era in which political authorities and administrative structures imploded made even federalists look to the aid of immediate and unconditional annexation to restore political order. Revolts and military conquests had made complete and rapid annexation imperative. It is the simple administrative breakdown in southern Italy that was itself a legacy of the Bourbon rule that made immediate and unconditional conquest necessary.[76] As Mack Smith argues, the Piedmontese viewed a rapid conquest of southern Italy not just as possible but as *necessary* for two reasons: "Annexation would restore law and order to the country and compel northern Italy to underwrite the revolution against a Bourbon restoration."[77] In short, it was Piedmont's political weakness (i.e., an inability to control developments) that made Piedmont pursue the unconditional conquest of southern Italy.

But this action had a decisive consequence for the future institutional development of Italy: the actions involved in the unconditional conquest of southern Italy instantly removed the institutionalized regional actors that might have negotiated the terms of national unification and that furthermore might have served as the basis of a decentralized organization of state authority after unification.

SECOND TASK OF NATION-STATE FORMATION: FORGING THE UNION

Just as Italy's first step of unification was shaped by institutional underde-velopment in its southern provinces, so too was the second step of nation-state formation (gaining the approval of the regions to be incorporated for annexation).[78] But this second stage of unification also reflected the manner in which the war of unification itself had been ended. Taken to-gether, both the preexisting institutional incapacity in Italy's south and the "self-reinforcing" logic of each stage of Italy's path of nation-state formation further reinforced the impulse toward political centralization.

How precisely did this "self-reinforcing" logic make itself felt? By end-ing the war of unification via unconditional conquest in southern Italy, the Piedmontese leadership destroyed the southern Italian monarchical leaders who might have served as diplomatic "negotiation partners" to seal a monarchical or negotiated unification of Italy's north and south—a process that would take place in Germany beginning in 1866. In re-sponse to this political vacuum, southern Italian *federalisti* advocated the creation of a new southern Italian parliament, as a kind of *ersatz* authority to negotiate the terms of unification with Piedmontese officials in order to achieve concessions for Italy's south. But this effort collapsed by Octo-ber 1860 when Cavour and Piedmont, in the face of the same massive political instability in southern Italy that induced an unconditional con-quest, began to advocate a more rapid route to unification than a parlia-mentary path of forging the union would allow. To achieve unification rapidly, Cavour advocated a direct plebiscite of the restricted Italian elec-torate. The aim of this plebiscite was not solely, as it might first appear, to guarantee a centralized political system for the new Italy. Rather, unifica-tion by plebiscite was more significantly a response to Piedmont's position of political weakness in southern Italy and in Europe. The aim was to assure the quickest possible path to unification in order to overcome the political instability of the fall 1860. That this decision led Italy further down the path toward a centralized state was, as George Trevelyan argued, "the necessary price Italy paid for her existence."[79] The central conse-quence of forging the union through a plebiscite rather than through dip-lomatic negotiation among the sovereign leaders of the Italian states was the founding of a revolutionary "myth" that was used to legitimate the centralization of the new Italian nation-state.[80]

But it was not preordained that a plebiscite rather than parliamentary approval would be used to have the annexed regions of Italy approve uni-fication. Rather, Cavour's choice to annex Italy's south via plebiscite repre-sented, according to Mack Smith, "the success of one set of ideas and one set of men over another. The limitations and incompleteness of this victory as well as the manner of its achievement, were to be of great importance for the future history of Italy."[81] The first stage of state building—unconditional conquest of Lombardy and Tuscany after Villafranca in 1859 as well as the unconditional conquest of the Kingdom of Two Sicilies in the summer of 1860—seemed to assure a fully united Italian peninsula. But events were driving at what Lord Palmerston at the time famously called a "railroad speed," making the institutional form that would emerge at the other end of the process still unclear to the political actors themselves. In September and October 1860 a new and important issue confronted the Piedmontese state-builders, an issue that confronts any state-building elite upon either negotiating or conquering new territory: what formal procedure should be used to incorporate the annexed territory? Put in other terms, how should the approval of southern Italians to carry out unification be determined? How is legitimacy for the new political entity to be achieved?[82]

The responses to these questions, as many of the political actors involved themselves recognized, would have an important impact on the institutional form that emerged at the end of the unification process. As a result, there were a range of opinions about the best way of gaining the approval of annexed populations: some advocated an immediate plebiscite, while others advocated careful deliberations between a southern Italian parliament and the Piedmontese crown. In the face of these disparate opinions, three features of the Italian political setting were decisive for the approach to national unification that was to be followed: First, the Piedmontese destruction of the Bourbon political leadership in the summer of 1860 eliminated a potential monarchical "negotiation partner" that could have sealed a monarchical national settlement between north and south Italy. Second, the collapse of the Bourbon regime and the flight of the Bourbon King heightened the level of political instability in southern Italy that demanded, according many Piedmontese officials in southern Italy at the time, immediate action. And third, without an already-existing parliament in Italy's south, there was no organized "voice" for southern Italian interests. As a consequence of all of these factors, events were prejudiced in one direction: the Piedmontese crown found itself turning to the option of using a "plebiscite"—a "citizen-wide" vote of southern Italians to settle the unification of Italy in a rapid manner. This would sidestep the problems of political instability in southern Italy and would also allow unification to go forward before foreign powers were tempted to intervene.

Yet events reveal that these two factors still did not automatically lead Italy to a path of unification by plebiscite. In the early weeks of October 1860 there still was a possibility of negotiating the terms of unification through an assembly rather than accepting unification wholly and immediately by plebiscite. On October 1, 1860, for example, a dozen prominent

Sicilians, including the director of the Bank of Sicily and the president of the Palermo civic council, wrote to the Piedmontese representative in Naples with a set of demands. As self-declared members of the dissolved 1848 parliament, they claimed that the institution had never "officially" been dissolved. The authors, whose positions were supported by a range of federalists such as Carlo Cattaneo and democrats including Mazzini and Crispi, advocated holding an election and forming an assembly, all with the purpose of allowing long and careful deliberation of the *terms* of unification with Italy's north. The authors sought a national unification but one accompanied by conditions—in their own words "by measures and restrictions which would ensure that the needs of each region and inveterate local customs, and the forces of tradition were all duly respected."[83] The aim of the proposal for a constituent assembly was to assure that regional political interests would be included in the process of national unification, thereby assuring that regions would be institutionalized in a decentralized or even a "federal" new polity.

What was the basis of these federalist ideas? And were the aims really federalist? The calls for annexation, but via careful and deliberate assembly approval rather than via a potentially hasty plebiscite, were partly based on the Sicilian economist Francesco Ferrara's memorandum to Cavour written earlier in the year, on July 8, 1860, which proposed alternative paths to achieving unification.[84] In the paper, Ferrara displayed extensive knowledge of different national systems of territorial governance throughout Europe. In his memo, Ferrara discussed and rejected "the Scottish" and "Swedish-Norwegian" systems as dangerous for Italy. Ferrara also rejected the centralism of the "French system." With a striking level of premonition, Ferrara wrote that a French-style centralization would require a "fusion" that "would make Sicily the Ireland of Italy and this, instead of making our nationality more compact and secure would be a real and perennial source of weakness from which an enemy could profit."[85] Instead of these various models, Ferrara embraced "the American system," which from Ferrara's view did not make "the common error of attributing more cohesion to a state whose central governments takes on tasks that subaltern bodies or individuals can do better."[86] With regards to the specific issue of annexation with or without conditions, Ferrara wrote, "Whoever knows Sicily well must be convinced that annexation, on conditions which Sicilians might later regret would soon generate sentiments not wholly Italian, which interested parties would not hesitate to nourish."[87]

Adding to the possibility of using an assembly to approve unification between south and north that might have led to a more decentralized polity was the fact that throughout 1860 Cavour himself advocated creating an assembly as the best means of gaining southern approval for unification. In June 1860 Cavour "thought it more honest and convenient to convene the Sicilian parliament" to gain approval of Sicily for unification.[88] Cavour and Victor Emanuel both resisted a plebiscite to seal their plans of national unification, hoping instead that a monarchical settlement could be reached between the Piedmontese king and his Bourbon "cousin."

Yet by October 1860, after the Bourbon king's departure from Naples, Cavour and his king recognized that events had taken a different course. In October 1860 Cavour called the Piedmont parliament in an important and special session to win approval for a new set of actions in southern Italy: In his speech in the Turin Chamber of Deputies on October 2, 1860, Cavour announced, "We must give it as our opinion that annexation ought not be accepted by our parliament if it were offered to us only under special conditions."[89] Cavour continued that an agreement between north and south that granted local autonomy would be "contrary to the trends of modern society and would constitute a relic of the Middle Ages."[90] To prevent such an outcome, and again in a turnaround from his earlier statements, Cavour called on the Piedmontese parliament to approve his plan to demand that a plebiscite by "universal suffrage" be held in Naples and Sicily, that no assembly be formed in southern Italy, that no conditions be attached, and that the ballots allow only for a "yes" or "no" vote.[91] By insisting on annexation without the approval of an assembly or without the possibility of conditions, Mack Smith argues, "Northerners were thus taking advantage of the fact that their own assembly was already in existence whereas the South so far had none."[92]

The Turin parliament approved Cavour's proposal for immediate annexation. Yet in the sitting of the Piedmontese parliament as well as in a series of debates in Naples in mid-October 1860, federalists throughout Italy denounced Turin's decision.[93] In the parliament itself, a northern Italian, Giuseppe Ferrari, voiced the concerns of federalists and southern Italians when he derided the "racial contempt" of the Piedmontese for other regions. He denounced the "Piedmontese system" as simply "imposing one single state upon all the other states of Italy . . . unconditional surrender of the south would mean that Piedmont could abolish all the Neapolitan laws and replace them with her own."[94] But despite such protests, on October 21, 1860, a vote was held in the former Kingdom of Two Sicilies in which 93 percent of the highly restrictive voting public in Sicily and on the mainland chose to be part of the new Italy under King Victor Emmanuel's rule. The fraud, police threats, and corruption necessary to generate this nearly unanimous support for unification without conditions have been well documented by historians.[95] If a monarchical settlement was not possible, the Piedmontese leadership would at least assure the success of its program with a guaranteed unanimous "mandate from the people."

More significant for our purposes of understanding why federalism did *not* emerge in Italy is to make sense of the puzzle of why Cavour switched from a strategy of allowing an assembly to approve unification—which might have led toward greater decentralization—to a strategy in which unification was accepted wholly and hastily by plebiscite. Was he aiming to establish as centralized a polity as possible? As Cavour's earlier statements about the desirability of a decentralized system of administrative make clear, this shift was in fact not the result of a long-standing and unwavering *ideological* commitment to the goal of political centralization. Rather the call for a plebiscite in the fall of 1860 represented what Cavour himself perceived to be a necessary change in strategy that was "unfortunately" demanded by the twisting Italian path of national unification. It can hardly be questioned that the ever-pragmatic Cavour, not to mention King Victor Emmanuel, would have preferred a carefully negotiated "pact" between the Bourbon and Piedmontese crowns like the monarchical settlement between the Bavarian and Prussian crowns that took place ten years later in Germany. To rely on plebiscites to achieve the political goal of unification was at best a second choice. Though Cavour was guaranteed a positive outcome to the vote, he and King Victor Emanuel would have preferred a compact among equal sovereigns to guarantee monarchical control over national unification.

Why, then, did Cavour adopt the strategy of gaining the approval of the newly incorporated regions via a plebiscite that would unintentionally deinstitutionalize the region in Italian politics, creating a myth of revolutionary change that would move Italy closer and closer to a centralized state? First, as already mentioned, the weight of earlier decisions made by Cavour forced him to reject an assembly-centered method of annexation. The unconditional conquest of southern Italy in the summer of 1860 and the displacement of established laws and state personnel led to violence and banditry in the southern parts of Italy in the late summer.[96] The arrival of Piedmontese troops did little to quell the violence. Even sympathizers with the federalist cause began to demand immediate annexation *without* an assembly. The established business and agricultural classes, though sympathetic to southern Italian independence, were made conservative by the disorder. The editorial of one paper *Il Plebiscito*, for example, proclaimed in October 1860, "For us annexation means order and justice . . . it will destroy any chance of the Bourbon's returning."[97]

But in addition to pressure from entrenched social interests, the Piedmontese officials themselves perceived that rapid annexation was necessary for their own state-building goals. There exists a massive record of correspondence between Piedmontese officials stationed throughout Italy and Cavour throughout the turbulent period of 1859–61.[98] In this correspondence, we see a record of increasingly nervous reports from Piedmontese and local officials about the growing civic unrest, ungovernability, and public finance crisis in Italy's south, especially beginning in the spring of

1860. Throughout the turbulent months of unification Count Cavour remained in Piedmont, keeping close watch on events via government reports. Immediately after Garibaldi's invasion with his "Thousand" in May 1860, for example, as the weak governance structures of the Kingdom of Two Sicilies imploded, news of Italy's south trickled into government ministries in Piedmont. In the summer of 1860 Piedmontese officials on assignment in southern Italy sent word to Turin of the difficulties of maintaining an orderly system of tax collection. Piedmontese Finance Ministry officials stationed in Italy's south in the early 1860s reported to Cavour on the "exhausted" state of public finances and the "collapse" of order and public safety.[99] There were frequent calls to Cavour from his officials in the south that mirrored the same sentiment—"Permit me, Excellency, to repeat to you the need for policemen (*carabinieri*) to save this country from ruin!"[100] To reassure those in the south, officials in Piedmont promised not only police forces but more administrative "staff" and "clerks" to maintain order.[101]

But the effort to maintain order was insufficient. For example, Piedmontese official and future prime minister Agostino Depretis, who was sent by the Piedmontese government to restore order in 1860, arrived optimistic that he could single-handedly reassert control over events. He was, however, soon overwhelmed by the popular unrest, lack of security forces, and unsustainable public finance situation. In letters to Bertani in July 1860 and to Garibaldi in September 1860, he announced that the only solution to the fiscal and social chaos was immediate annexation by Piedmont.[102] In short, by the summer and fall of 1860, Cavour and officials around him began to perceive that they had inherited a set of states incapable of doing the work of modern governance.

From the perspective of the new realist advocates of rapid annexation, the calling of an assembly to officially gain approval would require months of elections, debates, and decisions, during which time crime would overwhelm any hope of political stability. As Trevelyan summarizes the mind-set, "It would have been the height of unwisdom to waste two months in electing and calling together Neapolitan and Sicilian assemblies, and half a year more in bargainings and intrigues of every kind."[103] By evicting southern Italy's political leadership, Cavour eliminated a monarchical negotiation "partner" that could have granted a newly unified Italy a greater level of legitimacy. Instead of having this negotiation "partner" as Bismarck had with the kings of southern Germany, Cavour inherited a leaderless Bourbon regime that unleashed a political chaos demanding a rapid annexation via plebiscite rather than a careful annexation via assembly approval.

In addition to the force of his earlier state-building decisions, a second factor—the situation of foreign rule *within* Italy, demanded annexation by plebiscite. The continued presence of Austrian troops in parts of Italy made unrealistic the time-consuming negotiations that would be required by forming a southern Italian assembly. Military defeats in 1859 had not completely eliminated Austria from Italian political life in 1860. Cavour, aware of this instability, saw in October 1860 a rare political opportunity to complete the project of national unification. Di Scala writes, for example, "The threat of political disputes leading to foreign intervention and collapse made calling a constituent assembly impossible."[104] Or, as Trevelyan so aptly puts it, "A plebiscite for unconditional annexation could be held in a fortnight, but an assembly might sit until it was dispersed by Austrian bayonets"[105] In contrast to the German process of unification, the Italian unification was more delicate and precarious as a result of Italy's occupied status in Europe. Taken together, the Italian logic of state national unification and Italy's legacy as a foreign-occupied state made a plebiscite "regrettable but necessary." The consequences of this decision were critical. Trevelyan writes, even fifty years after Italian unification, that had an assembly rather than a plebiscite been the mode of approving unification, "Some of the evils that have actually resulted from a too close union might possibly have been avoided. Those who know South Italy of today deplore the rigid and mechanical application of the Piedmontese laws and administrative system . . . but that was the necessary price that Italy paid for her existence."[106] Because of Piedmont's inability to control events within the borders of the future Italy, Cavour and his king were forced to turn to a plebiscite to gain approval for unification. The unintended consequence of this decision was fateful: the establishment of a revolutionary myth for the new Italy that would be used by Piedmontese elites to justify greater and greater centralization throughout the early history of the new nation-state.

The Third Task of Nation-State Formation: Making the New Rules

In the third and final stage in forming the nation-state of Italy, Piedmontese officials faced a critical set of decisions involved with the constitutional questions of whether (1) regions should have direct parliamentary representation in the upper chamber of the national parliament, (2) regions ought to have any policy and fiscal autonomy, and (3) the new institutions of "national" public administration should allow the old regional actors and institutions some room for administrative autonomy.

The creation of the institutions of territorial governance took place in Italy over a five-year period between 1860 and 1865. In these early years of Italy's political life, as political leaders sought to establish new nation-wide state institutions, there was a strong consensus among the governing center-right coalition—in retrospect a surprising consensus—that some form of decentralization would be necessary. Not only had Cavour frequently appeased southern regional leaders in 1859–60 with reassuring words that the south would retain autonomy upon unification, but serious proposals were discussed across the political spectrum in the Piedmontese parliament before and after the events of 1860. On the left, intellectuals such as Cattaneo and Farrari had long been advocates of an Italian federalism. But on the right—in the seat of power—the Piedmont Interior Ministry, first under Minghetti and then under Farini, proposed and brought decentralization plans into the Piedmont parliament in 1860, 1861, and 1865. Yet all these plans foundered.

At the moment of unification, in the summer of 1860, before the conquest and annexation of southern Italy, there was an ideological consensus among many government officials in Piedmont that a decentralized political order in which "region" would play an important formal role in national politics should be an important feature of the new Italian state. Most political leaders rejected the notion that France's centralized model of government should simply be imposed on the Italian setting. From Cavour, on the right, to Mazzini, on the left, there was widespread consensus that a French prefectoral system for the regionally diverse Italy was simply inappropriate. But, by the summer of 1865, the "decentralist" ideological consensus of Piedmont's "center-right" government had failed to translate into actual institutional reforms of Piedmont's system of territorial governance. In fact, the French centralized model—with some small but important adaptations—was imposed onto the newly united Italy. To understand why federalism failed in this last stage of national unification, it is necessary to trace how earlier decisions shaped the fate of the efforts to create a federal political order for Italy between 1860 and 1865.

The question is particularly striking because beginning in the summer of 1860, the anticipated unification of Italy represented to the decisive Piedmontese political actors such as Interior Minister Farini and future interior minister Minghetti an opportunity to reform and decentralize the highly centralized Piedmontese system of center-periphery relations. Already in the summer of 1860, before Garibaldi's attack on southern Italy, the Ministry of the Interior under Farini recognized that institutional reforms might be necessary successfully to incorporate new territories. With this in mind, the Piedmontese government established a special commission, constituted by members of parliament and councilors of state, on June 24, 1860, to draft legislation on how to reorganize the 1859 act that had been the basis of Piedmont's centralized prefectoral system of governance. The central political aim of the important committee, according to Minister Farini, who wrote a memorandum to the committee in June 1860, was to create proposals that could be submitted to the new and first Italian parliament in March 1861.[107] The specific policy goal was the creation of new and effective explicitly "regional" level of government between the level of national government (*stato*) on the one hand, and provincial level of government, on the other hand.[108] These newly constituted regions with regional governors would maintain appointment authority over civil servants and a great deal of policy autonomy. Additionally, in the commission's report in August 1860, the members of the commission argued that these regions would not simply be "field offices" of the central government but rather an autonomous level of government with councils with oversight over a range of policy areas.

Even immediately after Garibaldi's conquest and the annexation of southern Italy in October 1860, the new minister of interior, Marco Minghetti, insisted that the special government committee have a finished legislative proposal in time for the first meeting of the Italian parliament in March 1861. In a meeting of the committee, Minghetti proclaimed, "It is necessary to form another aggregation, another corporate entity greater than the Provinces, such that the representatives of the Government may therein safely have the powers we have indicated."[109] The committee met Minister Minghetti's demands and submitted its proposal to the parliament on March 1861.

But that proposal as well as two additional proposals failed. The final defeat of all efforts at decentralization took place on March 23, 1865, when the parliament approved legislation that marked what Sabetti calls "the triumph of centralized government and administration."[110] That a centralized model of territorial governance won out even at this stage was not inevitable, as evidenced by the political struggles between 1860 and 1865. Yet a combination of factors associated with the prenational conditions of Italy and the process of national unification described so far seemed to make a federal outcome increasingly likely. Two factors above all mattered. First, because organized regional political actors were excluded from the process of conquest and annexation, no organized regional opposition existed to demand regional concessions in the critical stages between 1860 and 1865. Second, because of the prenational legacy of administrative weakness in Italy's south, Piedmontese officials viewed centralization as both desirable and necessary. In short, the Italian case of unification created neither the opposition nor the opportunities that would have favored a federalist settlement.

Conclusion: Nation-State Formation and the Making of a Unitary System

If national unification represented a critical juncture in the development of Italy's political institutions, then the way in which it was carried out represented a response to a particular set of prenational political conditions. More precisely, to understand why federalism or a decentralized political order was not constructed, we should not look to the configuration of ideas, culture, or even military power in a society—as most theories of federalism suggest.

Instead, we must look to the regional inheritance of infrastructural capacity. We must look to the question of how well developed the basic infrastructure of modern governments was before national unification. In Italy, we have seen that without the personnel, institutions, or the institutionalized practices of modern government, the Piedmontese leaders found themselves tempted—at each stage of national unification—to adopt a centralizing pattern of national unification. First, by ending the war of unification via unconditional conquest, second, by negotiating the terms of unification via plebiscite rather than via parliament, and finally, by making the new rules of the new polity absent regional actors, the Piedmontese leadership found itself with a unitary and centralized political system, having destroyed the regional governments that many in the center-right coalition had hoped might support a united but federal Italy.

Chapter Six

FROM STRONG REGIONAL LOYALTIES TO A FEDERAL SYSTEM: NATIONAL UNIFICATION BY NEGOTIATION AND THE CASE OF GERMANY

> The effort to violently conquer southern Germany would only create for us the same element of weakness that southern Italy has created for that state.
> —OTTO VON BISMARCK, 1866[1]

SIX YEARS after the events in Italy, the national unification of German was accomplished in two steps: the creation of the North German Confederation in 1866–67 and the German Reich in 1870–71. As earlier chapters have argued, the regional forces for and against national unification in Germany were very similar to those in Italy. Additionally, as this chapter will make clear, political debate among political and intellectual elites in Germany was similarly mixed between "centralizers" and "federalists." Finally, Prussia could have dominated a centralized German nation-state, even more easily than the militarily weaker Piedmont vis-à-vis the other Italian regional-states.

That the overbearing and powerful state of Prussia could create a federal system in the face of these similarities highlights an unexpected state-building irony: strong centers can make concessions that weak centers sometimes can not. The key issue in the establishment of a federation is not the strength of the center, but the relative institutional development of the subunits in a potential federation. With well-developed state structures throughout Germany, Prussia could adopt a negotiated or federal strategy of state formation that Piedmont tried to use but ultimately could not, a strategy that was designed simultaneously to deal with pressing international *and* domestic dilemmas of national unification.

Indeed, despite the broad similarities in context facing the nation-state builders of Piedmont and Prussia, the institutional outcome of German national unification diverged from the Italian outcome. Rather than a unitary state, the Prussian strategy of nation-state formation gave rise to an explicitly federal political system that was constructed for the new German Reich along three critical dimensions: (1) the regional governments had formal representative access in a national-level territorial chamber (Bundesrat), (2) the regional governments maintained a high level of public finance autonomy in which the Reich was reliant on the states for revenue (the so-called *Matrikularbeiträge* system), and (3) the regional governments maintained control over their own administrative structures, even implementing most federal legislation (a system called *Exekutivföderalismus*).[2] In Germany, the formerly independent regional states, though integrated into a larger political entity, persisted as important formal units within a new federal political system.

The Argument: Unification by Negotiation and Its Institutional Legacies

To understand this successful case of federalism that contrasts so starkly with the Italian case of unification, we see again the analytical weakness of ideological, cultural, and power-structural factors that most analysts have highlighted. Though these factors may have shaped which institutional formats were discussed and considered among elites in Germany and Italy, the presence of such factors was clearly not enough to guarantee a federal outcome in Italy. Instead, as the last chapter also argued, the most decisive difference between Germany and Italy was the higher level of *infrastructural capacity* of the regional governments Prussia inherited from the German regional states. While Piedmont's political leaders found themselves turning to a centralizing pattern of political authority in the critical years of national unification as a result of institutional incapacity in the non-Piedmontese states, Prussian political leaders faced institutionally developed and constitutional monarchical regional governments outside of Prussia with higher levels of institutional capacity. As a consequence, the Prussian political leadership had partners to negotiate with and, furthermore, could successfully and easily devolve fiscal, administrative, and political authority to the well-developed state structures outside of Prussia after national unification. In this sense, rather than seeking to maximize the absolute power of the center over the periphery via "conquest," Prussian and Piedmontese leaders both sought the path of least resistance to national unification. Confronted with different institutional settings, however, political leaders in Prussia were able to orchestrate a different strategy—an explicitly "federal" strategy—in response to the same tasks of national unification, institutionalizing a specific set of political actors, political norms, and formal rules that guaranteed federalism for a new Germany.

But why precisely were Prussian leaders and German state leaders outside of Prussia able to pursue a federal solution to the tasks of national unification? The well-developed German state structures outside of Prussia allowed political leaders both inside and outside of Prussia to take advantage of a preexisting feature of Germany's prenational institutional landscape in which state building at the subunit level *preceded* national unification, leaving politically developed subnational political units in place. As a consequence, the occupiers of the well-developed state structures outside of Prussia—in parliaments and state administrations—had both the means and motives to defend their political positions insisting upon being formally included as political actors in the new nation-state. Additionally, the well-developed state structures of Germany's regions allowed Bismarck simultaneously to achieve both foreign and domestic policy goals for Prussia: First, aware of French, British, and Austrian fears of an overly centralized and powerful Prussian Germany, Bismarck appeased these concerns by leaving monarchs in Bavaria, Baden, Saxony, and Württemberg in place.[3] But, second, even more important, the existence of well-developed regional state structures allowed Bismarck's to pursue a domestic agenda that Cavour sought but *could not* pursue for Italy: a negotiated unification in which existing domestic political structures and monarchical elites were left in place to assure a nonrevolutionary and gradual process of national unification. In fact, as some historians have argued, Bismarck took advantage of precisely these regional political elites and institutions to block the push for liberal democratic changes by entrenching monarchical leaders in power to serve as a counterweight to a powerful national parliament.[4]

The successful case of German federalism in 1866 and 1870, in this sense, not only highlights the weaknesses of cultural and ideological accounts of federalism's origins, but also highlights a gap in the classic Rikerian account that informs most contemporary approaches to federalism. Rather than assuming that the political leadership of the political center will always prefer as centralized a political system as possible, we discover that Prussian political leaders sought, as a first preference, an explicitly federal system in which regional governments maintained a high level of political authority. Well-developed regional state structures with a high level of institutional capacity were not merely "stumbling blocks" that constrained Prussian plans to create a Prussian-dominated German nation-state. Rather, such well-developed regional state structures also allowed Prussian state-builders to achieve their domestic goal of national unification within the constraints of an international system that feared Prussian power.

This chapter undertakes two tasks: First, I present original institutional-level data on the largest prenational German states to give an overview of the regional-state structures the Prussian government inherited from the rest of Germany with national unification. In this first section, I will highlight the higher level of political development and capacity of Germany's prenational regional governments when compared to Italy's. In the second part of the chapter, I trace the three stages of nation-state formation in Germany that I discussed in the last chapter, showing how well-developed institutional capacity in the regional-states of Germany provided an opportunity for the successful creation of a federal political system at each stage of national unification. By institutionalizing a specific set of political actors, political norms, and formal rules in the process of national unification, federalism was guaranteed for the new polity. Here, I will show that the "positive feedback" or "self-reinforcing" dynamic of nation-state formation, rather than further undercutting the institutional capacity of regional governments, as was the case in Italy, actually *reinforced* the institutional capacity and autonomy of regional governments, making efforts to centralize Germany in the 1870s and 1880s more difficult.

Inheritance of Institutional Capacity in Germany's Regions: Overview of the Prenational German Regional States, 1815–66

The post-1815 Napoleonic legacy of constitutional, parliamentary, and administrative reforms that had aimed to undo the old regime survived in the German states with greater success than in the Italian states of Europe. In the Italian states—from Lombardy to Piedmont and the Kingdom of Two Sicilies—the return of the ancien régime after 1815 meant that the restored monarchs embraced divine right rule, eliminated their parliaments, and purged their bureaucracies.[5] Additionally, despite brief flirtations with parliamentary and constitutional rule in 1848–49, Piedmont was the only Italian state to enter its last decade of independence in the 1850s with a constitution and parliament intact.

By contrast, most of the German states exited the Napoleonic age in 1815 with institutional reforms in place and actively pursued further projects of political development—the creation of new constitutions, parliaments, and modern systems of administration.[6] As this chapter will make clear, it was precisely this configuration of subnational institutions in the German states that assured the creation of a federal national polity upon unification. Indeed, in a majority of the states in Germany, the restoration in 1815, rather than undercutting Napoleonic reforms, reinforced them, generating a set of political institutions and practices that endured until national unification in 1866 and 1871, despite the period of "reaction" in the 1850s. As a consequence, as the evidence in this chapter will show, the preunification German states, most notably in Germany's southwest, were firmly embedded in German society, had greater legitimacy and visi-

TABLE 6.1
Political Development of the German States, 1855–65

	Rationalization of Authority (existence of constitution)	Parliamentary Development (parliament with access to budget process)	Administration Development (concentration and differentiation)	Cumulative Political Development Score
Prussia	1	1	2	4
Bavaria	2	2	2	6
Baden	2	2	2	6
Württemberg	2	2	2	6
Saxony	1	1	2	4
Mecklenburg	1	1	1	3
Hannover	2	1	2	4
Kurhessen	1	1	2	4
Nassau	1	2	2	5
Hessen Darmstadt	1	2	2	5

Note: In this table 0 = nonexistent, 1 = existent but contested, 2 = existent and effective. The data are drawn from the narrative account offered by Huber, *Deutsche Verfassungsgeschichte Seit 1789*, 182–223.

bility and as a result a higher levels of institutional capacity, and were harder to dissolve than their Italian counterparts.[7] In table 6.1, we can see an overview of the nine largest future states of the German Reich— constituting approximately 90 percent of its population in 1871—as they stood in the last decade before national unification (1855–65).[8]

As table 6.1 shows, along all three dimensions of political development—constitutional, parliamentary, and administrative—the nine largest states of the German Bund outside of Austria that Prussia would inherit after 1866 had constitutions, parliaments, and well-developed administrative structures in the 1850s, giving nearly all the German states higher scores than their Italian counterparts.[9] Most importantly, there was by and large no gap in the level of political development between Prussia and the states it inherited: Whereas Piedmont stood as the only constitutional state in Italy in the 1850s, Prussia was actually the only large state in Germany *not* to accept constitutional rule by 1848. But, as table 6.1 makes clear, by the mid-1850s, in all of the states, including Prussia, constitutions guaranteed that without parliamentary approval, "no law could be passed, no taxes raised, and no public debt undertaken."[10] Or, as Dieter Grimm puts it, by the 1850s "absolutism had definitively come to an end."[11]

To be sure, the German state parliaments and constitutions, embedded in monarchical systems, were by no means models of modern parliamentary rule. Indeed, the position of the monarch was predominant in the constitutional orders in all of the German states, but there were in fact important differences among the states in their last decade of independence: In the most progressive states of Baden, Bavaria, and Württemberg, concessions had been made to liberals even in the revised "reactionary" constitutions of the early 1850s to sustain state parliaments' right to veto budgets and legislation of the crown. Additionally, these parliamentary rights were frequently used by the late 1850s.[12] Furthermore, as public bodies, with publicly released transcripts of parliamentary debates and access by the press, the state governments of these three southwest German states were highly visible.[13]

By contrast, in the less progressive states of Hannover, Saxony, Darmstadt, Nassau, and especially Mecklenburg, the monarchs resorted to pre-1848 constitutions, often ignoring parliaments in their actions, dissolving parliaments, and calling for new elections when the parliament didn't support the monarch's proposals. And, finally, in Prussia, Nassau, Kurhessen, and Hanover, persistent constitutional conflict set the tone of politics throughout the 1850s, as parliaments and monarchs struggled over taxes and the setting of military budgets.[14] But despite this diversity, as James Sheehan has written, "With varying degrees of reluctance and self-consciousness, many German conservatives had come to accept the fact that constitutions and parliaments were here to stay."[15]

In addition to well-entrenched constitutional and parliamentary traditions, the German states, as table 6.1 shows, experienced quite uniformly high levels of administrative development by the 1850s. Unlike in Italy, where reforms were undone immediately after 1815, in many of the German states, monarchs and their ministers carried out administrative projects of *concentration* and *specialization* beginning in 1815. While in the Italian states the administrative institutions were better developed than parliamentary or constitutional institutions, they still suffered in absolute terms compared to the German states. Administrative reforms across nearly all the German states spawned concentrated, specialized, professional, and societally embedded bureaucracies across the German political landscape. First, in all states, monarchs and their civil servants installed centralized *prefectoral* models of administration between 1815 and 1820. In states such as Bavaria, Baden, and Württemberg, miniature provincial-level administrations were fused and staffed with an expanding civil service, not to serve as independent governments but as instruments of central state consolidation.[16] Though less directly influenced by the French model, the Prussian state also carried out a massive centralization of administrative organization after the 1806 defeat to establish a new administrative system constructed around the *Landratsamt*.[17] In states further from French influence, such as Saxony, the establishment of a centralized rule came later.[18] For example, even after the new constitution was imposed in Saxony in 1831, there were still regions such as Oberlausitz that maintained administrative autonomy. But, by the 1850s, though the main era of reform was over, the basic prefectoral-inspired institutions of modern administration were already in place throughout all of the German states.

Second, in addition to concentration within states, all of the German states pursued the *differentiation* of administrative structures. Traditionally, the absolutist states of Germany had fused all functions under the monarchical council (e.g., *Generaldirektorium*).[19] But beginning at the end of eighteenth century and especially in the period after 1815, the increasingly complex tasks of regulating society and raising revenue on a permanent basis presented new challenges to administrative actors. As a result, monarchs themselves proposed new administrative agencies, giving rise to a multiplication of administrative structures within each state to more effectively govern. In states such as Bavaria, Baden, and Württemberg, for example, authority was dispersed even before 1815 across five ministries: Justice, Finance, Interior, Foreign Affairs, and Church and Schools.[20] Similar differentiation of functions proceeded rapidly in Prussia immediately following Prussia's military defeat in 1806. But, the process of administrative differentiation—the creation of ministries potentially accountable to a parliament—was slower in Hessen, coming fully in the 1820s, in Saxony in 1831, and in Hannover over the course of the 1830s.[21] But in the important area of tax administration, nearly every state had already established an independent administrative finance ministry as early as 1817.[22]

Though the period before 1848 was a period of constitutional, parliamentary, and administrative innovation, the period *after* 1848 gave rise to what historians have conventionally dubbed the period of "reaction" in which the each state's coercive apparatus cracked down on civil society and the free press. Additionally, beginning in 1850, state monarchs used arbitrary measures to dissolve parliaments, impose decrees, undo election laws, and eliminate constitutional "basic rights" (*Grundrechte*) for citizens.[23] Like the Italian monarchs, the German monarchs sought a return to the pre-1848 political conditions. While this retrenchment in Italy meant a return to preconstitutional and nonparliamentary political arrangements that were predominant before 1848, in Germany this simply meant a return to the less progressive but nevertheless still constitutional and parliamentary orders of the pre-1848 period. Indeed, despite the po-

litical climate of retrenchment during the 1850s, only one of the German
states that had had constitutions by the 1830s removed constitutions entirely after the failed national revolution of 1848.[24] In this sense, parliamentary, and administrative developments before 1848 set the German
states on a trajectory of prenational political development that assured
the persistence of constitutions, parliaments, and modern administrative
structures at least until national unification.

But where did these pre-1848 state structures come from? Why did the
constitutional German states in 1848 already differ so markedly from the
Italian states, where absolutist nonparliamentary rule still monopolized
the peninsula? To answer these questions, we must look to developments
within Germany beginning in 1815. Indeed, all three dimensions of table
6.1—constitutional, parliamentary, and administrative—reflect the im-
print of two main "waves" of constitutional progress (1815–20 and 1830–
34) and one main period of constitutional retrenchment (1849–51)
within the German states.[25] In contrast to the constitutionally arid landscape of post-1815 Italy, there was a flowering of constitutions after 1815
guaranteeing parliaments to the individual German states. In 1814, the
Duchy of Nassau implemented a constitution.[26] In 1816, several small
states including Schaumberg-Lippe, Waldeck, Saxony-Weimar installed
constitutions. By 1818–19, the large southern states of Bavaria, Baden,
and Württemberg had adopted constitutions, as had Hessen, Darmstadt,
and a whole series of smaller states in 1820. By 1821, twenty-nine of the
forty-one states of the German Bund were governed as constitutional
states. By the 1830s, Kurhessen and the two conservative regimes of Saxony and Hannover joined the ranks of the constitutional parliamentary
states.[27] In contrast to the near universal embrace of constitutions in the
German states before 1848, the Prussian crown, as mentioned above, remained as always—excepting the Mecklenburgs—a uniquely recalcitrant
outlier. Though state reformers such as Hardenberg submitted constitutional proposals to the Prussian crown, by the 1820s plans of a constitution for Prussia had been defeated. Only in 1850, after the revolution of
1848, did the Prussian crown impose a constitution guaranteeing a role
for a parliament in the legislative process.[28]

But Prussia aside, the question still remains, why was such extensive
constitutional, parliamentary, and administrative reform undertaken in
Germany but not in Italy in the early years after 1815? Historians of the
period have focused on two distinctive features of the institutional landscape of prenational Germany. First, though independent like the Italian
states, the German states were members of the loose German Confederation. As a result, all of the German states were subject to Article 13 of the
German Confederation's founding document, which stipulated in famously vague language that all member states "will have . . . constitu-

tions."[29] But the existence of the German Bund, an organization without enforceable sanctions, did not automatically give rise to constitutions, nor did the Bund's founding document stipulate the nature of the constitutions within states. The driving force to adopt constitutions, as constitutional historians of Germany have argued, was a second factor: the fiscal requirements of the post-Napoleonic era.[30] The aim of the imposed constitutions in 1815–21 in Bavaria, Baden, and Württemberg, for example, was in large part the creation of centralized states with the capacity to collect revenues on a permanent basis.[31] Led by Minister Monteglas in Bavaria, Minister Friedrich Nebenius in Baden, and reform-minded ministers in Württemberg, the constitutions and parliaments were "revolutions from above" in which state bureaucrats, at the impetus of the crown, sought modernizing institutional reforms to provide a more consolidated basis for the financially strapped and territorially insecure southern German states. Whereas the Italian state entered the post-1815 period financially secure and with stable territorial borders, the German states—again especially in Germany's southwest—had much higher debts, driven by insecure borders and the absorption of new territory after 1815. In order to generate the fiscal resources to run a state apparatus constrained by high debts, the German state leaders viewed constitutions and parliaments as assuring a "bargain" to ease the process of taxation.[32] In Bavaria, as in other states, the creation of an upper parliamentary house reserved for the aristocracy was a "payoff" for removing the taxing privileges of the aristocrats themselves.[33] In short, Germany's unique position vis-à-vis the post-Napoleonic setting gave rise to institutional reforms that entrenched constitutions and parliaments in place even before 1848.[34]

Taking these events together, we see that just as the experience of the restoration regimes of Italy shows us that the reinstatement of rule by divine right accompanied the purging of state bureaucracies, the German states entered the restoration period with working constitutions, parliaments, and increasingly concentrated and specialized modern bureaucratic administrative structures. The process of political development in the German states after the restoration, just like the reverse process of the undoing of Napoleonic institutions in Italy, highlights the extent to which all three of these features of modern states—constitution, parliament, and administration—traveled hand in hand in the nineteenth century. In fact, German reformers, liberals, and advocates of state authority themselves viewed these three features of state organization as critical to expanding their capacity to extract resources, regulate social life, and provide services for the population.[35] In this period, *Verfassung* (constitution) and *Verwaltung* (administration) were both conceived as part of the same project of consolidating state structures.

TABLE 6.2
Institutional Capacity of the German Regional Governments, 1850–66

	Extractive Capacity (state revenue per capita, in thaler)	Coercive Capacity (conscription rate: military personnel as % of male population)	Regulative Capacity (road density: km roads per 1,000 km²)
Prussia	5.5	2.2%	66
Bavaria	6.1	4.3%	112
Baden	6.2	1.1%	136
Württemberg	6.0	1.4%	148
Saxony	5.4	2.3%	228
Hannover	5.2	2.8%	141
Kurhessen	6.0	2.1%	143
Darmstadt	5.2	2.8%	229
Ratio of Prussia to average of remaining states	1:1.04	1:1.09	1:2.45

Source: State revenue data, population data, and road density data are drawn from Borchard, "Staatsverbrauch," 42–43 and 274; military personnel data from Singer and Small, *National Materials Capabilities Data*.

If the aim of these reforms was in fact increased state capacity, how did the outcome measure up? And how did the German states differ from the Italian states? As chapter 5 discussed, constitutions, parliaments, and modern systems of administration have long been hypothesized to increase institutional effectiveness of the state.[36] Scholars of the history of state capacity have long argued that, taken together, constitutions, parliaments, and systems of administration create more effective patterns of governance. In table 6.2, I present an overview of the institutional capacity of the German regional states disaggregated into the same three dimensions used in the last chapter: extractive capacity, conscription capacity, and regulative capacity. The purpose of using measures as similar as possible to those in chapter 5 is to assess the extent to which each of the German states could extract resources from its population, coercively construct a military, and penetrate and transform society.

The data on the German states in table 6.2, when compared to the data on the Italian states presented in chapter 5, highlight two major points. First, in terms of *absolute* level of institutional capacity, the German states by the 1850s were far more developed than their Italian counterparts. Second, and perhaps even more importantly for the future development of federalism in Germany, the *relative* gap in institutional capacity between Prussia and the states it would inherit in 1867 and 1871 was much smaller than the institutional gap between Piedmont and the states it would inherit in 1861. Whereas Piedmont was twice as developed along all three dimensions as the states it inherited, Prussia inherited states that actually had *higher* levels of institutional capacity than Prussia itself. This institutional fact was critical in shaping the perceptions and strategies of Prussian political elites as they negotiated national unification.

First, in terms of *extractive capacity*—a central dimension of capacity that encompasses the ability of the state to raise revenue from its population—there were generally even levels of revenue per capita across the largest German states. In contrast to Italy, where the initiator state (Piedmont) had the highest levels of extractive capacity, in Germany some of the states most hostile to national unification (Bavaria and Württemberg) had among the highest rates of extractive capacity. These rates of revenue per capita may reflect, among other things, the different systems of fiscal administration across the German states. As the above discussion made clear, the early formation of systems of fiscal administration in response to the debt crises early in the century promoted well-developed state structures above all in the parliamentary constitutional states of Germany's southwest. A central contention of this chapter is that the high and even levels of extractive capacity across the German states, in contrast to Italy's experience, explains to a very large degree Prussia's willingness to allow the states to maintain fiscal autonomy upon national unification.

Second, as table 6.2 also shows, the *conscription rates* of the German states were twice as high, on average, as the Italian states (2.5 percent for the German states versus 1.6 percent for Italian states). Not only suggesting more effective capacity to construct a military, these data also reflect the greater coercive capacity of the German states to maintain civic order. Indeed, in comparison to the Papal States and Kingdom of Two Sicilies, where foreign troops were often required to quell violence, the German states, again especially in the largest anti-Prussian state of Bavaria, possessed the coercive capacity to maintain stability in its own population.[37] Finally, most importantly, rather than a gap between the initiator state and the rest, as we found in Italy, in Germany, Prussia and the states it would annex maintained nearly identical capacity to conscript a military. Again, this high level of infrastructural capacity outside of Prussia set the terms for Prussian plans upon national unification, making it easier for Prussia to devolve authority in this area to the states.

Finally, in terms of the *regulative capacity* of the states to initiate societal change, we see further evidence that the German states maintained high

and evenly distributed institutional capacity. While data on elementary
school enrollment rates are not sufficient to make a direct comparison
between the Italian and German states, available accounts confirm that in
contrast to most of the Italian states, elementary school reform was a major
success for the German states in this period.[38] To assess relative levels of
regulative capacity within the German states, we can use an alternative
measure that is more reliable in the German setting—the ability of states
to construct roadways. Beginning in the 1820s in many German states,
state-led road-building, along with the creation of statewide systems of
public schools, were socially revolutionary programs that aimed to create
more economically vibrant and connected societies. Furthermore, by constructing schools and roads, the leaders of Germany's states sought to
expand their zones of influence and control over society.[39] Though road
building was at the center of state building in Europe, little comparative
attention has been given to the implementation of this socially transforming project.[40] In contrast to Italy, where huge regional variations existed in road density, the German states—with the exception of Prussia
itself—experienced relatively even levels of state-sponsored road development in the nineteenth century.[41]

The evenly developed structures of the German monarchical states governed by constitutions, parliaments, and well-developed systems of administration presented different challenges for nation-state builders of
Germany. In contrast to Italy, where Piedmontese leaders faced states experiencing revolutionary conditions of instability induced by lack of state
capacity, the Prussian political leaders encountered a starkly different institutional environment when they undertook the three tasks of national
unification: ending the war of unification, forging the new union, and
writing the new rules for the new polity. As Prussian political leaders undertook these three tasks within the context of well-developed state structures, a specific set of *political actors* came to be institutionalized, along
with a set of *political norms* and *formal rules* that generated a federal polity.
Taken together, the three responses to the tasks of national unification
established the main federal contours of the German polity. But how precisely did the German institutional landscape—dominated by well-entrenched monarchical parliamentary governments—affect Prussian strategies of national unification? What opportunities and problems did the
Prussian leadership find in this setting? And how is it that the prenational
institutional landscape of well-developed state structures translated into
the actors, norms, and rules that would form the basis of a new federal
polity? These are the questions the following sections explore as we examine how the three stages of national unification undertaken between 1866
and 1871 transformed the loose confederation of German states into a
federal nation-state.

First Task of Nation-State Formation:
Ending the War of Unification

The first stage of national unification in Germany, like in Italy, was the task of ending the war of unification. The situation was essentially quite similar. Like Piedmont in 1860, Prussia found itself in the early summer of 1866 victorious and able to make territorial demands but also apprehensive about Austrian and French perceptions of its domestic plans. Yet Prussia's political leadership adopted a different set of policies toward its German neighbors than Piedmont did to its Italian neighbors in 1859–60. The aim was not to form a new centralized German nation-state on the French or Italian model that would have begun with an unconditional conquest of the German territories of Europe and the expulsion of existing and sovereign monarchical leaders and their administrative and parliamentary institutions. Instead, the Prussian leadership was content with what scholars have called a "negotiated peace" that was marked by a series of state-building concessions and accommodations.[42] Above all, the negotiated peace contained two elements: first, direct annexation of Hannover and some small states of Germany's north and center and indirect control over Saxony (forming the basis of the North German Confederation); and second, leaving intact and independent the entrenched monarchical political leaders and their state structures of Germany's south. This twofold strategy of annexation *plus* concession laid the foundations of German federalism by institutionalizing actors (the monarchical states of the south and Saxony) that would form the constituent states of a German federal state.

Put in brief, the central contention of this section is that the terms upon which the war of unification is ended institutionalizes the main political actors in a new polity: If, as in Italy, complete annexation of the periphery leads to the elimination of regional monarchical leaders and subsequently to a more unitary political structure, then an annexation project limited by concessions and pragmatic accommodations is most likely to lead to the institutionalization of regional monarchical leaders and the construction of a federal political structure. The key first step toward these two different state structures was the issue of how the war of unification was ended.

What determines when accommodation is possible? While complete annexation was perceived to be necessary in Italy, in Germany the possibility of achieving a negotiated ending to the war of unification was viewed as an opportunity. Six years after the events in Italy, the Prussian government found itself also at war with Austria, wrestling for control of the German states to create what would eventually be a smaller but united Germany.

Like the Piedmontese leadership in 1860, the Prussian king and his advisors confronted in July 1866 the question of how to end their war of unification. Ironically, given the final outcome of unification, King Wilhelm and his closest military advisors at first pushed for the immediate and unconditional conquest of the three southern German states of Baden, Württemberg, and Bavaria, which had allied with Austria.[43] In a memorandum written to the Prussian ambassador to France on July 9, 1866, Bismarck dubbed this a "maximalist annexation strategy."[44] It displays striking similarities to Cavour's war-ending strategy, and not just in retrospect. Even in 1866, Bismarck himself recognized and criticized the Prussian king's plan as being too similar to the Piedmontese crown's flawed unification designs from six years earlier.[45]

In the light of the rapidity of the victory over Austria at Königgrätz in July 1866, the atmosphere in Berlin was not surprising: "Prussian headquarters was filled with talk concerning the necessity of acquiring Saxony and parts of Bavaria, the advantages of taking the Bohemian districts of Reichenberg, Karlsbad . . . and of making other attractive annexations."[46] More surprising than that, especially when contrasted to the experience of Piedmont in Italy in 1860, is the restraint shown by Bismarck. Rather than conquering Austria or the southern German states, as Bismarck knew Piedmont had done in its project of national unification in 1860, Bismarck implemented a unification policy that directly annexed the states of Hannover, Kurhessen, the Duchy of Nassau, and Frankfurt but left the largest states of Bavaria, Baden, Württemberg, Saxony, and Austria untouched to remain as independent states.[47] The actions of Prussia in July 1866 had, according to the Bismarck's biographer, Lothar Gall, "the look of a retreat in the very moment of victory."[48] Gall summarizes the Prussian restraint: "In the moment of its greatest triumph, seen in traditional absolutist and military terms, the Prussian monarchy imposed a two-fold restraint on itself."[49] More precisely, over the next several weeks, Bismarck self-consciously rejected the path of "maximalist annexation" and pursued what he himself called a "minimalist annexation" strategy.

But, if this delicate strategy of state-building accommodations was so difficult to achieve in the Italian context, what allowed it to succeed in Germany? Several factors were behind the realpolitik restraint that contrasts with the Italian experience. First, the contingencies of war—military miscalculations and miscommunications—undermined Chief of the General Staff Moltke's bold plans of encirclement, and the Austrians retreated in July 1866 back to Vienna beyond the Danube River, opening the question of whether Prussia should move on to Vienna.[50] In an exercise in historical counterfactual, one can ask what would have happened if Prussia's encirclement plans had been effective? Would maximalist annexation strategies, favored by the Prussian king, have been pursued? Would conquest have already been achieved before all threats of French intervention?

But beyond mere contingency, a second factor, Bismarck's vision of the importance of a strategy of negotiated annexation to achieve Prussia's dominance in a united Germany, has to be considered as a weighty factor in its own right. Indeed, despite the failure of Moltke's encirclement plans, the alternative of pursuing a maximal strategy of annexation continued to carry great weight in government circles. As of June 15, 1866, Prince Friedrich Karl wrote to Bismarck outlining his plans for an attack on Saxony and Bavaria.[51] Even in July 1866, the military councils involving the king, the generals, and Bismarck that met in Berlin in the weeks after the war were marked by frequent and heated discussions of plans to pursue the Austrians into Hungary and onto Constantinople.[52] In a letter to his wife, Bismarck identified himself as having "the thankless task of pouring water into the bubbling wine and making it clear that we don't live alone in Europe but with three other Powers who hate and envy us."[53]

Bismarck's reluctance to pursue a maximalist strategy of annexation throughout all of Germany and his willingness to make territorial concessions especially in the south came under criticism, after the fact, by his domestic opponents and even by his closest allies. The General Staff was outraged and promised that in the future politicians would not be allowed to meddle in "professional" matters.[54] But his allies, too, questioned the wisdom of Bismarck's minimalist territorial annexation strategy. His trusted ambassador to Bavaria, Freiherr von Werthern, frustrated with the slow pace of postwar negotiations with Bavaria, secretly wrote to his own brother in 1868, "It is a shame that we did not march on to Munich and Stuttgart immediately after [Königgrätz]."[55] Likewise, in 1868, the Prussian ambassador to Paris confided to Lord Clarendon, the British foreign secretary, that he regretted the Prussian failure to complete the unification of Germany after Königgrätz.[56] Even the German nationalist historian Heinrich Treitschke, along with both liberals and leaders of the workers movement in Prussia, praised the annexations of the northern German states but thought such a strategy should be used in all German states outside of Prussia.[57] In 1866 the possibility of maximalist strategy of annexation, similar to Piedmont's in Italy, was not only advocated by a wide range of important actors in Prussia, it also stood as the most likely course of action.

If other policy choices were possible, what precisely was the minimalist strategy of annexation and why, in contrast to Italy, did it win out and with what consequences? Three sets of treaties constituted the centerpiece of the postwar "minimalist" settlement: the Nikolsburg Preliminary Treaty, June 26, 1866; the Prague Peace Treaty, August 23, 1866, and the seven bilateral treaties between Prussia and Württemberg, Baden, Bavaria, Hessen, Reuss Ältere Linie, Saxony, and Saxony-Meiningen, August 13–

October 21, 1866.[58] In all of these treaties as well as in official wartime memorandum between Bismarck and military officers in the field, it is clear that Prussia pursued a state-building strategy marked by accommodations and concessions to achieve what Bismarck conceived of as "minimalist" territorial demands. Three features were central: The three southern German states (Baden, Württemberg, and Bavaria), south of the Main River, were to remain "independent";[59] all midlevel administrative and political actors even in the six annexed territories (Hannover, Kurhessen, Nassau, Frankfurt, Schleswig, and Holstein) were to be left in place to assure, in Bismarck's own words, "as little interruption of administration as possible";[60] and Austria, though forced to pay war retributions, was to be left in intact and independent in exchange for the disbanding of the German Confederation and the self-removal of Austria from the sphere of the German states.[61] Unlike Piedmont's conquest of southern Italy, Prussia's negotiations and concessions with southern Germany arranged a peace marked above all by self-restraint.[62]

To understand why Prussia did not conquer Austria or Germany's south to impose maximalist or unconditional terms of annexation on these defeated states but did directly annex some states in the north, we should not refer, as Riker (1964) might suggest we do, to the military incapacity of Prussia. First, as the brief quantitative discussion of the constellation of power in Italy and Germany in chapter 1 made clear, Prussia was a first-tier dominant military and political force in Europe, having displayed its military superiority in 1866, and yet pursued a strategy of military conquest only in the northern part of Germany. Piedmont was a second-tier, comparatively weaker power that nevertheless unconditionally conquered *all* of Italy. Second, those in Prussia who best knew if Prussia had the military capacity to conquer the south were in fact the main advocates of immediate annexation. A careful look at the coalition of interests within Prussia pushing for conquest in the south, reveals that if anything, it was military officers who sensed their clear military superiority to Austria, who developed plans for an invasion beyond the Danube, and who were very serious advocates of a well-planned total annexation of Saxony, southern Germany, and Austria.[63] Yet despite the capacity to conquer, Prussian leaders, under Bismarck's advice, did not pursue the strategy predicted by a strictly power-centered account.

Similarly, an account of the events that focuses solely on the impact of ideology confronts some difficulties. It is true that Bismarck possessed an extraordinary strategic vision in his dealings with the southern German states. His willingness to abandon traditional Prussian policies toward Europe as a whole and the German states has received a great deal of attention from scholars, who call Bismarck "the White Revolutionary."[64] Moreover, some scholars have attributed these concessions and all subsequent institutional choices as a reflection of Bismarck's pursuit of personal power. Yet attribution of the negotiated settlement of Germany's unification entirely to Bismarck's coherent and self-contained ideological framework is plagued by two problems. First, by insisting that the *actual* history of Germany is solely a consequence of Bismarck's own vision of Germany, we would repeat a mistake of early German historiography that grants Bismarck an unrealistic degree of Machiavellian far-sightedness and self-awareness, that is overly reliant on Bismarck's own idealized memoirs, and that ignores the extent to which real political decisions depend on the contingencies of the moment.[65] Second, and even more important, an insistence on Bismarck's coherent and self-contained ideology as the determinant of Prussia's concessions ignores the fact that Cavour, like Bismarck, wanted a negotiated settlement to end the war of unification. Yet circumstances intervened to prejudice history in two different directions for the two great state-builders of the nineteenth century.

Though we can correctly call Bismarck's vision of Germany "revolutionary," his vision was anchored in a very specific political reality and set of circumstances. Bismarck's realpolitik vision of annexation of the north combined with negotiation vis-à-vis the south and Saxony did not develop in a vacuum. The most typical explanation of Bismarck's caution, however,—the influence of French and other international concerns—only tells part of the story. Though Bismarck was clearly concerned with foreign perceptions, the "negotiated peace" represented a simultaneous solution—in a two-level game—to two separate goals: the first a matter of foreign policy and the second a matter of domestic governance.[66]

The foreign policy goal was clear: to carry out a massive project of political expansion for Prussia without arousing the suspicions of its neighbors. Against Riker's expectations, Prussia's status as a first-tier power in Europe ironically made this task even more difficult, assuring that negotiations with the southern German states would be a more desirable route of unification.[67] Indeed, upon Prussia's unexpected victory in the beginning of July 1866, France shifted its policy toward Prussia. On July 4, 1866, as Prussia's victory seemed assured, Napoleon III sent a memo to King Wilhelm that initiated France's turn away from impartiality in the war. Napoleon begins his correspondence with the careful words, "Your successes . . . force me to depart from my role of complete abstention."[68] Following the July 4, 1866, memo, French policy did change and Napoleon's interventions increased, shaping the desirability of a negotiated end to the war: Napoleon insisted upon the continued independence of Saxony and the states south of the Main River, but Napoleon also revealed his willingness to allow Prussia's direct absorption of the other states of the north.[69]

But the domestic governance goal was also clear: to carry out the same massive project of political expansion while maintaining monarchical con-

trol without awakening resistance and unrest in the newly annexed territories. It was the intersection of these domestic and international concerns
and the institutional reality of well-developed state structures in Germany's southern states that led Bismarck to a strategy of negotiation: By
being able to leave the Bavarian, Baden, and Württemberg monarchs in
place, Bismarck could achieve his foreign policy and domestic governance
goals simultaneously. He could appease foreign concerns and simultaneously address his concerns about monarchical control, legitimacy, and stability for the new nation-state. The contrast with Italy is clear. Cavour also
sought domestic stability, monarchical control, and the appeasement of
international concerns, but had to abandon the Bismarck-like cautious
negotiations with the Neapolitan king because of institutional weakness
and the revolutionary circumstances of southern Italy. For Cavour, institutional underdevelopment in southern Italy meant an abandoning of a
strategy of negotiation for the purposes of assuring Piedmontese control
over unfolding events. In this sense, to say that the source of Bismarck's
famous caution is to be found only in the constraints of international politics is to underestimate the monumental task facing Bismarck and Cavour:
to unify their new nation-states while both appeasing international concerns and maintaining control over unfolding domestic events.

Indeed, domestic concerns were tightly linked to international considerations and were hence central to Bismarck's thinking. For example, in justi-
fying his minimalist annexation plans to the French ambassador, Goltz,
for example, Bismarck wrote in July 1866, "I believe it is impossible to
incorporate the Bavarian south German Catholic element [because] . . . the
effort to violently conquer it would only create for us the same element of
weakness that southern Italy has created for that state."[70] To what kind of
weakness was Bismarck referring? He outlined it one month later when, in
the face of pressure to conquer and rapidly unify Germany, Bismarck in a
special sitting of the Prussian Assembly in August 1866 rejected bold plans
of rapid annexation and conquest and presented his grand plan for Germany's south. As Bismarck outlines three possible ways of coming to terms
with the south Germans, the Italian experience of national unification once
again serves as the negative model. In his speech Bismarck highlights the
domestic considerations of his plans for integrating Germany's south:

> One [method] is the integration and complete merger with Prussia itself even
> in the face of popular resistance—resistance, in particular, by civil servants
> and officers (officer estates) who feel duty-bound to the previous govern-
> ments. The Prussian government intends to overcome the difficulties of these
> [groups] in a German way, through indulgence for [their local] particularities
> and through gradual habituation, and not—as is customary for a Romanic
> [Italian] peoples—all at once.[71]

Bismarck, like any state leader, feared the domestic instability and unrest that might accompany the monumental undertaking of German unification. Also, like any state leader, Bismarck drew on the lessons from what he perceived to be analogous political scenarios. But it was not only well-organized "localist" resistance to state building that led Bismarck to adopt a negotiated strategy. Instead, Bismarck sought to take advantage of the legacy of well-governed, politically developed, and effective institutions in the soon-to-be-acquired states of southern Germany; Bismarck saw in these well-developed political structures of Bavaria and southern Germany an opportunity for achieving greater state legitimacy and effectiveness by establishing a system of territorial governance that would grant formal recognition and autonomy to the constituent parts, which also were monarchical. After the fact, of course in his memoirs, his strategy of pursuing negotiation gains a retrospective logic that many historians dismiss. The fact that in retrospect Bismarck would provide a coherent intellectual framework to his actions is not surprising. More striking, then, is that, when one looks at his correspondence in the summer and fall of 1886, even the midst of the peace negotiations, Bismarck articulated a position that recognized the benefits of concessions for the future development of a united Germany. In September 1866, for example, as the final treaties with the southern states were being settled, Bismarck wrote, "If we were to attack now, then the annexation would always be viewed as a result of war and victory, as an act of violence."[72] Likewise, in October 1866, Bismarck wrote to the Prussian king that it made sense not to offer the south German states admission to the North German Confederation because they would accept such an offer "out of fear, not out of conviction."[73]

In short, we see that the Italian and German cases of ending the war of unification are two experiences with apparently similar starting points but very different end points. In the last chapter, we saw that in Italy, Cavour faced a regionally divided territory but had no "partners" with well-developed state structures with whom to negotiate unification. As a result, his strategy turned toward the elimination of the remaining but weak regional political leaders, making a sharp break with the past. By contrast, Bismarck—learning from the Italian experience and reacting to different circumstances—recognized that he had the opportunity of negotiating with regionally embedded political actors that, taking advantage of institutional and personnel continuities, would avoid the disorder of the experience in southern Italy. The consequences for German state-building trajectory was the institutionalization of a specific set of preexisting actors—regional monarchical leaders in both Prussia and the other German states—who would eventually serve as the critical social base that insisted upon the construction of a federal political order between 1866 and 1871.

SECOND TASK OF NATION-STATE FORMATION: FORGING THE UNION

The task of forging national unity established a different founding myth for the new nation-state of Germany. Rather than being pushed, as in Italy, by circumstances toward an unwanted plebiscite that might have given rise to a founding myth of revolutionary change, the entrenchment of the German monarchs and the well-developed states they governed gave rise to a different route of forging the union. The well-embedded constitutional monarchies outside of Prussia gave Bismarck a set of negotiation partners with whom to establish a new nation-state "from above" in which the German monarchs would set the terms of a gradual and diplomatically negotiated process of national unification.[74] In Italy, events had intervened to force the Piedmontese crown to accept a national unification via a plebiscite and thereby established the Risorgimento myth of "revolutionary" change that was used, at times intentionally and at times unintentionally, by Piedmontese political elites to crystallize diverse regional commitments and to legitimate the new centralized polity.[75]

In Germany, by contrast, the monarchical leaders of the German states did not need to resort to revolutionary rhetoric and instead could act on behalf of their states' autonomous interests to guarantee a carefully crafted set of diplomatic agreements among the German states that was very much rooted in the norms of the long-standing German Bund. Rather than decisively replacing prenational patterns of political authority, the German leaders adapted to and recast existing state structures. Indeed, because the state structures of the annexed states were more developed, more effective, and hence less dissolvable, an important norm of *Verhandlung* (negotiation) among constituent parts was reinforced in the process of national unification that proved to be a critical ingredient in the new federal political system.[76] Scholars have tended to emphasize the antidemocratic dynamic of this negotiated unification but in doing so have ignored the norm of *Verhandlung*, which was in fact just as critical a feature of this political founding.[77]

At the heart of the agreements that brought the North German Confederation and German Reich into existence were the notions of *Vertrag* (contract) and *Bund* (compact) that represented a symbolic continuity with the pre-1867 past. Rather than "revolution" or even the Risorgimento myth of "renewal" that represented a break from the prenational past, the German monarchs who sat atop well-developed state structures could set the terms of national unification through diplomatic negotiation. As a result, the mode by which the German states granted approval for annexation was what German constitutional thinkers have called a diplomatic "compact among sovereigns," or what has come to be known in one Bavarian interpretation as the *Fürstenbund* (Federation of Princes) or even by later and more unitarian scholars as a practice of bargaining and compromise.[78]

The precise nature of these "compacts" among the sovereigns has been subject to much debate among scholars of German constitutional history.[79] But the competing interpretations of the founding of the Reich among scholars provided much of the symbolic glue that held the Reich together during its earlier years. Indeed, it was arguably precisely the ambiguity of the core concepts of the founding of German federalism—contract, treaty, bargain—that contributed to their effectiveness as means of providing cohesion to the new nation-state.[80] Some "federalist" theorists, for example, tended to see the Reich as a "confederation." These scholars, usually found in Germany's south, emphasized what they regarded as the "contractual" foundation of the North German Confederation in 1866–67 and the German Reich in 1870–71. For example, constitutional thinkers such as the Bavarian Max von Seydel were influenced by the American states' rights advocate John Calhoun and insisted that the German Reich was a "contract" (*Vertrag*) between twenty-three equal and independent sovereign states that could be undone at any time. Other more moderate unitarian thinkers such as the Prussian Paul Laband agreed with von Seydel that the national political entity came into existence through the political decisions of twenty-three independent and parallel subnational state leaders. But Laband diverged from the "states' rights" radicalism of von Seydel insofar as he recognized the ultimate supremacy of the German Reich. Yet even for Laband, the locus of this political supremacy was neither in the lower national parliamentary chamber (as in France) nor in the national crown (as in Great Britain) but rather in the Bundesrat, the chamber that represented the monarchs of the constituent states in what scholars call a "kind of collective monarch."[81] Despite this rich debate in German constitutional scholarship, what is striking is the degree of consensus that runs throughout German constitutional thought: the North German Confederation and the German Reich were formed not "from below" nor strictly "from above" by a single monarch but were instead created in a series of diplomatic treaties between sovereign, unelected leaders of the independent German states—establishing the norm of negotiation that underpinned nineteenth-century German federalism.

In fact, if we turn to the historical record, eight separate public treaties were signed between August 18, 1866, and November 25, 1870, between the Prussian monarch and the monarchs of the other German states to bring the Reich into existence. First, beginning after the war with Austria, a treaty was signed on August 18, 1866, by the Prussian king and the kings of sixteen north German states that committed the states to a "defensive and offensive union" that aimed to preserve the "independence" and "integrity" of the members of the new North German Confederation. Two critical state-building features were contained in the treaty: the call for the creation of a north German parliament; and the statement that the sovereigns all agreed to allow their troops to be under the leadership of the Prussian crown.[82] With this treaty, the monarchs of the northern German states gave birth to a new political entity—the North German Confederation—that lasted for three years until fused with the southern German states. An important consequence of this treaty was that the monarchs of even the northern states were promised inclusion in the process of writing a new constitution for the North German Confederation. Since that constitution served as the model for the German Reich's constitution three years later, in 1870, historians normally regard 1867 and not 1871 as the decisive turning point. But these negotiated terms of unification were further reinforced four years later in 1870–71, as seven additional treaties were signed by the Prussian king—always "in the name of the North German Confederation"—and by the monarchs of Baden, Hessen, Württemberg, and Bavaria.[83] In each of the six main treaties and one secret agreement between the Prussian and Bavarian kings, the monarchs of each of the states agreed to "union" with the German Federation.

After national unification was negotiated, the notion of "diplomatic negotiation" as the basis of the new political entity came to be formalized in the new constitution in 1867 and in 1871. Both constitutional documents begin in section 1 with the statement that the "monarchs of the member states join in everlasting union."[84] In contrast to the failed 1849 constitution, which made no such claims of having its origins in a "union" of states, the constitutions of the North German Federation and the German Reich displayed a self-conscious continuity with the 1815 German Bund's structure by insisting upon the importance of the member states as founding members of the larger political entity. Additionally, political leaders looking for a "contractual" or "diplomatic" basis of the new German federation also point to Article 10 of the 1871 constitution, in which diplomatic immunity rather than parliamentary immunity is guaranteed to the members of the Bundesrat as if members were from a foreign land. Finally, the continued existence of diplomatic envoys for member states of the new Reich in Berlin was also evidence of this deeper tendency to conceive of it a compact among sovereign governments. All of this together suggests the extent to which the new union of states not only institutionalized regional actors but also did so in terms that emphasized the symbolic importance of the federation as a "compact" among monarchical leaders of the German states.

But, why precisely did Prussia carry out unification via a set of treaties rather than through a plebiscite, as did Piedmont, giving rise in Germany to this symbolic norm of "compact" and "negotiation"? Again, it was not solely an ideological commitment to federalism, nor was it simply a story of Prussia's inability to impose its will on the rest of Germany. In Germany, political leaders simply confronted a different institutional landscape in which states were not so easily dissolvable as in Italy. In Germany, the "negotiated" terms of national unification were informed by what Max Weber and more recently Reinhard Bendix have dismissed as a "feudal ideology"—the notion that the seat of sovereignty is found with the monarch of states rather than the citizens of states.[85] The experience of the non-Prussian German monarchs contrasted with the non-Piedmontese Italian monarchs insofar as they were still in existence upon unification and could sign treaties with the Prussian crown between 1866 and 1871. Though in some instances parliamentary approval within the German states was demanded to ratify the actions of each state's crown, the decisive feature of this process was that national unification was achieved by a set of eight formal treaties between the unelected leaders of each of the independent German states. In contrast to Italy, where sovereignty could be interpreted to lie with the Piedmontese crown or with the populations that voted by plebiscite to join Piedmont in the absence of negotiation partners, in Germany, "neither the united German people nor the people of the individual German states, but rather the individual and implicitly sovereign monarchs had ceremonially called the entity into existence."[86]

But why was this so-called feudal ideology sustainable in Germany and not Italy? It is true that Cavour had sought precisely such a diplomatic relationship between his monarch and the Neapolitan monarch in the waning days before Italian unification. The feudal ideology survived more successfully in the German context because of the firmly developed state structures of the German states, in which monarchs were not removed from power; parliaments that passed legislation and budgets continued to do so; and empowered administrative actors carried out modernizing reforms for their societies. Whereas in Italy the fragile and ineffective state structures without parliaments or constitutions collapsed upon unification, in Germany these parliamentary monarchies were the driving impetus behind unification, negotiating the terms of unification at each stage. Even the 1849 constitution retained many federal features despite the fact that it was the product of a revolutionary interlude in which control was wrestled away from the German monarchs.[87] We can ask, in another historical counterfactual: if the constitutional proposals of 1849 had been successful, how federal would the German nation-state have remained? Looking at the constitutional document itself, we see that first, under the 1849 constitution, more powers were granted to the national parliament, removing powers from the territorial body of the upper house. Second, though Article 5 of the 1849 constitution left all rights and privileges not explicitly granted to the federal government to the states, one crucial feature of the 1849 constitution retained the right of the federal government at any time to alter the rights of the states by altering the constitution. More to the point, the 1849 constitution is federal, but the underlying ideology of that constitution abandons the monarchical notion of a "compact" among sovereigns and hence is the most centralized German constitution of the nineteenth century. We see that the firmly entrenched state structures that became even more entrenched during the "reactionary" 1850s resisted their dissolution and were a source of sovereignty that could only be absorbed through the long-standing practice of negotiation among states. The insertion of a *norm* of "compact" or "negotiation" into the new state structures after 1866 nearly assured federalism for the new German nation-state.

THIRD TASK OF NATION-STATE FORMATION: MAKING THE NEW RULES

Though the *political actors* (regional monarchs) and *political norms* ("compact" or "negotiation") institutionalized and formalized by Germany's negotiated path of nation-state formation might have guaranteed that the new nation-state would never be a unitary state on the Italian model, the question remains: what determined what *type* of federal structure would be established? How centralized would it be? How much autonomy would the constituent parts retain? And, how did Germany's prenational legacy of well-developed regional-state structures shape the process of making the new rules? In particular three questions of institutional design were crucial: (1) How much formal access via a chamber representing territorial interests would the formerly independent regional governments have in the new nation-state? (2) How much discretion would they have in public finance? and (3) How much administrative autonomy would they have? The following section traces the politics of institutional design of the German Reich through three critical periods—the internal government-level discussions in the summer of 1866 surrounding various proposals for a new constitution; the process of seeking approval from the member states in the fall and winter of 1866–67; and the process of extending the north German constitution to the southern German states in 1870–71. By 1871, a particular *type* of federalism (*Exekutivföderalismus*) was adopted in Germany that reflected the effort to impose national integration onto a subnational context of well-developed state institutions.

The first period in the development of the German constitution that began in the summer of 1866, as the war with Austria was ending, was a period in which proposals for a new constitution were discussed across various government ministries in Berlin. In this first period, it is striking that among federalist advocates of a decentralized state structure and the liberal nationalist advocates of a more centralized state, the need for a new written constitution for the new German Reich went unquestioned. Rather than imposing Prussia's constitution on the rest of Germany, as Piedmont had done in Italy, all actors assumed that a new constitution would be necessary to encompass the existing German constitutional monarchies even if only extended to the north German states. But, importantly even after the war of 1866 had ended, Bismarck and officials in the Prussian ministries who would design the North German Confederation constitution remained divided on the future shape of Germany's institutions. As in Piedmont, there was a range of ideological positions within the Prussian government. At one end were close advisors to Bismarck such as high-ranking officials in the Foreign Ministry such as Lothar Bucher and Robert Hepke and other civil servants such Max Duncker who all advocated what the actors themselves called a "unitary" federal vision of Germany, often based on the failed 1849 Frankfurt constitution.[88] Many of these advisors' ideas were inspired by the nationalist liberal movement in Germany. Frustrated with Germany's fragmented parochialism (*Kleinstaaterei*) and the weakness they believed the German Confederation generated for the nation, liberal nationalists saw in France's prestigious and successful centralized unitary state a model for what a modern Prussian-led modern Germany might look like. Moreover, many viewed the prospect of integrating Germany's legal codes as a surrogate for national unification. During the summer of 1866, Bismarck's advisors, influenced by this view, prepared drafts of a German constitution and were in frequent contact with Bismarck.[89]

Their constitutional proposals varied from each other in significant ways, but they shared a unitary tendency insofar as they advocated an expanded role for a new national-level legislature elected via expanded franchise to supersede the monarchical states' parliaments. For example, Max Duncker's proposals would have vested less authority in the states. In Duncker's proposal, the territorial house (*Bundesversammlung* in Duncker's draft) would have had much more limited scope of authority; rather than the authority to initiate legislation, the territorial chamber would have only had the authority to approve or disapprove of legislation.[90] Additionally, Duncker's constitutional draft gave the national government the ability to impose direct taxes, a move that would in fact not come to the fiscally decentralized Germany until after 1900. Pushing still further, in March 1867, the liberal leader of the Progressive Party, Dr. Benedikt Waldeck, expressed a sentiment widespread among national liberals that sought an explicitly unitary (*Einheitsstaat*) organization for the new German state that would dismantle the monarchical "particularistic" and "feudal" prenational states.[91] The unitary tendency was still quite strong even in the summer and fall of 1866.

But, by October 1866, Bismarck, who had specifically commissioned Max Duncker to draft his constitutional proposal, rejected Duncker's broad unitary proposal as unrealistic. The prospect of imposing a unitary model on a set of states that had already undergone far-reaching state-building presented a challenge to these unitary thinkers. But certain key elements of what Gerhard Lehmbruch (2002) calls the 1848 unitary "discourse" that informed Duncker's proposal would nevertheless leave important institutional legacies for German federalism.[92] In particular, Germany's "executive federalism" beginning in 1866 was marked by two core characteristics: active national legislation coupled with state-level administrative primacy in the implementation of national legislation. This unique combination, which made German federalism distinct from its nineteenth-century American or Swiss counterparts, has been read by some scholars as an effort to reconcile the entrenched interests of German state monarchies and bureaucracies, on the one hand, with the important unitary vision of men like Duncker, on the other.[93] Moreover, the development of German federalism after 1871 would reflect the same unitary impulse, facilitated by Article 2 of the 1871 constitution, which stipulated that the Bund's legislation superseded member state legislation. Indeed, during the 1870s, the Reichstag became the site of a highly active project of legal and judicial unification, as a Reich commercial code, civil code, and criminal code were created, alongside the creation of a federal-level court in 1877–79.[94] Similarly, with the creation of the Bismarckian welfare state, what has come to be known a "unitary federalism" was created.[95] In short, though Duncker's unitary vision of Germany may have been formally defeated in 1849 and 1867, it did not disappear, but continued to shape the German political landscape.[96]

How precisely did the Duncker unitary constitutional proposal come to be rejected, leading to the creation of a federal constitution? In September 1866, after the tumultuous events of the summer, Bismarck left Berlin for the rural island of Rügen in the Baltic Sea, where he examined the proposed constitutional drafts of his Prussian advisors.[97] Here, Bismarck wrote two famous "dictates" that would serve as the basis of the final constitution of 1866 and 1870.[98] Though scholars have remained understandably divided on the extent to which Bismarck foresaw in the winter of 1866 an immediate unification with Germany's south, the contents of the two dictates reveal that Bismarck's goal of an eventual unification with the south was at the forefront in his mind even at this early stage, and accommodating the southern states was a main motivation in his rejection of Duncker's centralized constitutional proposals. First, in the dictates, Bismarck writes that Duncker's proposal was "too centralized for the eventual accession of the south Germans."[99] Reflecting a recognition that what contemporary social scientists now call "pathbreaking" institutional change often requires a rhetorical strategy that emphasizes path-dependence, Bismarck writes in the dictates, "In form, we shall have to stick more to the confederation of states while in practice giving it the character of a federal state with elastic, inconspicuous but far-reaching form." Additionally, he displayed his sensitivity to southern concerns by arguing that the "central authority" of the Reich ought to be "not a single Ministry but a Federal Diet, a body consisting of delegates from the individual governments."[100] Finally, Bismarck admonished his advisors that a more "elastic" set of institutions was necessary that would display as much continuity with those of the loose pre-1866 German Confederation. Again, showing a remarkable appreciation for issues of path-dependence, Bismarck wrote, "The more we link the institutions to the old forms, the easier things will be."[101]

In this first period that ended in the fall of 1866, various proposals for constitutions were considered. The unusual combination of a proposed constitutional change justified by a rhetorical strategy that emphasized continuity had its roots in the peculiarities of the German institutional landscape, in which regional political actors and norms of cooperation were intact and state structures were well developed and effective. Like Cavour in Italy, Bismarck was very aware of the "particularistic" regionalism of his divided nation-state. Yet this regional resistance led to a new constitution in Germany, but not in Italy, not because of the military incapacity of Prussia. Rather, the crucial difference was threefold: the political actors involved, the political norms underpinning the process of constitutional approval, and the institutional context in which a new constitution was to be approved in the new Germany. In Italy, as the discussion in the last chapter made clear, regional governments were eliminated from the process of national unification, no norms of negotiation among the states existed, and the Piedmontese constitution was simply extended to the rest of Italy to fill the institutional vacuum left behind by the poorly developed and now extinct regimes. Bismarck, by contrast, advocated a new constitution that could be federal because existing regional governments were *included* in the process of national unification, a norm of negotiation had been established at the end of the war of 1866, and the German states through their well-developed parliamentary and administrative structures had already penetrated and embedded themselves in their societies in arenas such as education, religion, transportation, and public finance. Rather than placing new structures atop these already existing structures, it made sense, as other analysts have also noted, to simply devolve authority to these already existing and effective structures.[102] With the creation of a national parliament that would pass legislation to be implemented by the

states, we see that executive federalism emerged as a solution to the particular path of German state formation, in which state consolidation had
preceded national integration.

The second period of constitutional developments in Germany that
began in the fall of 1866 was dominated by the pursuit of approval for the
new constitutional design that Bismarck had drawn up during the late
summer 1866. The terms for this process of approval were set in the August 1866 treaties with fifteen kings of the north German states—treaties
in which the Prussian government had assured that the approval by a majority of the monarchs of the north German states was a requirement for
the Prussian constitutional proposals to be implemented.[103] Any future
extension of a constitution to the even more regionalist southern states
would—and did—require approval of the monarchs and parliaments of
each of those southern states. As a result, it is not surprising that Bismarck
was concerned with the opinions of the monarchs and parliaments of other
German states, including his own state of Prussia, where Bismarck accurately sensed that the creation of too "centralized" a government with
power vested in a nationally elected parliament rather than a federal diet
(Bundesrat) would be perceived by conservative Prussian leaders as removing too much power from Prussia itself.[104] Because Prussian political leaders were confident they would dominate a federal structure, they advocated granting concessions to the other states, thereby creating a federal
structure of governance. It is this irony that has made scholars such as
Manfred Rauh argue that German federalism was merely a "fig-leaf for
Prussian hegemony."[105] But it is also this irony that made political leaders
in other German states agree with Prussian "particularists" that federalism
was the most effective way of leaving the structure of the existing states
intact and preventing their state structures from being entirely subsumed
by a new national political entity.[106]

With these preemptive considerations in mind, Bismarck met in a sum-
mit on December 15, 1866, in Berlin with the monarchical leaders and
the representatives of all of the German states to approve his constitutional
proposal that had been finished in the Prussian Royal Council (Kronrat)
on December 13, 1866. The process for putting the constitution into
effect required first the approval of the monarchs of the German states
(achieved in February 1867) and second the approval a majority of the
new North German Reichstag (achieved in April 1867). Though the new
and first North German democratically elected parliament (Reichstag)
would still follow in April 1867, the North German constitution was in
fact largely finalized over the course of nearly two months of negotiations
between the heads of each of the German states when discussions were
ended on February 7, 1867.

A whole range of both symbolically ideological and pragmatic issues became immediately contentious.[107] When one considers that the project of forming the North German Bund was asking the member states for the first time in their history to voluntarily hand over their long-standing sovereignty to a new and untested larger "national" entity, it is not surprising that leaders responded with dismay, at the first meeting on December 15, 1866, to Bismarck's proposed new constitution.[108] At the center of the debates were three federal issues: First, what should the chamber representing territorial interests look like? Bismarck's proposed institution of the Bundesrat was modeled after the pattern that had dominated inter-German relations under the Holy Roman Empire. Since 1666, the "Permanent Diet" (Immerwährende Reichstag) served as a congress of ambassadors where the heads of the 160 German states met to negotiate issues of war and peace. After 1815, the number of German states was reduced, but the institution of the Bundestag was established on that model. Undoubtedly basing it partly on his experience as Prussia's representative in that body in the 1850s, Bismarck adapted it to the new North German Confederation, changing its name to Bundesrat, and thereby also rejected proposals for an upper house modeled on the British House of Lords.

First, in reaction to Bismarck's Bundesrat proposal a coalition of smaller states—Oldenburg, Saxony-Coburg, Saxony-Weimar, Braunschweig, and Hamburg—formally proposed that the Bundesrat be replaced with a more traditional upper chamber on the British model to assure that Prussia would not dominate it.[109] Second, even after accepting the Bundesrat, the leaders of smaller states disputed the planned power balance between the "federal" Bundesrat and the "national" Bundespräsidium, once again insisting that too much power located in the "federal" Bundesrat would result in a nation-state dominated by Prussia.[110] Finally, an issue of contention remained the distribution of seats in the Bundesrat. With more than two-thirds of Germany's population, Prussia would dominate a chamber based on population. To walk a fine line between the "particularists" of the larger states of Mecklenburg, Saxony, and Hessen, and the "unitarian-oriented" smaller states, Bismarck's solution gave smaller states greater representation but left Prussia and several other larger states with the most seats. After negotiations among the state representatives, the Bundesrat came into existence, guaranteeing that all state leaders would have direct and important access to the federal legislative process.[111]

A second issue that was contentious in the process of approval was how much administrative autonomy the states should have. Over the course of the debates, states such as Braunschweig and Hamburg displayed reluctance to give up control of their own postal systems. The state leaders of Weimar, Meiningen, Lippe-Detmold, Altenburg, Coburg, and Reuss found excessive the terms of fusion of their militaries with the Prussian military. States sought to protect their zones of administrative autonomy, and Bismarck and Prussian negotiators easily consented, recognizing that concessions would give Prussia greater autonomy over its own administrative life.[112] Though Prussia might have dominated policy at the national level, the administration of most policy areas were left in the hands of state-level administrations.

Third, how should the system of public finance be organized? With effective systems of tax administration already in place in every single state, the notion of starting from scratch and imposing a new "national" or Bund-level tax administration made little sense. The new North German Confederation would be funded through contributions from the states, depending on state size. The leaders of Mecklenburg insisted to Prussian representatives in bilateral negotiations that Mecklenburg not be required to enter all of the terms of the German customs union. Similarly the Hanseatic cities of Hamburg and Bremen insisted on extra financial transfers since they were not members of the German customs union. In short, nearly every state had a different position on every issue as each state government sought to secure its own interests in the new political entity.

The task of finding a consensus among the conflicting interests of each of the fifteen state governments entailed granting many concessions, including special public finance arrangements for some states and granting some states more representatives in the Bundesrat than initially planned. But, in the end, the revisions left the federal structure of the state intact and furthermore once again reinforced the element of diplomatic bargaining and negotiation in federal relations that would slowly be institutionalized into Germany's political system. To successfully create a federal structure out of these long, heated, and conflict-ridden negotiations, Bismarck displayed, according to one account, his "greatest achievement in the art of state-making."[113] The proposed constitution passed with the unanimous approval of the state representatives. In the first Reichstag, again it was approved with few amendments. By April 1867, the new Norddeutsche Bund was created as a federation, laying the groundwork for the creation of the federal German Reich in 1871.[114]

CONCLUSION

The creation of an explicitly federal German nation-state, in which all member states had (1) access to national political institutions via the Bundesrat, (2) high levels of public finance discretion, and (3) continued administrative autonomy, was a direct outcome of a particular prenational institutional environment in which the constituent states of Germany already had constitutions, parliaments, and well-developed administrative structures long before national unification. At the most practical level, the highly developed state structures gave Prussia a set of negotiation partners with whom to seal unification and, furthermore, a set of states upon which authority could be devolved *after* unification. Put in other terms, this preexisting institutional setting translated into a federally organized nation-state because this setting assured that national unification could be achieved through a careful and gradual process of *negotiation* among monarchs rather than conquest or direct annexation that might have led to a much more centralized or even unitary state in Germany.

But how precisely did "unification by negotiation" give rise to Germany's federalism? It was the inclusion of a particular set of actors, norms, and formal rules that were an inherent part of this process of negotiation that guaranteed federalism for Germany. By achieving unification by negotiation, the existing actors, norms, and formal rules that constituted the prenational pattern of political authority in Germany were neither cast entirely aside nor marked by a wholesale continuity. Rather, some features of the old patterns of authority persisted, some were recast, and others were entirely redone. In particular, existing regional political actors stayed in power, long-standing norms of diplomatic *Verhandlung* (negotiation) among states were reinforced, and new formal rules that guaranteed public finance and administrative and political autonomy in the new political construction but that allowed for national integration were created from scratch. We see, then, that the manner in which federalism emerged after 1867 and 1871 in Germany challenges the way we often think about how institutions are created in moments of critical juncture. Rather than a clean break from the past, federalism was a multilayered product of new formal rules but also of long-standing actors and norms, giving rise to the central irony of nineteenth-century German federalism. Compared to the constitutional continuity that marked Italy's national unification in the same time period, the transformation from the German *Bund* to German *Reich* between 1815 and 1871 was marked by an apparent continuity with the past in terms of the actors, institutions, and political norms involved. Yet this continuity with the past—and the success of federalism itself—was possible only because it was accompanied by a sharp constitutional break from the past, in which a new constitution, without historical precedent, was negotiated for Germany.

In this sense, the federal structure of Germany's state emerged not solely because of deep-seated cultural, ideological, or even power-structural characteristics of German society as most theories of federalism might suggest. Nor can Germany's federalism be attributed merely to Bismarck's prescient genius, as so many historians have implied. Rather, federalism emerged out of a particular logic of prenational state structure and as an outcome of a particular path of state formation in which state-building preceded national unification. The mechanism by which this sequencing of state formation and nation-state formation led to federalism was through the multilayered process of institutional change that this chapter has identified. Because state building was completed at the regional level before nation-state formation even began in Germany, a set of old actors could use a set of old norms to develop new rules that would give rise to a distinctive "executive federal" polity.

Chapter Seven

CONCLUSION: THE POLITICS OF FEDERALISM AND INSTITUTION BUILDING IN THE NINETEENTH CENTURY AND BEYOND

THE PUZZLE that motivated this study is embedded in two historical cases of national unification: why did Prussia, a military heavyweight, make concessions to southern Germany to establish a federal state, while the much weaker Piedmont conquered southern Italy to establish a unitary state?

For several reasons this very specific empirical puzzle has proven to be a fruitful starting point from which to rethink federalism's origins. First, Italy and Germany, as the two great parallel west European cases of late unification, experienced starkly different institutional outcomes. Second, the two cases, as this study has also made clear, shared a set of prenational cultural and historical similarities that might have led us to expect similar institutional outcomes after national unification. But, above all, the Italian and German cases have been such a useful comparative pair because they run directly against the intuitively appealing expectations of Rikerian theories of federalism, which assume that, unless constrained by a countervailing military power, the political center in a new polity will always adopt a unitary institutional solution to the task of national integration.

When we look more closely at the puzzle of why Prussia made concessions to establish a federation while Piedmont did not, we discover that the actual institutional outcomes in each case do not simply reflect the "congealed tastes" or the intentions and institutional designs of the main political actors.[1] Why? First, in both the German and the Italian context, though key state-building elites were goal-driven, purposive actors, they had multiple, shifting, and sometimes contradictory goals as they designed political institutions. Not only concerned with maximizing military power on the international stage, achieving national unification, and assuring a monarchical control over the unfolding events, the political leadership was also motivated by concerns with domestic governance, primarily that of maintaining social stability in the newly unified states. As a result, the actions and state-building strategies of Prussian and Piedmontese political leadership, as they considered which broad institutional "solution" to adopt, were mediated not only by military and security threats but also by the domestic governance structures that emerged from each state's pathway of national political development.

In particular, in instances where the pattern of prenational state formation had left effective regional political institutions in place at the moment of national unification, political leaders viewed such institutions not as constraints on their power but as useful means of achieving national unification rapidly and without social upheaval. The lesson of the two cases is that if effective regional political institutions are in place, federalism is viewed as the path of least resistance to national unification. In this sense, for these two particular cases, the conventional causal account of federalism's origins is backwards: federalism was not a second-best strategy adopted when necessary. Instead, federalism emerged when possible, while it was unitary structures that were viewed as necessary.

Given the usual disclaimers about the limits of a focused two-case comparison, to what extent do these conclusions represent an amendment to traditional theories of federalism's origins? How well do the findings travel to other national cases? This final chapter will make the case that with some small refinements, the proposed state-centered perspective highlights a set of factors, usually overlooked by traditional theories, that can make sense of a range of cases beyond Germany and Italy. In the following, I first summarize the central theoretical innovation offered in my study. Second, I refine and test my argument by applying it to a broader set of seventeen national cases. Finally, in the last part of this chapter I articulate the broader implications of my account for theories of institutional change.

THE CENTRAL ARGUMENT SUMMARIZED: A SUPPLY-SIDE THEORY OF FEDERALISM

Because the various theories frequently used to explain the origins of federalism are not usually subjected to rigorous and systematic empirical testing, what normally passes for theory is in fact a set of intuitively appealing but flawed propositions that conflate analytically separate questions. For example, the Rikerian contention that the impulse behind the formation of federations is the presence of external security threats might tell us a great deal about the causes of political unification but tells us very little, as it purports to do, about the causes of the specific political institutions (unitary or federal) in a newly formed polity. Similarly, the more recent notion that federations are formed in order to take advantage of larger-scale zones of economic integration also might answer the question, "Why unify?" but again tells us little about the answer to question, "Why unify as a federation?"[2] In short, there is a tendency among scholars to mistake the causes of national unification for the causes of federalism.

It is with this distinction in mind that this study has answered two separate questions: First, why do states join or merge together to form larger political units? Second, why, when forming larger political units, do they sometimes form federations and other times unitary state structures? Chapters 2, 3, and 4 answered the first question. I argued that national unification was driven by both economic and political motivations that shaped the dominant ethos of political expansion and centralization that were hallmarks of Europe's national age. The long-standing debate between neo-Marxists and statists on the causes of state formation has been fruitful but is ultimately diversionary; both the "state-centered" security concerns of state leaders interested in raising revenue to support militaries and the economic motivations of an emerging commercial class drove national unification. The issue, as chapters 2, 3, and 4 made clear, is the relative weight and interaction of the two factors highlighted by statist and Marxist accounts.[3]

The central argument of this study, as developed in chapters 5 and 6, has focused on the second question: Under what conditions does federalism emerge as the mode of political integration for state elites seeking to integrate economically and politically diverse territory? To explain why new polities take on federal political structures, scholars usually make use of one of three propositions that should by now be familiar to the reader; at first glance, all three propositions are not only logical but also seem to find some scattered support. For example, the first proposition, that deeply *culturally* or *economically divided* societies are likely to give rise to federal states, appears to be sustainable with cases such Switzerland and India, two divided societies that are also federal states. Similarly, the second proposition, that federations emerge when political elites are *ideologically* committed to a federal state structure, also seems to find some evidence when one notes the ideological commitments of political leaders in the United States in 1787 or any federalist thinkers who author a federal constitution for a new state.[4] Finally, the most influential proposition, that *militarily weak* founding political centers, in contrast to strong founding political centers, tend to "negotiate" federal "bargains" with their periphery appears to explain federal states such as Australia, Switzerland, and the United States.

Despite their differences, all of these approaches portray federalism either as a second-best option of a powerless political center too weak to penetrate recalcitrant localities or as nearly automatic once a political leadership becomes ideologically converted to federalist institutional designs. A central finding of this study is that both these portrayals are flawed in their assumption that institutions neatly "fit" the farsighted designs of powerful political actors: To assume, first, that a political center will always adopt a strategy of unification that *maximizes* military control vis-à-vis subnational actors and will compromise to establish indirect rule only when too militarily weak to establish direct rule ignores a great deal of empirical evidence that political leaders frequently embrace federal structures even when possessing the military prowess to penetrate recalcitrant regions. Second, to assume that an ideological commitment to federalism guarantees federal state structures is to focus too exclusively on the "demand side" of institutional creation. A theory of institutional creation that looks only at the ideas of political actors is bound to be disappointed as political leaders try convert their plans into actual institutions in the far more complicated reality of a moment of institutional creation. This study finds that the most decisive factor in such a moment of institutional creation is the preexisting supply of regional political institutions, shaping which strategies of institutional creation are possible and desirable. Put in the simplest of terms, to achieve a federal rather than a unitary structure, there must exist not only a *demand* for federalism but also a *supply* of well-developed regional political institutions with high levels of institutional capacity that can be used both to negotiate the terms of polity formation and to govern after the polity has been formed. In table 7.1, I present the main contours of the argument applied to the two cases.

As table 7.1 makes clear, I first argue that the key "background" factor that made federalism succeed in Germany and fail in Italy despite the common ideological preference for it was an uneven legacy of the German and Italian prenational regional period, which reflected a different sequencing of national unification and political development. While state building and political development in the constituent states of Germany *preceded* national unification, leaving a set of well-developed states in place, state building and political development was not yet complete in the constituent states of Italy before national unification, leaving a set of absolutist states without parliaments, constitutions, or effective administrative structures. As a consequence, Piedmont inherited absolutist states that were brittle and ineffective without constitutions, without parliaments, and with only partially modernized state administrative structures. By contrast, Prussia inherited a set of much more embedded (though not liberal), institutionally dense, and effective regional states with constitutions, with parliaments, and with much more fully developed and differentiated administrative structures. Furthermore, this study finds evidence to suggest that the states Piedmont inherited had much less institutional capacity to do the work of modern governance—tax, conscript a military, and educate the population—than the German states did that Prussia inherited six years later.

TABLE 7.1
Summary of Findings: From Strong Regional Loyalties to Two Institutional Outcomes

	Federal Path of State Formation	Unitary Path of State Formation
1. Conditions at moment of polity formation	1. High regional institutional capacity	1. Underdeveloped regional institutional capacity
	Parliaments	No Parliaments
	Constitutions	No Constitutions
	Systems of public Administration	Weak systems of public administration
2. Strategy of unification	2. Unification by negotiation	2. Unification by conquest
3. Process of institutional change	3. Layering	3. Conversion
	Old actors included	Old actors excluded
	Old norms reinforced	New norms created
	Creation of new formal rules from scratch	Extension of pre-existing formal rules
4. Outcome	4. A decentralized federal state	4. A prefectoral unitary state

As a consequence, as the second step in table 7.1 also makes clear, national unification was carried out in different ways in the two otherwise similar cases: In the moment of national unification (1859–60) Piedmontese leaders and provisional leaders outside of Piedmont were tempted, despite their "decentralist" inclinations, to carry out the direct annexation of central and southern regions, or what I call "unification by conquest." This strategy centralized political authority in the face of institutional incapacity and the threat of civic instability in the newly annexed regions. Given the aim of assuring geopolitical weight and monarchical control, the collapsing revolutionary states outside of Piedmont were not promising partners. Indeed, the preexisting institutional weakness and the decisions made during these critical moments created a self-reinforcing dynamic that further undercut the capacity of Italy's regional governments to carry out the work of modern governance: social regulation, taxation, and the maintenance of civic stability. By 1865, the presence of troops and Piedmontese officials throughout Italy made the prospects of federalism increasingly infeasible and improbable. The strategy of unification by conquest ultimately entailed a dislodging of existing political elites and structures, justified by a "myth" of revolution and supported by the extending of the Piedmontese constitution to the rest of Italy; monarchical control was assured via Italy's highly restrictive franchise.

By contrast, Prussian leaders—in the face of well-developed and "modernized" states in Germany's south—could carry out national "unification by negotiation" in 1866 and 1871 and could leave large areas of state activity in the hands of highly capable, preexisting monarchical but parliamentary governments, all creating a self-reinforcing dynamic that gave regional governments greater institutional autonomy in a federal German Reich. Not only were there organized regional parliaments in place to negotiate national unification on behalf of non-Prussian regions, but Prussian leaders could devolve power to states that were in fact more effective than Prussia at carrying out the work of governance. Since formal agreements were in place to assure that Bavaria and other large German states would contribute troops and resources to Prussia in case of war, establishing indirect rule was the path of least resistance for Prussia. While established theories of federalism might suggest that Prussia, as a militarily powerful state, should have sought the "maximalist" strategy of a unitary state, the existence of highly capable parliamentary monarchical governments throughout Germany gave rise to a shift in strategy, assuring that federalism would be created in the decisive moment of national unification. Here, existing political elites were left in place, a long-standing norm of "negotiation" among state leaders was reinforced, and a new constitution was written to make room for these still-standing regional political structures. We see, in short, that federalism's fate in Italy and Germany was shaped by the institutional legacies of the prenational context: where effective regional governments were in place *before* the national government was formed, federalism was created.

Two broader points may be gleaned from this supply-side institutional argument on federalism's origins. First, national political leaders, though goal-oriented, often have multiple goals and do not always seek only to maximize their short-term military power vis-à-vis subnational governments, as most theories of federalism assume. Rather, state-building elites often willingly follow the path of least resistance to national unification, exchanging national unification for indirect federal rule, but only when the subnational institutions already in place can effectively extract taxes and human resources for conscription and can maintain civil order. Second, simply weakening the center does not strengthen the subnational regions. While the decentralization of power might be a consequence of federalism, the sources of federalism are found elsewhere. The effort to decentralize political power founders without regional governments with high levels of institutional capacity because political leaders in the center are tempted to intercede to take on the tasks that a failed subnational government cannot manage. In this sense, the greatest threat to the successful construction of federal structures is subnational institutions *without* the basic capacity to govern; such institutional weakness prompts the central government to unilaterally intervene, institutionalizing a set of centralizing pathologies that can eventually undermine the sustainability of federal structures.[5]

BEYOND THE NINETEENTH CENTURY? REFINING THE ARGUMENT IN LIGHT OF EVIDENCE FROM SEVENTEEN CONTEMPORARY EUROPEAN NATION-STATES

The proposed state-centered and developmental theory of federalism's origins explains political developments in nineteenth-century Italy and Germany. But as I made explicit in chapter 1 of the study, I intentionally held "ideology" constant across the two cases; both Piedmontese and Prussian state-builders were ideologically committed to federalism as an institutional goal. The questions that thus remain unanswered are the following: What happens when ideology is not held constant? Or put more precisely, how do the two factors my account highlights—federalist ideology and strong regional institutions—interact across a broader and more diverse set of cases? And, finally, how would we go about assessing how well the account presented here can travel beyond the structured and focused comparison I have made?[6]

If we systematically look at the seventeen largest contemporary nation-states of western Europe, we discover that my argument, with some small but important refinements, does indeed work quite well.[7] Following the lead of other recent prominent analyses, we can use Derbyshire and Derbyshire's coding scheme to code the seventeen largest democracies in western Europe as federal or unitary.[8] Each nation-state presented in table 7.2 is coded dichotomously in terms of its *contemporary* federalism score. But it is important to note that our search for the potential causes focuses on a set of *historical* causes. Why? As chapter 2 noted, one of the strongest predictors of a nation-state's federalism score in the 1990s was its institutional form immediately following the creation of its first constitution. Indeed, this striking correlation between the distant past and present highlights the enduring causal impact of the national critical juncture on the nature of contemporary political institutions. Furthermore, it compels

TABLE 7.2
Eighteen Cases in Western Europe, 1996

National Case	Institutional Outcome	National Case	Institutional Outcome
Austria	Federal	Italy	Unitary
Belgium before 1993	Unitary	Netherlands	Unitary
Belgium after 1993	Federal	Norway	Unitary
Denmark	Unitary	Portugal	Unitary
Finland	Unitary	Spain	Unitary
Germany	Federal	Sweden	Unitary
Greece	Unitary	Switzerland	Federal
Iceland	Unitary	United Kingdom	Unitary
Ireland	Unitary	France	Unitary

us to explore which precise factors present at the national constitutional founding shape institutional outcomes today.

What "historical" causes associated with the constitutional founding of modern nation-states explain the variation in patterns of territorial governance presented in table 7.2? How does my argument, which focuses on the supply of regional institutions at the moment of constitutional founding, intersect with the other factor held constant in my focused comparison—ideology? That is, what happens in other settings when ideology is present but regional institutions are absent? And what happens when ideology is present but regional institutions are not? How can we determine how well my argument—that both factors are necessary but neither is sufficient—works in a broader context? In table 7.3, I present an overview of *all* the possible logical combinations of the two independent variables (strong federalist ideology and effective regional institutions), including an assessment of which combinations would be theory-confirming and which would be theory-disconfirming.[9]

The benefit of presenting the logical possibilities in this way is that we can specify the conditions under which my account would be confirmed or disconfirmed, an exercise too infrequently done in qualitative analysis. First, when cases fit into scenarios 1, 4, 5, and 7, the theoretical expectations are confirmed. If, for example, a strong ideology of federalism exists as do strong regional institutions, and we find federal state structures (scenario 1), this would be confirming evidence of the main proposed theoretical framework. Similarly, if we find cases where there exists no strong ideology of federalism in the founding moment and no strong regional

TABLE 7.3
The Range of Possible Combinations

Scenario	Strong Ideology	Strong Regional Institutions	Federalism	Confirming/ Disconfirming
1	Yes	Yes	Yes	Confirming
2	Yes	Yes	No	Disconfirming
3	Yes	No	Yes	Disconfirming
4	Yes	No	No	Confirming
5	No	No	No	Confirming
6	No	No	Yes	Disconfirming
7	No	Yes	No	Confirming
8	No	Yes	Yes	Disconfirming

institutions, and we find a case without federal state structures (scenario 5), this would also be theory confirming. Finally, if we find a case where either strong federalist ideology or strong regional institutions are absent, and there are no federal state structures (scenarios 4 and 7), then the theory would also find confirmation.

By contrast, we can also specify the conditions under which the evidence disconfirms the main theoretical expectations. When we find cases, for example, where both independent variables are present, yet federalism fails to take root, this is disconfirming evidence (scenario 2). Likewise, if we find cases where neither factor is present and federalism successfully is created, this also suggests my account is focusing on the wrong independent variables (scenario 6). Finally, if either factor is absent but federal structures nevertheless emerge, then again, the theory is disconfirmed (scenarios 3 and 8). In short, we see that a federal pattern of organizing the state ought to be predictable based on the configuration of ideology and regional institutional structures at the moment of national founding. How do the two variables hold up? In table 7.4, I present a summary of the findings based on a review of the secondary literature.

As table 7.4 suggests, the broader set of national cases provide confirming evidence for the proposed framework. The national cases, which are coded according to their status when the first national constitution was adopted, are the largest nation-states in western Europe. With the important exception of post-1993 Belgium, the evidence highlights the importance of the intentions of political actors as well as the overlapping institutional landscapes they faced when designing national institutions.[10]

TABLE 7.4
Summary of Findings

Scenario	Strong Ideology	Strong Regional Institutions	Federalism	Nation-States and Year of Founding	Confirms/ Disconfirms
1	Yes	Yes	Yes	Austria (1920) Germany (1871) Switzerland (1848)	Confirms
2	Yes	Yes	No	No cases	
3	Yes	No	Yes	No cases	
4	Yes	No	No	Italy (1861) Netherlands (1814)	Confirms
5	No	No	No	France (1791) Finland (1917) Iceland (1944) Ireland (1937) Sweden (1809) Portugal (1822) Norway (1905) Pre-1993 Belgium (1831)	Confirms
6	No	No	Yes	Post-1993 Belgium (1831)	Disconfirms
7	No	Yes	No	Denmark (1849) Spain (1812) United Kingdom (1707)	Confirms
8	No	Yes	Yes	No cases	

More specifically we see that for seventeen of the eighteen cases, the absence of either ideologically committed actors or effective regional institutions means that federalism is *never* constructed. Furthermore, in five important national cases (scenarios 1 and 4), political leaders often ideologically preferred federal designs to unitary designs irrespective of the military prowess of the political center. In this sense, the assumption that political leaders will always prefer to "overawe" the periphery in the absence of a countervailing military power has very little empirical validity or explanatory utility.

But, finally most revealing of all are the divergent fates of the five cases in scenarios 1 and 4. In all five cases, an ideological commitment to federalism was present. Yet in the three cases in scenario 1—Austria (1920), Switzerland (1848), and Germany (1871)—political designers in the constitutional moment confronted an institutional landscape in which state structures were already rationalized and consolidated at the regional level.[11] By contrast, political leaders in the two cases in scenario 2—Italy (1861) and the Netherlands (1815)—faced a set of underdeveloped, unconsolidated states without constitutions and parliaments.[12] Though the task of integrating a diverse set of formerly independent states was similar across both groups of states, the internal structure of the states in each group differed in their degree of institutional rationalization and consolidation.[13] As a result, national unification proceeded along two different trajectories in the two groups of states: in one instance a federal solution was possible, while in the other federal plans were abandoned and unitary constitutions were adopted.

In short, we see that among seventeen of the largest nation-states in western Europe, a state-centered approach to federalism's origins that focuses on the motivations of actors and the institutional constraints they face is quite fruitful. While most theories of federalism's origins assume a close "fit" between the intentions of powerful political actors and the institutions they design, the broader cross-national evidence largely confirms that political actors adapt their strategies to forces beyond their control. But importantly, the evidence from the larger sample of west European states also confirms that the main constraint is not external military weakness of the political "center," but is rather a lack of effective regional domestic governance capacity in the states of the "periphery." In both the sparse and underdeveloped prenational southern states of Italy and in the densely populated and wealthy provinces of post-Napoleonic Netherlands, this study surprisingly discovers a similar dynamic overlooked by traditional theories of federalism's origins: in the face of poorly developed regional capacity for governance, the aspirations of even the most committed federalists founder.

BROADER IMPLICATIONS AND CONCLUDING THOUGHTS

The creation of the two central cases in this study—Germany and Italy—represented a turning point in European history in which "territorially defined, fixed, and mutually exclusive enclaves of legitimate domination" had finally and decisively replaced an older, overlapping, and more diverse array of political structures.[14] Furthermore, national unification represented a moment in which the basic state structures of two new polities were created. The central purpose of this study has been to provide a glimpse into the process of establishing internal sovereignty for new nation-states. In exploring this issue, the focus has been on the institutional dynamics of national integration. How are new political institutions constructed within a new polity? Why is it that federalism is the mode of political integration in some instances but not others?

The answers I have proposed run against the conventional wisdom of existing theory and deepen our understanding of the origins of federalism by highlighting the often-overlooked institutional structures that must be in place for the successful creation of federal states. A common assumption is that institutional development is an orderly, self-contained unfolding of state structures that reflect "optimal" solutions to a singular set of short-term problems for the main political actors involved. The account I have offered to make sense of Germany, Italy, and a broader range of west European states cuts against this conventional view by focusing on the processes by which state structures develop; I have shown that when designing new political institutions, political actors often find themselves constrained by a complex web of preexisting norms and formal institutions that require different forms of adaptation—for example, the layering of new rules and formal institutions atop old actors and norms, and sometimes the converting of old rules and institutions to new purposes.[15]

Indeed, a central finding is that the precise mode by which political institutions develop often forecloses what would otherwise be desirable institutional choices for political actors. If, for example, regional governments experience the rationalization and consolidation of state structures before constitutionally protected national political institutions are created, then federalism becomes a viable route to establishing internal national sovereignty. If, by contrast, rational and consolidated regional political institutions either are dismantled or do not develop before a constitutionally governed national government is created, then federal institutional solutions are regarded as a nonviable solution to the task of national integration. In short, the findings suggest a perspective on federal institutions that combines a focus on the multiplicity of short-term motivations of purposive political actors with the deep institutional legacies such political actors confront when designing and redesigning political institutions. It is only by looking at when and how different subspheres within the state develop that we can begin to understand why states take on the wide range of institutional forms that they do.

Appendix A

PRENATIONAL GERMAN AND ITALIAN

STATES, 1850s–1860s

THIS APPENDIX discusses issues of conceptualization and measurement as well as data and data sources involved with the analysis presented in chapter 2. I first provide commentary on the dependent variable, followed by a discussion of explanatory variables.

DEPENDENT VARIABLE: LEVEL OF REGIONAL
SUPPORT FOR NATIONAL UNIFICATION

The level of regional support for national unification captures the orientations and political actions taken by the political leaders vis-à-vis the project of national unification for each of the twenty-four regional states in Italy and Germany for which data is available. The time frame of each Italian regional state's score is the last ten years before national unification (1850–60). In Germany, I likewise coded the orientations and political actions of political leaders for the last ten years before that country's national unification (1860–70). I coded each of the twenty-four regions on its orientation toward national unification, using an ordinal scale: 1 = hostile, 2 = resistant, 3 = supportive, 4 = initiator.

My data are drawn from an extensive review of the German, Italian, and English-language secondary literature for each of the twenty-four regional states for the time periods under study. I coded for positions taken by the executive of each state—monarch or mayor—with respect to two specific issues: (1) the rise of the leading nationalist organization in each country, and (2) proposals for an explicitly "national" political and economic unification. I rely on the evaluations of the secondary sources of the orientations and political actions of political leaders, expressed usually via (1) correspondence between the leaders of the regional states, or (2) positions taken by the leaders of regional states in summits or official meetings of the political leaders. It is true that some political leaders may have shifted their positions, or at times made contradictory statements or took contradictory positions, creating problems of reliability and validity. Similarly, use of secondary sources, though extensive, presents the usual problems of selection bias that confront all historical analysis. I have attempted to counteract this potential methodological pitfall by (1) using as wide-ranging a selection of sources as possible and (2) using the qualitative case material presented in chapter 3 and chapter 4 to check on the validity of the ordinal measures in chapter 2.

Data and Scores for Twenty-Four German and Italian Regional States on Dependent Variable

1. Bavaria (score = 1).   For a useful discussion of Bavarian hostile resistance to national unification, see Hans Rall, "Die politische Entwicklung von 1848 bis zur Reichsgründung 1871," in Max Spindler, ed., *Handbuch der Bayerischen Geschichte, 1800–1870*, vol. 4 (Munich: C. H. Beck'sche Verlagsbuchhandlung, 1974), 228–82. For a discussion of the mobilization of Bavarian troops on May 10, 1866, against Prussia, see Rall, 259. On constitutional developments and relations between Prussia and Bavaria, Prussia, see Ernst Rudolf Huber, *Deutsche Verfassungsgeschichte Seit 1789*, vol. 3 (Stuttgart: W. Kohlhammer Verlag, 1963), 531–42. For a discussion of the anti-Nationalverein policies of the Bavarian government, see Huber, 392. For a discussion of Bavaria's tendency to take an independent stand vis-à-vis the Bund, starting with the Würzburger Congress of 1859, see Huber, 402.

2. Oldenbourg (score = 3).   Typically the *Fürst* of Oldenbourg during the 1850s and 1860s was regarded as the "Nationale Fürst" for his open support of Prussian plans for a "small" Germany. See Otto Becker, *Bismarcks Ringen Um Deutschlands Gestaltung* (Heidelberg: Quelle und Meyer, 1958), 358. But more nuanced accounts have recently been offered to highlight the Oldenbourg crown's harsh policies toward the Nationalverein. See, for example, Albrecht Eckhardt, "Der konstitionelle Staat (1848–1918)," in Albrecht Eckhardt, ed., *Geschichte des Landes Oldenburg: Ein Handbuch* (Oldenburg: Heinz Holzberg Verlag, 1988), 333–402. For the most detailed account that shows the Oldenbourg government's "reluctance" toward the national movement, especially between 1859 and 1863, see also Peter Klaus Schwarz, *Nationale und Soziale Bewegung in Oldenburg im Jahrzehnt von der Reichsgründung* (Oldenburg: Heinz Holzberg Verlag, 1979), 43–65.

3. Hannover (score = 2).   For a description of King George's post-1859 antagonism to the Nationalverein and the nationalist agenda in general, see Margaret Anderson, *Windthorst: A Political Biography* (New York: Oxford University Press. 1981), 66; for a discussion of policies towards the

Nationalverein, see pp. 79–82; for a discussion of passive reluctance towards Prussia, see pp. 98 and 98n. See also Huber, *Deutsche Verfassungsgeschichte Seit 1789*, 392, for a discussion of the harsh "extra" legal measures taken by the Hannover government towards the Nationalverein.

4. Bremen (score = 3).   For a discussion of Bremen city government's relationship to the Nationalverein, see Herbert Schwarzwälder, *Geschichte der
Freien Hansestadt Bremen*, vol. 2 (Bremen: Verlag Friedrich Röver, 1976),
274. For a discussion of the sympathy of Bremen mayor Duckwitz in 1863
for Prussian positions at the Frankfurter Fürstentag, see Schwarzwälder,
276. For support for Prussian agenda among Bremen representatives at
the Baden-Baden conference in 1863, see also pp. 276–77.

5. Baden (score = 3).   For a characterization of Baden leadership's orientations and actions, in particular of Grand Duke Friedrich after his 1856
accession to the throne in "a national liberal state" supportive of Prussian
"small-Germany" plans, especially at the Würzburg Conference in November 1859, see Harm-Hinrich Brandt, *Deutsche Geschichte, 1850–1870.
Entscheidung über die Nation* (Stuttgart: Kohlhammer, 1999), 131. That
a free-market orientation and calls for increased trade ties between the
German states was advocated by the "liberal" ministry in the 1860s is
documented by Lothar Gall, *Der Liberalismus als regierende Partei. Das
Grossherzogtum Baden zwischen Restauration und Reichsgründung* (Wiesbaden: F. Steiner, 1968), 180. See also Huber, *Deutsche Verfassungsgeschichte Seit 1789*, 392, for a discussion of the Baden ruler's sympathies
for the Nationalverein.

6. Weimar-Saxony (score = 3).   The orientations and actions of Weimar
Saxony's Grand Duke Carl Alexander vis-à-vis national unification are
characterized by Brandt, *Deutsche Geschichte, 1850–1870*, 131, as "national
liberal." See also memoirs of Ernst II, Herzog von Sachsen-Coburg-
Gotha, *Aus meinem Leben und aus meiner Zeit*, vol. 3 (Berlin: Verlag von
Wilhelm Herz, 1889), 275–545.

7. Coburg-Saxony (score = 3).   The orientations and actions of Saxon-Coburg's Duke Ernst II are characterized by Brandt, *Deutsche Geschichte,
1850–1870*, 131, as "national liberal." See also memoirs of Herzog von
Sachsen-Saxon-Coburg, *Aus meinem Leben*, 275–545. See also Huber,
Deutsche Verfassungsgeschichte Seit 1789, 392, for a description of the leadership's sympathies for the Nationalverein.

8. Württemberg (score = 2).   For Württemberg's anti-Prussian vote in the
German Bund in 1866, see Huber, *Deutsche Verfassungsgeschichte Seit*

1789, 541. King Wilhelm's rule until 1864 was marked by a strong antinational and anti-Prussian streak, as was King Karl's after 1864. Nevertheless, neither leader took the lead and instead followed Bavaria's positions. For a discussion of the anti-Nationalverein policies of the government, see Huber, *Deutsche Verfassungsgeschichte Seit 1789*, 391–92.

9. Kurhessen (score = 2).   While not as "conservative-particularist" as Hessen Darmstadt, the duke of Kurhessen, Friedrich Wilhelm, was more "particularistic" than the leadership of Hessen Nassau. At most important critical votes and junctures, the leadership supported Austrian and Bavarian notions of a loose confederation rather than a Prussian-led nation-state. For many decades politics in Kurhessen was dominated by the Hassenpflug, and especially during the 1850s, Hassenpflug oversaw a virulently anti-Prussian set of policies. Though in the 1860s, the policies were tamed, nevertheless, Kurhessen qualifies as a "passive resistor" to national unification. See Hans-Werner Hahn, *Wirtschaftliche Integration im 19. Jahrhundert: Die hessischen Staaten und der Deutsche Zollverein* (Göttingen: Vandenhöck und Ruprecht, 1982), 285. See also Nicholas Martin Hope, *The Alternative to German Unification: The Anti-Prussian Party, Frankfurt, Nassau, and the Two Hessens, 1859–1867* (Wiesbaden: F. Steiner Verlag, 1973). See also Huber, *Deutsche Verfassungsgeschichte Seit 1789*, 392, for a description of repressive policies towards the Nationalverein.

10. Schleswig Holstein (score = 2).   The resistance to Prussian annexation in these two provinces is discussed briefly in Huber, *Deutsche Verfassungsgeschichte Seit 1789*, 593–94.

11. Hessen Darmstadt (score = 3).   For a thorough review of the positions taken by Hessen Darmstadt leadership, especially Minister Dalwigk, with regard to the competition between Prussia and Austria in the 1860s, see Hahn, *Wirtschaftliche Integration*, 277–306. For a characterization of Hessen Darmstadt's leadership as the "most particularistic" among the three Hessen states, especially with regard to expanding the Prussian-led Zollverein, see Hahn, 298. For a description of the harsh policies of the Hessen Darmstadt government against the Nationalverein, see Huber, *Deutsche Verfassungsgeschichte Seit 1789*, 392.

12. Nassau (score = 3).   Though frequently opposed to Prussian plans and often sympathetic to Austrian and Bavarian resistance to Prussia in the mid-1860s, most accounts agree that Nassau's political leadership gently shifted its orientations away from "particularism" and towards greater small-German national integration. In August 1862, for example, while the duke of Hessen Darmstadt and the duke of Kurhessen rejected the

Prussian-initiated proposal for closer ties with France, the duke of Nassau accepted the treaty "as a friendly gesture to Prussia" (Hahn, *Wirtschaftliche Integration*, 290). This "gesture" was paradigmatic of a generally friendlier stance of Nassau towards Prussian "national" unification plans.

13. Hamburg (score = 3).   See discussions in Detlef Rogosch, *Hamburg im Deutschen Bund 1859–1866: Zur Politik eines Kleinstaates in einer mitteleuropaischen Föderativordnung* (Hamburg: R. Kramer, 1990).

14. Prussia (score = 4).   One of the best discussion of Prussian efforts from the late 1850s to 1871 to reorganize the German Bund by excluding Austria to make an explicitly *kleindeutsch* "national" entity that it could dominate is offered by Helmut Böhme, *Deutschlands Weg Zur Grossmacht* (Cologne: Verlag Kiepenheuer, 1966). See also Becker, *Bismarcks Ringen*, 68–81.

15. Saxony (score = 2).   For a discussion of Saxon efforts to ban the Nationalverein, see Huber, *Deutsche Verfassungsgeschichte Seit 1789*, 391–92, 401. For a discussion of active anti-Prussian policies of the Saxon foreign minister, Beust, after the failure of 1860 Bund reforms, see Huber, 409–10.

16. Mecklenburg-Schwerin (score = 2).   The best discussion of the shifting resistance of the two Mecklenburg states to Prussian unification plans is found in Otto Vitense, *Geschichte von Mecklenburg* (Gotha: Friedrich Andreas Perthes, 1920). For a discussion of early reluctance towards Zollverein plans, see pp. 480–81; for a discussion of the neutrality of the two Mecklenburg states in the Prussian Holstein war (1863–64) and the policy formulated by Minister Derzen, see p. 481. Finally, regarding negotiations between Prussia and Schwerin regarding a potential mobilization against Austria, Vitense reports that the Schwerin government declared in a March 1866 meeting that it had no "antagonistic" (*feindseliges*) plans vis-à-vis Prussia but was not inclined to join Prussia's plans of war with Austria (Vitense, 483). In sum, the position of Schwerin was quite ambivalent towards Prussia.

17. Mecklenburg-Strelitz (score = 2).   According to Vitense, *Geschichte von Mecklenburg*, 485, the government of Strelitz, under the leadership of Friedrich Wilhelm, displayed greater resistance to Prussia's demands than Schwerin, but like Schwerin, Strelitz entered the war of 1866 on Prussia's side. Vitense's work also notes that the Mecklenburg aristocracy was critical of war with Austria, given that a significant portion of the aristocracy's sons had served in the Austrian army (486).

18. Piedmont (score = 4).   According to all accounts, Piedmont played a decisive initiating role in the unification of Italy. Not only do events speak for themselves, the key liberal-conservative coalition in the Piedmontese parliament displayed the most prounification orientation of any political leadership in Italy. For some examples of this, see Denis Mack Smith, *Italy: A Modern History* (Ann Arbor: University of Michigan Press, 1969), 17–25.

19. Kingdom of Two Sicilies (score = 1).   The greatest opponent to Piedmontese plans of national unification remained the king of Naples, who despite frequent overtures for an alliance with Piedmont, rejected any such plans. Along with the Papal States, the Kingdom of Two Sicilies was the main militarily hostile opponent of Piedmontese expansionism. For a discussion of Garibaldi's attack on the Kingdom of Two Sicilies and the military response, see Denis Mack Smith, *Cavour* (London: Weidenfeld and Nicholson, 1985), 209–35.

20. Tuscany (score = 2).   The "liberal" Grand Duke Leopold was supported by Austrian troops until late into his rule. But after Austrian troops left Tuscany, Cavour sought cooperation between Piedmont and Leopold-ruled Tuscany. But these efforts failed in March 1859 when the Tuscan duke firmly refused to join the anti-Austrian coalition led by Piedmont. As a consequence, Cavour turned to Ricasoli and aristocratic nationalists. For a discussion, see William Keith Hancock, *Ricasoli and the Risorgimento in Tuscany* (London: Faber and Gwyer, 1926), 190–92, 196–200; see also the discussion of Tuscany vis-à-vis Piedmontese plans in J.A.R. Marriott, *The Makers of Modern Italy* (Oxford: Clarendon Press, 1931), 116–17.

21. Modena (score = 2).   As an Austrian-sponsored regime in Italy, it is clear that Modena was an opponent of national unification. But, in contrast to the leadership of the Papal States and the Kingdom of Two Sicilies, Francis V and the leadership of Modena passively waited for Austria to secure its regime and fled the country upon Austria's defeat. See Hanns Faber, *Modena-Austria: Das Herzogtum und das Kassereich von 1814 bis 1867* (Frankfurt am Main: Peter Lang, 1996), 197–207.

22. Parma (score = 2).   For an assessment of Parma's policy as "hesitant" and a discussion of the duchess of Parma's orientation towards Piedmont's and Cavour's plans, see Marriott, *Makers of Modern Italy*, 115.

23. Lombardy (score = 3).   Because Lombardy-Veneto was under direct Austrian rule, the coding of the Lombard case is difficult since it is unclear which political leadership should be coded. However, what emerges from a close reading of the secondary literature is a picture of a domestic political elite in Lombardy, centered in Milan, that was quite sympathetic to Piedmontese plans of unification, especially in Italy's northern and central regions, as a route to evicting Austrian rule. For some examples, see the discussion in Mack Smith, *Cavour*, 167.

24. Papal States (score = 1).   For a discussion of the resistance of the leadership of the Papal States, especially Pope Pius IX and his prime minister, Giacomo Antonelli, to overtures from Piedmont for national unification, see Frank Coppa, *Cardinal Giacomo Antonelli and Papal Politics in European Affairs* (Albany: State University of New York, 1990), 115–27. When King Victor Emannuel offered in 1859 to "buy" the Romagna lands from the Papal States, his offer was rejected by Pius IX. Similarly, an offer to have Piedmontese troops stationed in Romagna in exchange for preserving the Papal authority—a kind of bargain that might have occurred among the German states—was also rejected outright. An account of the conquest of the Papal States with strong military resistance is offered also by John Mack Smith, *Victor Emanuel, Cavour, and the Risogimento* (London: Oxford University Press, 1971), 237; and Coppa, *Cardinal Giacomo Antonelli*, 120–21, see also the extremely detailed and still classic account by R. De Cesare, "The Holy See Prepares for Defense," in *The Last Days of Papal Rome* (Boston: Houghton Mifflin, 1909), 268–78.

INDEPENDENT VARIABLES

Level of Regional Economic Modernization

The concept of "level of regional economic modernization" refers to the extent of economic commercialization within each of the prenational political units of Germany and Italy. To assess this, I use the best and most recent estimates of regional GDP per capita in the last decades before national unification. My source for the Italian data is Alfredo Giuseppe Esposto, "Estimating Regional per Capita Income: Italy, 1861–1914," *Journal of European Economic History* 26 (1997): 589. Because the German data are only available at the provincial level, I aggregate the provincial-level data for each state, adjusting for population of each province to estimate the average GDP per capita of each state. For data on provincial level GDP per capita, see Harald Frank, *Regionale Entwicklungsdisparitäten im deutschen Industrialisierungsprozess, 1849–1939* (Münster: Lit Verlag, 1996), appendix 8, p. 30.

State Size

The concept of "state size" in this analysis refers to the total size of state and uses the measure of total budget of each prenational state. Italian data is drawn from Luigi Izzo, *La finanza pubblica: Nel primo decennio dell'unita italiana* (Milan: Dott. A. Giuffre-Editore, 1962) and German data is from Karl Borchard, "Staatsverbrauch und Öffentliche Investitionen in Deutschland 1780–1850," dissertation, Wirtschafts- und Sozialwissenschaftlichen Fakultät, Göttingen, 1968.

ORIGINS OF FEDERALISM DATA ON SEVENTEEN
LARGEST WEST EUROPEAN NATION-STATES

THIS APPENDIX summarizes indicators, data, and sources for the cross-national analysis conducted in chapter 7. The universe of cases includes the seventeen largest countries in western Europe.

The coding procedure included three steps: First, I coded cases for date of first constitution, using the country profile handbook by J. Denis Derbyshire and Ian Derbyshire, *Political Systems of the World*, 2nd ed. (New York: St. Martin's Press, 1996). For purposes of measurement reliability, I conducted the some coding procedure using the country profile handbook by Joel Krieger, ed., *The Oxford Companion to Politics of the World*, 2nd ed. (Oxford: Oxford University Press, 2001). Second, I coded the dependent cases as either federal or unitary, using Derbyshire and Derbyshire, *Political Systems*, 5. Third, to code the independent variables, I used the country profile handbooks (i.e., Derbyshire and Derbyshire, *Political Systems*, and Krieger, *Oxford Companion*); when data were not available, I used secondary sources listed below.

The first independent variable—"strong federalist ideology," was coded dichotomously (i.e., presence vs. absence). For this variable, the indicators used in reviewing the secondary literature were twofold: (1) did at least one of the major political parties advocate a federally organized polity in the decisive years of constitution adoption, (2) was a draft of a federal constitution proposed in the same era? If the answer to either of these questions was "yes," I coded the case as possessing a strong federal ideology. The second independent variable—"regional parliaments"—is also coded dichotomously: Were there modern parliaments in the constituent regional states at the moment of constitution adoption? If the answer to this question was "yes," I coded the case as possessing developed regional institutions.

AUSTRIA

First constitution: 1920
Strong federalist ideology: Yes

Regional parliaments: Yes (created in 1861)
Data sources: Wilhelm Brauneder, *Deutsch-Österreich 1918* (Vienna: Amalthea, 2000); Herbert Schambeck, *Föderalismus und Parlamentarismus in Österreich* (Vienna: Verlag der Österreichischen Staatsdruckerei, 1992).

BELGIUM

First constitution: 1831
Strong federalist ideology: No
Regional parliaments: No
Data sources: J.C.H. Blom and E. Lamberts, eds., *History of the Low Countries* (New York: Berghahn, 1994); E. H. Kossman, *The Low Countries, 1780–1940* (New York: Oxford University Press, 1978).

DENMARK

First constitution: 1849
Strong federalist ideology: No
Regional parliaments: Yes (provincial parliaments after 1830)
Data source: W. Glyn Jones, *Denmark: A Modern History* (London: Croom Helm, 1986).

FINLAND

First constitution: 1917
Strong federalist ideology: No
Regional parliaments: No
Data source: Osmo Jussila, *From Grand Duchy to Modern State: A Political History of Finland since 1809* (London: Hurst, 1999).

FRANCE

First constitution: 1791
Strong federalist ideology: No
Regional parliaments: No
Data sources: Samuel Scott and Barry Rothaus, eds., *Historical Dictionary of the French Revolution, 1789–1799* (Westport, Conn.: Greenwood

Press, 1985); Suzanne Berger, *The French Political System* (New York: Random House, 1974).

GERMANY

First constitution: 1871
Strong federalist ideology: Yes
Regional parliaments: Yes (since at least 1815)
Data source: James Sheehan, *German History, 1770–1866* (Oxford: Clarendon Press, 1989).

GREECE

First constitution: 1829
Strong federalist ideology: No
Regional parliaments: No
Data sources: Richard Clogg, *A Concise History of Greece* (Cambridge: Cambridge University Press, 2002); Richard Clogg, ed., *Balkan Society in the Age of Greek Independence* (Totowa, N.J.: Barnes and Noble, 1981).

ICELAND

First constitution: 1944
Strong federalist ideology: No
Regional parliaments: No
Data sources: Byron Nordstrom, *Scandinavia since 1500* (Minneapolis: University of Minnesota Press, 2000); Gunnar Karlsson, *History of Iceland* (Minneapolis: University of Minnesota Press).

IRELAND

First constitution: 1937
Strong federalist ideology: No
Regional parliaments: No
Data source: John Ranelagh, *A Short History of Ireland*, 2nd ed. (Cambridge: Cambridge University Press, 1994).

ITALY

First constitution: 1861
Strong federalist ideology: Yes (1848 and afterwards)
Regional parliaments: No (none outside of Piedmont)
Data source: Lucy Riall, *The Italian Risorgimento: State, Society, and National Unification* (London: Routledge, 1994).

NETHERLANDS

First constitution: 1814
Strong federalist ideology: Yes (1798 debates)
Regional parliaments: No
Data sources: Blom and Lamberts, *History of the Low Countries*; Kossman, *The Low Countries.*

NORWAY

First constitution: 1905
Strong federalist ideology: No
Regional parliaments: No
Data source: Nordstrom, *Scandinavia since 1500.*

PORTUGAL

First constitution: 1822
Strong federalist ideology: No
Regional parliaments: No
Data sources: Douglas Wheeler, *Historical Dictionary of Portugal* (London: Scarecrow Press, 1993); R.A.H. Robinson, *Contemporary Portugal: A History* (London: Unwin, 1979).

SPAIN

First constitution: 1812
Strong federalist ideology: No
Regional parliaments: Yes

Data sources: Robert Kern, *A Historical Dictionary of Modern Spain, 1700–1988* (New York: Greenwood Press, 1990); Raymond Carr, *Spain, 1808–1975* (Oxford: Clarendon Press, 1982).

SWEDEN

First constitution: 1809
Strong federalist ideology: No
Regional parliaments: No
Data sources: Byron Nordstrom, *The History of Sweden* (Minneapolis: University of Minnesota Press, 2002); Nordstrom, *Scandinavia since 1500*; Nils Stjernquist, "The Creation of the 1809 Constitution," in Steven Koblik, ed., *Sweden's Development from Poverty to Affluence, 1750–1970* (Minneapolis: University Minnesota Press, 1975).

SWITZERLAND

First constitution: 1848
Strong federalist ideology: Yes
Regional parliaments: Yes (in sixteen of twenty-five cantons)
Data sources: Georges Andrey, "Auf der Suche nach dem neuen Staat, 1798–1848," in Beatrix Mesner, ed., *Geschichte der Schweiz und der Schweizer*, 2nd ed. (Basel: Helbing and Lichtenhahn, 1983); Thomas Maissen, "The 1848 Conflicts and Their Significance in Swiss Historiography," in Michael Butler, Malcolm Pender, and Joy Charnley, eds., *The Making of Modern Switzerland, 1848–1998* (London: Macmillan, 2000), 3–34.

UNITED KINGDOM

First constitution: 1707[1]
Strong federalist ideology: No
Regional parliaments: Yes (in Scotland)
Data sources: Linda Colley, *Britons: Forging the Nation, 1707–1837* (New Haven: Yale University Press, 1992); W. A. Speck, *A Concise History of Britain, 1707–1975* (Cambridge: Cambridge University Press, 1993).

NOTES

CHAPTER ONE
INTRODUCTION: HOW NATION-STATES ARE MADE

1. Heinrich Treitschke, *Cavour: Der Wegbereiter des neuen Italiens* (Leipzig: Wilhelm Langeweische-Brandt, 1942), 207.

2. For a useful conceptualization and discussion of the novel characteristics of this post-1830 "territorial regime," see the important work by Charles Maier, "Consigning the Twentieth Century to History: Alternative Narratives for the Modern Era," *American Historical Review* 105 (2000): 807–31; see also Charles Maier, "Transformations of Territoriality, 1600–2000," manuscript, September 12, 2002. For another discussion of this period, see Robert Binkley, *Realism and Nationalism, 1852–1871* (New York: Harper and Row, 1935). In addition to the two examples above, the following countries were also created in the same time frame: Brazil (1822), Bolivia (1825), Colombia (1830), Ecuador (1830), Venezuela (1830), and Canada (1867). Additionally, previously looser confederations or federations were transformed into more centralized federal states, including Switzerland (1848) and the United States.

3. This paradox of federalism's *origins* draws on work that emphasizes a similar set of dilemmas that makes federalism, once established, inherently unstable. For the clearest statement of this, see Rui de Figueiredo and Barry Weingast, "Self Enforcing Federalism," Hoover Institution, manuscript, March 2002. For a summary of the broader literature, see Jenna Bednar, "Formal Theory and Federalism," *Newsletter of the Comparative Politics Section, American Political Science Association* 11, no. 1 (2000): 19–23.

4. This definition of "infrastructural capacity" borrows from Michael Mann, *The Sources of Social Power*, vol. 2 (Cambridge: Cambridge University Press, 1993).

5. See Barry Weingast, "The Economic Role of Political Institutions: Market-Preserving Federalism and Economic Development," *Journal of Law, Economics, and Organization* 11, no. 1 (1995): 1–31.

6. Jonathan Rodden, "The Dilemma of Fiscal Federalism: Grants and Fiscal Performance around the World," *American Journal of Political Science* 46 (2002): 670–87; Jonathan Rodden, "Reviving Leviathan: Fiscal Federalism and the Growth of Government," *International Organization* 57 (2003): 695–729; Jonathan Rodden and Erik Wibbels, "Beyond the Fiction of Federalism: Macroeconomic Management in Multitiered Systems," *World Politics* 54 (2002): 494–531.

7. Michael Hechter, *Containing Nationalism* (Oxford: Oxford University Press, 2000); Nancy Bermeo, "The Merits of Federalism," in Nancy Bermeo and Ugo Amoretti, eds., *Federalism and Territorial Cleavages* (Baltimore: Johns Hopkins University Press, 2004), 457–82.

8. For some examples, see Christopher Garman, Stephen Haggard, and Eliza Willis, "Fiscal Decentralization: A Political Theory with Latin American Cases," *World Politics* 53, no. 2 (2001): 205–34; Peter Ordeshook, "Federal Institutional Design: A Theory of Self-Sustainable Federal Government," California Institute of Technology, manuscript, 2001; Jose Afonso and Luiz de Mello, "Brazil: An Evolving Federation," paper presented to the Conference on Fiscal Decentralization, International Monetary Fund, Fiscal Affairs Department, November 20–21, 2000.

9. On the sustainability of federalism, see de Figueiredo and Weingast, "Self Enforcing Federalism."

10. See Thomas Ertman, *Birth of the Leviathan: Building States and Regimes in Medieval and Early Modern Europe* (Cambridge: Cambridge University Press, 1997); Barrington Moore, *Social Origins of Dictatorship and Democracy: Lord and Peasant in the Making of the Modern World* (Boston: Beacon Press, 1966); Gregory Luebbert, *Liberalism, Fascism, or Social Democracy* (Oxford: Oxford University Press, 1991); Alexander Gerschenkron, *Economic Backwardness in Historical Perspective* (Cambridge: Harvard University Press, 1962); Carles Boix, "Setting the Rules of the Game: The Choice of Electoral Systems in Advanced Democracies," *American Political Science Review* 93 (2000): 609–24.

11. Definitions of nationalism, the nation-state, or "national state" abound. For this study, a sample of some of the most influential and useful works on nationalism and the nation-state include Charles Tilly, "Reflections on the History of European State-Making," in Charles Tilly, ed., *The Formation of National States in Western Europe* (Princeton: Princeton University Press, 1975), 3–83; Ernest Gellner, *Nations and Nationalism* (Oxford: Oxford University Press, 1983); Mann, *Sources of Social Power*, and Ernst Haas, *Nationalism, Liberalism, and Progress* (Ithaca: Cornell University Press, 1997). My definition borrows from Ken Jowitt, "Nation-Building as Amalgam of State, Civic, and Ethnicity," manuscript, 2001.

12. See conceptual discussion in Ronald L. Watts, "Federalism, Federal Political Systems, and Federations," *Annual Review of Political Science* 1 (1998): 117–37.

13. See Alfred Stepan, "Toward a New Comparative Politics of Federalism, Multinationalism, and Democracy: Beyond Rikerian Federalism," in *Arguing Comparing Politics* (Oxford: Oxford University Press, 2001), 318.

14. It should be noted that for purposes of broader cross-national comparison, the categories "federal" and "unitary" are dichotomous; they are mutually incompatible and exhaustive (i.e., all modern states are either federal or unitary). Within each of these broad categories occur, however, important distinctions in the degree of centralization or decentralization. My study's primary focus on the broader dichotomous difference between federal and unitary state structures. For a discussion of patterns of centralization and decentralization *within* federal systems, see Arend Lijphart, *Patterns of Democracy* (New Haven: Yale University Press, 1999).

15. Other largely compatible and influential conceptualizations of federalism can be seen in Carl Friedrich, *Trends of Federalism in Theory and Practice* (New York: Praeger Press, 1968); K. C. Wheare, *Federal Government* (New York: Oxford University Press, 1964); Ivo Duchacek, *Comparative Federalism: The Territorial Dimension of Politics* (New York: Holt, Rinehart, and Winston, 1970); and David McKay, *Federalism and the European Union* (Oxford: Oxford University Press, 1999). For an effort to develop measures of federalism for cross-national comparison, see Lijphart, *Patterns of Democracy*.

16. Michael Burgess, "The European Tradition of Federalism: Christian Democracy and Federalism," in Michael Burgess and A. G. Gagnon, eds., *Comparative Federalism and Federation* (Toronto: University of Toronto Press, 1993).

17. Maiken Umbach, *Federalism and Enlightenment in Germany, 1740–1806* (London: Hambledon Press, 2000). Umbach's account, though more sophisticated than this stark causal claim, is nevertheless reflective of the broader school of thought that views federalism as a product of long-standing cultural divisions.

18. William Riker, *Federalism: Origins, Operation, Significance* (New York: Little, Brown, 1964).

19. See, for example, de Figueiredo and Weingast, "Self Enforcing Federalism."

20. It has been argued that this formal centralization of Italy in part explains the emergence of patronage politics and the existence of "unofficial" governments in parts of south-

ern Italy. See Sidney Tarrow, *Between Center and Periphery: Grassroots Politicians in Italy and France* (New Haven: Yale University Press, 1977), 61–63.

21. An example of a quite sophisticated cultural analysis of Italy's path of political development during the Risorgimento can be seen in Luigi Barzini, *The Europeans* (New York: Penguin, 1983), 174–81.

22. Though admittedly not at the center of his analysis, Robert Putnam (1993) in his classic and important study refers to the work of Italian historians who have explained Italy's turn to a unitary state in 1860 as a product both of the prominence of Franco-Napoleonic model and the "backwardness" of Italy's south. See Robert Putnam, *Making Democracy Work: Civic Traditions in Modern Italy* (Princeton: Princeton University Press, 1993), 18. It is a central contention of this study that such claims ought to be subjected to systematic comparative research.

23. See Herbert Jacob, *German Administration since Bismarck* (New Haven: Yale University Press, 1963).

24. In his important recent work on the history of governance in Italy, *The Search for Good Government: Understanding the Paradox of Italian Democracy* (Montreal: McGill-Queen's University Press, 2000), Filippo Sabetti concludes that by 1860 a federal Italy "could not be established" (49). My study seeks to build on Sabetti's insights by systematically exploring a set of hypotheses that might explain why a federal Italy was impossible by 1860.

25. For the most thorough and systematic English-language discussion of ideological developments in the Italian context, see Sabetti, *Search for Good Government*; and Filippo Sabetti, "The Liberal Idea in Nineteenth Century Italy," paper presented to the Annual Meeting of the American Political Science Association, August 2001. Additionally, see a discussion of the "liberal project" of the Risorgimento in Raffaele Romanelli, *Il comando impossibile* (Bologna: Il Mulino, 1988). For a discussion of the ideas of federalism in the nineteenth century in Germany, see Rudolf Ullner, "Die Idee des Föderalismus in Jahrzehnt der deutschen Einigungskriege," *Historischen Studien* 393 (1965): 5–164; Hermann Wellenreuther, ed., *German and American Constitutional Thought* (New York: Berg, 2000); and Stefan Oeter, *Integration und Subsidiarität im deutschen Bundesstaatsrecht: Untersuchungen zu Bundesstaatstheorie unter dem Grundgesetz* (Tübingen: Mohr Siebeck, 1998).

26. Oeter, *Integration und Subsidiarität*, 29. It must be noted, however, that in nationalist and liberal circles, opinion was different and reflected the position of the influential historian Heinrich von Treitschke, who advocated a unitary-centralized model for Germany.

27. Binkley, *Realism and Nationalism*, 197.

28. Stuart Woolf, *The Italian Risorgimento* (New York: Barnes and Noble, 1969), 7.

29. Spencer Di Scala, *Italy: From Revolution to Republic* (Boulder, Colo.: Westview Press, 1995), 71.

30. Clara Lovett, *Carlo Cattaneo and the Politics of the Risorgimento, 1820–1860* (The Hague: Martinus Nijhoff, 1972); Sabetti, *Search for Good Government*.

31. Lucy Riall, *Sicily and the Unification of Italy: Liberal Policy and Local Power, 1850–1866* (Oxford: Clarendon Press, 1998); see also Rosario Romeo, *Il Risorgimento in Sicilia*, 2nd ed. (Bari: Editori Laterza, 1970).

32. Denis Mack Smith, *Cavour* (London: Weidenfeld and Nicolson, 1985).

33. Ibid., 249.

34. A. William Salomone, *Italy in the Giolittian Era: Italian Democracy in the Making, 1900–1914* (Philadelphia: University of Pennsylvania Press, 1960), 13. It should be noted that Salomone notes that these political leaders gradually abandoned their confederative principles. The question of why this occurred is critical to understanding the failure of federalism in Italy.

35. Dieter Langewiesche, "Föderativer Nationalismus als Erbe der deutschen Reichsnation: Über Föderalismus und Zentralismus in der deutschen Nationalgeschichte," in Dieter

Langewiesche and G. Schmidt, eds., *Föderative Nation: Deutschlandkonzepte von der Reformation bis zum Ersten Weltkrieg* (Munich: Oldenbourg Verlag, 2000); Umbach, *Federalism and Enlightenment*; Alon Confino, *The Nation as a Local Metaphor: Württemberg, Imperial Germany, and National Memory, 1871–1917* Chapel Hill: University of North Carolina Press, 1997).

36. As chapter 5 will demonstrate, the repeated efforts at alliances among Italian states broke down in the 1850s because of the internal structure of the absolutist states themselves. See the discussion on pp. 91–94.

37. Riker, *Federalism*, and more recent formal analyses in the same tradition such as de Figueiredo and Weingast, "Self Enforcing Federalism," argue that federalism persists if the center is not so powerful as to "overawe" the periphery (which would create a unitary system) but not so weak as to be undone by the constituent parts (which would result in political disintegration).

38. Riker, *Federalism*, 12. In this same analysis, Riker notes that a second factor that may thwart the political center's aim of establishing a unitary system is "ideological distaste." Riker's own identification of this potentially constraining cause calls into question the utility of Riker's initial assumption that a political center's first preference will always be a unitary system.

39. These figures are based on my own calculations. The relative power of Piedmont and Prussia is calculated by estimating each state's control over population, territory, and military expenditures (before unification) as a proportion of the future territory of each unified nation-state (i.e., excluding Austria in both cases) after 1871. Italy's population figures are from 1861, and taken from Vera Zamagni, *The Economic History of Italy, 1860–1990* (Oxford: Clarendon Press, 1993), 14; Italy's territory figures are from 1857, and taken from Robert Fried, *The Italian Prefects: A Study in Administrative Politics* (New Haven: Yale University Press, 1963), 54; German population figures are for 1865, and taken from Thomas Nipperdey, *Germany from Napoleon to Bismarck, 1800–1866* (Princeton: Princeton University Press, 1996), 86; Germany's territory data is from Rolf Dumke, *German Economic Unification in the Nineteenth Century: The Political Economy of the Zollverein* (Munich: University of the Bundeswehr, 1994), 55; Germany's expenditures on military are from Karl Borchard, "Staatsverbrauch und Öffentliche Investitionen in Deutschland, 1780–1850," dissertation, Wirtschafts und Sozialwissenschaftlichen Fakultät, Göttingen, 1968, 183–85. The data on military personnel is from J. David Singer and Melvin Small, *National Material Capabilities Data, 1816–1985* (Ann Arbor: Inter-university Consortium for Political and Social Research, 1993), computer file.

40. The general insight that effects of institutions are frequently mistakenly used to explain the origins of institutions is made in Paul Pierson, *Politics in Time: History, Institutions, and Social Analysis* (Princeton: Princeton University Press, 2004).

41. Because the aim is to produce as generalizable a theory as possible, it is critical to specify the "scope conditions" that bound a framework. Here, the proposed framework is informed by Alfred Stepan's useful distinction between "coming together" and "holding together" pathways to federalism. Borrowing from Stepan, "New Comparative Politics," the proposed framework recognizes the different causal logic underlying the process of a new nation-state forming out of a smaller collection of constituent states ("coming together"), the process of a unitary state decentralizing power to constituent states ("holding together"), or even new postcolonial states emerging out of a colonial setting. Though all three pathways to federalism are important, the proposed framework, like William Riker's classic work, is intended *exclusively* for the first, the "coming together" class of cases, and hence has a particular amenablility to the European context of state formation.

42. This definition of "infrastructural capacity" borrows from Mann, *Sources of Social Power.*

43. This finding that parliamentary states tend to be willing to negotiate while autocratic states are not conforms with recent work in international relations. See, for example, James Fearon, "Domestic Political Audiences and the Escalation of International Disputes," *American Political Science Review* 88 (1994): 577–92.

44. See, for example, Jonah Levy, *Tocqueville's Revenge: State, Society, and Economy in Post-Dirigste France* (Cambridge: Harvard University Press, 1999); Theda Skocpol, "How Americans Became Civic," in Theda Skocpol and Morris P. Fiorina, eds., *Civic Engagement in American Democracy* (Washington, D.C.: Brookings Institution Press and Russell Sage Foundation, 1999); Marc Morje Howard, "The Weakness of Postcommunist Civil Society," *Journal of Democracy* 13, no. 1 (2002): 157–69.

45. In the Weberian terminology, patrimonialism is the application of patriarchal authority to the imperatives of large political communities, assuring that the government remains as the "ruler's private domain." For a useful discussion, see Reinhard Bendix, *Max Weber: An Intellectual Portrait* (Berkeley and Los Angeles: University of California Press, 1977), 334.

46. These are the three defining attributes of comparative historical analysis as identified by James Mahoney and Dietrich Rueschemeyer, "Comparative Historical Analysis: Achievements and Agenda," in James Mahoney and Dietrich Rueschemeyer, eds., *Comparative Historical Analysis in the Social Sciences* (Cambridge: Cambridge University Press, 2003), 6. See the important piece by Theda Skocpol and Margaret Somers, "The Uses of History in Macrosocial Inquiry," *Comparative Studies in Society and History* 22, no. 2 (1980): 174–97; more recently, see Evan Lieberman, "Causal Inference in Historical Institutional Analysis: A Specification of Periodization Strategies," *Comparative Political Studies* 34 (2001): 1011–35.

47. Edward L. Gibson and Tulia Falleti, "Unity by the Stick: Regional Conflict and the Origins of Argentine Federalism," in Edward L. Gibson, ed., *Federalism and Democracy in Latin America* (Baltimore: Johns Hopkins University Press, 2003).

48. Ibid., 226–54.

49. See Riker, *Federalism*; Chad Rector, "Federations in International Politics," Ph.D. diss., Department of Political Science, University of California, San Diego, May 2003.

50. Among the many excellent accounts that link conceptualization as a central part of the process of creating good research designs, see David Collier and James E. Mahon, "Conceptual Stretching Revisited: Adapting Categories in Comparative Analysis," *American Political Science Review* 87 (1993): 845–55; David Collier and Robert Adcock, "Measurement Validity: A Shared Standard for Qualitative and Quantitative Research," *American Political Science Review* 95 (2001): 529–46; Giovanni Sartori, "Concept Misformation in Comparative Research," *American Political Science Review* 64 (1970): 1033–53; Andrew C. Gould, "Conflicting Imperatives and Concept Formation," *Review of Politics* 61 (1999): 439–63.

51. Some classic statements of the comparative method are Arend Lijphart, "Comparative Politics and the Comparative Method," *American Political Science Review* 65 (1971): 682–93; Adam Przeworski and Henry Teune, *The Logic of Comparative Social Inquiry* (New York: Wiley Interscience, 1970); David Collier, "Letter from the President: Comparative Methodology in the 1990s," *APSA–Comparative Politics Newsletter* 9, no. 1 (1998): 1–5.

52. John Stuart Mill, "Two Methods of Comparison" (1888) reprinted in Amatai Etzioni and Frederic L. DuBow, eds., *Comparative Perspectives: Theories and Methods* (Boston: Little Brown 1970), 205–13.

53. Skocpol and Somers, "Uses of History," 183.

54. One of the central claims of this study is that the Italian and German nation-states both emerged as part of the broader set of changes that Charles Maier in "Transformations of Territoriality" describes as having given rise to a new "territorial regime" that replaced imperial and dynastic forms of territorial organization.

55. Skocpol and Sommers, "Uses of History"; Richard Snyder, "Scaling Down: The Subnational Comparative Method," *Studies in Comparative International Development* 36, no. 1 (2001): 93–110.

56. The third question—the *type* of federalism—is systematically explored in the German case with a diachronic comparison that contrasts the proposed centralized federal institutional outcome of the 1848 constitution with the actual decentralized federal institutional outcome of the 1871 constitution. This diachronic comparison receives more complete discussion in chapter 6.

CHAPTER TWO
THE NATIONAL CRITICAL JUNCTURE: AN OVERVIEW OF THE
DYNAMICS OF REGIONALISM AND NATIONAL UNIFICATION

1. Karl Polanyi, *The Great Transformation* (New York: Farrar and Rinehart, 1944), 65.

2. Otto Hintze, "The State in Historical Perspective," in Reinhard Bendix, ed., *State and Society: A Reader in Comparative Political Sociology* (Berkeley and Los Angeles: University of California Press, 1968), 164.

3. The concept of a "national critical juncture" draws on the developmental framework originally conceptualized by Seymour Martin Lipset and Stein Rokkan, eds., *Party System and Voter Alignment* (New York: Free Press, 1967), who identified four historical critical junctures in the development of all polities: church versus state, land versus industry, owner versus labor, and center versus periphery. Recently, work by David Collier and Ruth Berins Collier, *Shaping the Political Arena: Critical Junctures, the Labor Movement, and Regime Dynamics in Latin America* (Princeton: Princeton University Press, 1991), has focused on the institutional consequences of different patterns of labor incorporation. Yet little comparative empirical work has examined the institutional consequences of different pathways of center-periphery conflict or what this study calls the "national" critical juncture—the moment in which a polity incorporates new territory. It is this gap that this study seeks to fill.

4. My concept of "national constitutional founding moment" refers to the first adoption of a nationwide constitution, the body of rules that formally or informally regulates the government of a state. In the Italian and German contexts, national unification and the formation of a national constitution occurred *simultaneously*, while in other national settings, national unification or national independence preceded the national constitutional founding moment. For a cross-national application of these ideas, see chapter 7.

5. Since these categories—initiating, supportive, resistant, and hostile—are important for this chapter, they deserve immediate definition. By *initiating* I mean regional governments that through military conquest and political negotiation successfully expand their borders to attempt an explicitly "national" unification. By *supportive* I mean regional governments that express support for the "national" unification of independent states in official statements, and that when granted the opportunity, take the side of the "initiating" regional governments on the issue of national unification, though the supportive regional governments never themselves seek to expand their *own* borders. By *resistant*, I mean regional governments that express, in public statements, their opposition to national unification and when given the opportunity, take the side of "hostile" regional governments. Resistant regional governments, however, never *themselves* initiate military or organized political action against national unification. Finally, *hostile* refers to regional governments that actively initiate and undertake political and military action to protect the autonomy of the regional governments and to resist efforts at national unification.

6. This point is also made in the important case study of Italian state-building by Riall, *Sicily and the Unification of Italy.*

7. By "commercialization" I refer here both to the specific set of legal changes and to changes in economic practice that transformed the basic factors of production—land, labor, and capital—into commodities. As classic treatments of the subject make clear, the "commercial" revolution followed different trajectories in different regions of Europe. In Britain, the commercialization of land occurred earliest and most intensively between 1760 and 1810. On the European continent, the process occurred slightly later. In those regions, closest to France (e.g., Piedmont, Lombardy, the Rhineland), under the direct rule of Napoleon, traditional land-tenure systems and guilds were rapidly and effectively dismantled by 1815. By contrast, in regions outside of French rule or under less direct Napoleonic rule or influence (e.g., Bavaria, southern Italy, Sicily), the process of eliminating feudalism and guild systems progressed more slowly after 1815. For a discussion of the early British case of commercialization of land in Britain, see J. H. Plumb, *England in the 18th Century* (Middlesex: Penguin, 1950), 77–90. For a discussion of the uneven processes of commercialization in Europe, see E. J. Hobsbawm, *The Age of Revolution: Europe, 1789–1848* (London: Weidenfeld and Nicolson, 1962), 149–67.

8. For general discussions of the geographically uneven impact of Napoleon's rule on Italy and Germany, see Stuart Woolf, *Napoleon's Integration of Europe* (New York: Routledge, 1991), 40–41; and David Laven and Lucy Riall, eds., *Napoleon's Legacy: Problems of Government in Restoration Europe* (Oxford: Berg, 2000), 8–12.

9. For a discussion of the orientations and actions of Saxon-Coburg vis-à-vis Prussia and national unification between 1859 and 1866, see Ernst II, Herzog von Sachsen-Coburg-Gotha, *Aus meinem Leben und aus meiner Zeit*, vol. 3 (Berlin: Verlag von Wilhelm Herz, 1889), 275–545. Since the Lombard political elite was dominated by an occupying Austrian military and administration, the Lombard leadership was politically and militarily incapacitated.

10. For a concise and useful account of the Württemberg crown's and political leadership's attitudes toward Prussia beginning in 1866, see Ernst Rudolf Huber, *Deutsche Verfassungsgeschichte Seit 1789*, vol. 3 (Stuttgart: W. Kohlhammer Verlag, 1963), 669–70.

11. On tensions and open conflict between Bavaria and Prussia, see Huber, *Deutsche Verfassungsgeschichte Seit 1789*, 531–42; on the end of the Bourbon regime in Naples and its effort at military resistance against Piedmont in 1860, see Alfonso Scirocco, *L'Italia del Risorgimento* (Bologna: Il Mulino, 1990), 401.

12. Such an impression emerges if one examines the colorful memoirs of participants in the German Bund negotiations between the monarchs of the German states in the 1860s. See, for example, Herzog von Sachsen-Coburg-Gotha, *Aus meinem Leben*, 275–545. In the Italian context, the importance of personal relations between the monarchs can be seen in the personal correspondence between representatives of the Piedmontese and Bourbon kings in 1859–60. See a small collection of translated correspondence in John Santore, *Modern Naples: A Documentary History* (New York: Italica Press, 2001), 166–79.

13. The classic statement of the opposed forces of nationalism and regionalism is articulated by Heinrich Treitschke, who derides "regionalism" as a "fairy-tale world of particularism." See *Historische und Politische Aufsätze* (Leipzig: Verlag von Hirzel, 1867), 448. This conception clearly influenced the classic statement of modernization theory by Lipset and Rokkan, who write that "the growing nation state developed a wide range of agencies of unification and standardization and gradually penetrated the bastions of *primordial* local culture" (*Party System*, 13).

14. Parallel revisionist English-language historical accounts have recently developed on national unification in Italy and Germany to highlight the importance of regionalism and regional identity as an important "integrative" force. Significant examples in the German context include Celia Applegate, *A Nation of Provincials: The German Idea of Heimat* (Berkeley and Los Angeles: University of California Press, 1990); and Confino, *Nation as*

174   NOTES TO CHAPTER TWO

Local Metaphor, and in the Italian context Riall, *Sicily*. My chapter seeks to synthesize, in a comparative framework, the insights of both of these recent historiographic trends.

15. For an example of this argument in the German context, see the classic work by Theodore S. Hamerow, *The Social Foundations of German Unification, 1858–1871* (Princeton: Princeton University Press, 1969); and more recently a collection of essays edited by Lothar Gall and Dieter Langewiesche, *Liberalismus und Region* (Munich: R. Oldenbourg Verlag, 1995). In this same tradition is Jonathon Sperber, *Rhineland Radicals: The Democratic Movement and the Revolution of 1848–1849* (Princeton: Princeton University Press, 1991), who calls his approach "history from below." For early examples of this argument in the Italian context, see Kent Greenfield, *Economics and Liberalism in the Risorgimento: A Study of Nationalism in Lombardy, 1814–1848* (Baltimore: Johns Hopkins Press, 1965).

16. In the German context, see Liah Greenfeld, *Nationalism: Five Roads to Modernity* (Cambridge: Harvard University Press, 1992); in the Italian context see Raymond Grew, *A Sterner Plan for Italian Unity: The Italian National Society in the Risorgimento* (Princeton: Princeton University Press, 1963).

17. In the German context, see Helmut Böhme, *Deutschlands Weg Zur Grossmacht* (Cologne: Kiepenheuer und Witsch, 1972); and Richard Tilly, "The Political Economy of Public Finance and the Industrialization of Prussia, 1815–1866," *Journal of Economic History* 26 (1966): 484–97. For the Italian context, see Lucy Riall, "Elite Resistance to State Formation: The Case of Italy," in Mary Fulbrook, ed., *National Histories and European History* (Boulder, Colo.: Westview Press, 1993), 58. For an explicitly state-centered account that rejects "economic determinism," see Luciano Cafagna, *Cavour* (Bologna: Il Mulino, 1999).

18. Dumke, *German Economic Unification*. For a tentative exploration of this thesis in Italy, see Rupert Pichler, *Die Wirtschaft Lombardei als Teil Österreichs* (Berlin: Duncker und Humblot, 1996).

19. The benefits of a "subnational" comparative method have increasingly been noted by scholars of comparative politics. For the best recent methodological discussion, see Richard Snyder, "Scaling Down: The Subnational Comparative Method," *Studies in Comparative International Development* 36, no. 1 (2001): 93–110. Snyder cites Gary King, Robert Keohane, and Sidney Verba, *Designing Social Inquiry: Scientific Inference in Qualitative Research* (Princeton: Princeton University Press, 1994), 219, to argue that since theories usually have observable implications at many levels of analysis, a theory focused on a national case can be tested in subnational units of that case (95).

20. This point is made by Thomas Nipperdey, *Germany from Napoleon to Bismarck, 1800–1866* (Princeton, Princeton University Press, 1996), 130.

21. See, for example, Gary Herrigel, *Industrial Constructions: The Sources of German Industrial Power* (Cambridge: Cambridge University Press, 1996); Nipperdey, *From Napoleon to Bismarck*.

22. See Eric Dorn Brose, *German History, 1789–1871* (Providence: Berghahn, 1997), 153–64; Harm-Hinrich Brandt, *Deutsche Geschichte, 1850–1870. Entscheidung über die Nation* (Stuttgart: Kohlhammer, 1999), 20–51, 79–128. See also my own discussion in chapter 6.

23. Italian historiography has long noted the large economic differences between "north" and "south." In recent years, this division has been even further disaggregated as scholars have increasingly noted that there never has been one single "south." Rather, within the south, there have always been huge disparities that are lost with analysis that centers exclusively around the north-versus-south distinction. For recent important literature on this topic, see Adrian Lyttleton, "A New Past for the Mezzogiorno?" *Times Literary Supplement*, October 4, 1991, 14–15; and the Italian-language journal *Meridiana*, which in recent years has become a forum to discuss the long-hidden "diversity" of southern Italy.

24. On this point in the German context, see Confino, *Nation as Local Metaphor*, and Alon Confino, "Federalism and the Heimat Idea in Imperial Germany," in Maiken Umbach, ed., *German Federalism: Past, Present, and Future* (London: Palgrave, 2002); and in the Italian context, see Riall, *Sicily*, 29.

25. For a discussion of the methodological pitfalls associated with having as many or fewer cases than potential independent variables, see King, Keohane, and Verba, *Designing Social Inquiry*, 119–22.

26. This theoretical insight was most explicitly articulated by Theda Skocpol and her colleagues in a series of essays during the 1980s. For the most direct statement, see Peter Evans, Dietrich Rueschemeyer, and Theda Skocpol, eds., *Bringing the State Back In* (Cambridge: Cambridge University Press, 1985).

27. To measure each of the twenty-four regions along these two dimensions, I utilize the following measures: For my measure of "regional level of economic modernization" or "commercialization," I utilize data on regional GDP per capita for each region from 1861 in Italy and 1850 in Germany. For my measure of "state size" or "state strength" I use data on the total state expenditures (i.e., size of state budget) in Italy and Germany between 1850 and 1852. For a complete discussion of measures, original data, and data sources, see appendix A.

28. Any effort to quantify complex historical processes will generate resistance from historians who know the cases well. Conversely, for quantitatively minded social scientists the reliability and validity problems inherent in my historical data may prove equally frustrating. My account treads precisely in this treacherous domain of applying basic statistical techniques to historical data by using the admittedly problematic though best available data on this period. By coupling my quantitative analysis with a more detailed narrative account in later chapters, I believe my approach can sidestep many of the criticisms of both historians and quantitatively minded social scientists.

29. For a similar methodological approach that uses secondary literature to construct a quantitative historical dataset, see Eric Schickler, "Institutional Change in the House of Representatives, 1867–1998: A Test of Partisan and Ideological Power Balance Models," *American Political Science Review* 94 (2000): 271–72, 284.

30. For the German data, see Borchard, "Staatsverbrauch." For Italian data, see Luigi Izzo, *La finanza pubblica* (Milan: Dottore a Giuffre Editore, 1962), 123.

31. My estimates on Italian regions are aggregated from provincial/regional GDP per capita data estimated by Alfredo Esposto, "Estimating Regional per Capita Income: Italy, 1861–1914," *Journal of European Economic History* 26 (1997): 589. The GDP per capita scores for the German states are estimated by aggregating provincial-level data provided by Harald Frank, *Regionale Entwicklungsdisparitäten im deutschen Industrialisierungsprozess, 1849–1939* (Münster: Lit Verlag, 1996), appendix 8, p. 30.

32. Lipset and Rokkan, *Party System*, 13.

CHAPTER THREE

THE NATIONAL MOMENT IN GERMANY: THE DYNAMICS OF REGIONALISM
AND NATIONAL UNIFICATION, 1834–1871

1. As cited by W. O. Henderson, *The Zollverein* (Cambridge: Cambridge University Press, 1939), 94.

2. It is important to note that though my argument identifies these three steps as critical stages of the process of national unification in Germany, my argument by no means contends that each stage inevitably led to the next. In the past, German historiography often suffered from a pro-Prussian bent that viewed the unification of Germany in 1871 as the inevitable

pinnacle of all political developments up until that point. See for example Heinrich Treitschke's *History of Germany in the Nineteenth Century*, trans. Eden Paul and Cedar Paul (London: Jarrold and Sons, 1918). Furthermore, such accounts, using Bismarck's notoriously unreliable memoirs as evidence, often claim that all Bismarck's political actions before 1871 were aimed at German unification. For a summary and critique of such approaches, see Lothar Gall, *Bismarck: The White Revolutionary* (London: Allen and Unwin, 1986).

3. The "regions" in this analysis include not only independent region states but provinces within Prussia for which data are available. Sources: data on regional Nationalverein membership, Andreas Biefang, *Politisches Bürgertum in Deutschland, 1857–1868. Nationale Organisationen und Eliten* (Düsseldorf: Droste Verlag, 1994), 104; data on regional population, Wolfgang Köllmann, ed., *Quellen zur Bevölkerungs-, Sozial- und Wirtschaftsstatistik, 1815–1875*, vol. 1 (Boppard am Rhein: Harald Boldt verlag, 1980), 34–327; estimates of GDP per capita, Frank, *Regionale Entwicklungsdisparitäten*, appendix 8, 30.

4. Prussia as a single region was, of course, itself economically, socially, and culturally split: The western provinces of Prussia that serve as the focus here were highly developed, early commercializing, and early industrializing parts of Germany where social support for national unification was strong. By contrast, the economically backward and largely agrarian regions of eastern Prussia, dominated by the antinational conservative Junkers, were a source of regional "particularism" that was either indifferent or even resistant to the perceived "liberal" agenda of national unification. This pattern confirms my hypothesis on the relationship between economic modernization and support for national unification. For a discussion of the antinationalism of these groups, see Eugen Anderson, *The Social and Political Conflict in Prussia, 1858–1864* (Lincoln: University of Nebraska Press, 1954), 134–35. My discussion of regional resistance to national unification focuses on southern German resistance and intentionally excludes these Prussian groups because as Martin Shefter, *Political Parties and the State: The American Historical Experience* (Princeton: Princeton University Press, 1994), has argued, these Prussian regions were "governed by the state whose institutions were extended over the newly unified nation," and a result this "most important segment of Germany's landed classes had been integrated into and had acquired a stake in the integrity of the nation's administrative apparatus" (52). The task of melding a coalition of pronational liberals and antinational conservatives will be discussed below.

5. This argument about internal trade that asserts that the "early" commercializers tended to support free trade while the "late" commercializers did not finds a parallel with Peter Gourevitch's argument in *Politics in Hard Times* (Ithaca: Cornell University Press, 1986) about the determinants of policy toward international trade that asserts that "early developers" are more likely than "late developers" to support free trade (88–89).

6. This "economic" explanation of why the most commercialized regions supported unification is by no means analytically exclusive and can be complemented by a "cultural" explanation by borrowing from classic modernization theory and recent culturalist insights on the relationship of regions and nation building. If we argue that economic modernization is a process that gradually replaces exclusively "corporate" identities with "individual" identities, it makes sense that in regions of economic modernization and cultural "individuation" we see national loyalties develop. Recent historiography on regions and nation building has emphasized the extent to which national identities and local identities were not opposed to each other during nation building but rather complemented each other—the "nation as local metaphor," in Confino's provocative phrase in the title of his work. In short, it was in the most economically commercialized regions of Germany that the "cultural leap" of national invention was most possible.

7. Sidney Pollard, *Peaceful Conquest: The Industrialization of Europe, 1760–1970* (Oxford: Oxford University Press, 1981). I make this claim about the early geographical dispersion of Germany's commercialization notwithstanding the important findings of Gary Her-

rigel that by century's end a distinctive mode of capitalism had in fact emerged in Germany's southwest. See Herrigel, *Industrial Constructions.*

8. It should be noted that by century's end, this gradient had transformed as southern manufacturers developed a distinctive market-oriented set of organizational strategies. My discussion focuses on the pre-1866 period. See Hal Hansen, "Caps and Gowns," Ph.D. diss., University of Wisconsin–Madison, 1997, 348–49.

9. Arnold Price, *The Evolution of the Zollverein: A Study of the Ideas and Institutions Leading to German Economic Unification between 1815 and 1833* (New York: Octagon Books, 1973), 185.

10. The following account of Rhineland business interests is based on Jeffry M. Diefendorf, *Businessmen and Politics in the Rhineland, 1789–1834* (Princeton: Princeton University Press, 1980) and my own review of the three-volume collection of archival material collected by W. von Eisenhart Rothe and A. Ritthaler, eds., *Vorgeschichte und Begründung des Deutschen Zollvereins 1815–1834* (Berlin: Verlag von Reimar Hobbing, 1934) on the occasion of the one hundredth anniversary of the founding of the Zollverein.

11. Source: Frank, *Regionale Entwicklungsdisparitäten,* appendix 8, p. 30.

12. For a description of these institutional developments, see Brose, *German History, 1789–1871,* 46–76; and Wolfram Fischer, *Wirtschaft und Gesellschaft im Zeitalter der Industrialisierung* (Göttingen: Vandenhöck und Ruprecht, 1964), 296–314. For a discussion of Saxony, see Hubert Kiesewetter, *Industrialisierung und Landwirtschaft. Sachsens Stellung im regionalen Industrialisierungsprozess Deutschlands im 19. Jahrhundert* (Cologne: Böhlau Verlag, 1988).

13. As Paul Bairoch put it in his classic work on the industrial revolution, the commercialization of agriculture is the *conditio sine qua non* of all economic development. See Paul Bairoch, *Révolution industrielle et sous-développement* (Paris: Societe d'edition d'enseignement superieur, 1963), 73.

14. The commercializing legislation that reduced the authority of the guilds took place incrementally in the other German states: Austria (1809), Prussia (1811), Nassau (1814), Bavaria (1825), Hesse-Darmstadt (1827), Württemberg (1828), Saxony (1840), and Hannover (1846). Significantly, despite this legislation, other informal and formal restrictions on free enterprise continued to exist in many of the southern German states. See Brose, *German History, 1789–1871,* 112.

15. Woolf, *Napoleon's Integration of Europe,* 128.

16. Franklin F. Mendels, "Proto-industrialization: The First Phase of the Industrialization Process," *Journal of Economic History* 32 (1972): 241–61.

17. For a statement and comparative study of this thesis on the firm-level determinants of protectionist and free-trade policy in the twentieth century, see Helen Milner, *Resisting Protectionism: Global Industries and the Politics of International Trade* (Princeton: Princeton University Press, 1988).

18. Kiesewetter, *Industrialisierung und Landwirtschaft,* 158.

19. The transformation of Rhineland manufacturers from their pro-French leaning in 1815 to their patriotic German orientation by 1834 is the subject of Diefendorf's *Businessmen and Politics.*

20. Dumke, *German Economic Unification,* 58.

21. These leaders have also attracted much attention as a result of the fact that many of them would eventually participate in the "failed" parliament of 1848. The much-debated "failure" of 1848 by no means reduces the importance these social leaders would have in transforming Prussian official policy away from an antinational restoration position toward a pronational position in the 1860s. Though the Prussian crown rejected the Frankfurt parliament's offer of the imperial crown in 1848, it was the very existence of this new commercialized and largely liberal social elite, most significantly in Rhineland but also in other parts

of Prussia, that spawned the success of the liberal parties in the Prussian Assembly, generated the constitutional crisis of the 1850–1860s, and induced Bismarck to turn to a policy of national unification to solve his Prussian "domestic" problems. For a useful discussion that links the liberal challenge in the Prussian Assembly to Bismarck's increasingly prounification stance in the 1860s, see Nipperdey, *From Napoleon to Bismarck*, 643.

22. For a discussion of this "conservative" coalition, its ability to dominate government, and its anti-industrial policies, see Tilly, "Political Economy," 484–97.

23. Letter from manufacturers to King Friedrich Wilhelm III, Berlin, April 27, 1818, in Eisenhart Rothe and A. Ritthaler, *Vorgeschichte und Begründung des Deutschen Zollvereins 1815–1834, Akten der Staaten des Deutschen Bundes* (Berlin: Verlag von Reimar Hobbing, 1934), 69–70.

24. The Rhineland manufacturers were not alone in their calls for the creation of a single "national" market. Manufacturers from Thüringen also wrote to the king of Prussia calling for the creation of a single national market (ibid.). Likewise, one liberal leader spoke to the Baden Chamber of Deputies in the spring of 1818: "The German nation calls loudly and in unison for the creation of completely free commerce between the states of the Federation without the limits that have until now only weakened the people and that have alienated the common sons of Germany from each other" (ibid.). Finally, in perhaps one of the most famous statements of the "nationalist" call for a single market, Friedrich List spoke on behalf of the newly created German Trade and Industrial Association (Allgemeine Deutsche Handels- and Gewerbeverein) to the German Federal Assembly to call for the unification of an internal German national market. In his petition, List stated, "Thirty-eight separate tariff zones in Germany paralyze both internal trade and movement. This has the same highly dangerous consequence as would the dividing up of the human body to prevent blood flowing from one limb to another. In order to conduct trade between Hamburg and Austria or from Berlin to Switzerland, one must travel today through ten states, one must study ten separate sets of tariff laws, and one must pay ten separate sets of tariffs. It is clear that he who must do this has no fatherland." For partial text of List's speech, see Wolfram Siemann, *Vom Staatenbund zum Nationalstaat: Deutschland 1806–1871* (Munich: Beck, 1995), 337.

25. Cited by Diefendorf, *Businessmen and Politics*, 322.

26. Cited by Diefendorf, *Businessmen and Politics*, 321.

27. For a discussion of the effect of Napoleon's reforms on Germany, see Michael John, "The Napoleonic Legacy and Problems of Restoration in Central Europe: The German Confederation," in Laven and Riall, *Napoleon's Legacy*, 93–96.

28. Jürgen Kocha, "Germany," in Ira Katznelson and Aristide Zolberg, eds., *Working-Class Formation* (Princeton: Princeton University Press, 1986), 290.

29. Additionally, it is not surprising that manufacturing economies where "guilds" were still predominant were hostile to free trade with other regions, insofar as guilds usually maintained two rules: First, no guild member could trespass on the economic territory of another guild member; second, no person who was not a guild member could operate in a geographical area where a guild member already worked. As a result, outsiders were known as *Bönhasen* (ground rabbit), *Pfuscher* (bungler), and *Störer* (intruder or disturber). See Barrington Moore, *Injustice: The Social Bases of Obedience and Revolt* (White Plains, N.Y.: M. E. Sharpe, 1978), 129.

30. Hans-Werner Hahn, *Wirtschaftliche Integration im 19. Jahrhundert: Die hessischen Staaten und der Deutsche Zollverein* (Göttingen: Vandenhöck und Ruprecht, 1982), 341.

31. Brose, *German History, 1789–1871*, 173.

32. Ibid., 171.

33. Ibid., 172.

34. Heinrich Treitschke, *Historische und Politische Aufsätze* (Leipzig: Verlag von Hirzel, (1867), 448.

35. Preussisches Handelsarchiv (1865) as cited by Hamerow, *Social Foundations*, 102.
36. Ibid.
37. Ibid.
38. See discussion in note 3 above.
39. Wilhelm Marr, "Selbständigkeit und Hoheitsrecht der freien Stadt Hamburg Sind ein Anachronismus geworden" (Hamburg, 1866), 52–53, as cited by Hamerow, *Social Foundations*, 388.
40. The data in figure 3.2 are from Kiesewetter, *Industrialisierung und Landwirtschaft*, 387.
41. Heinrich Best, *Interessenpolitik und nationale Integration 1848/1849 Handelspolitische Konflikte im frühindustriellen Deutschland* (Göttingen: Vandenhöck und Ruprecht, 1980), 149–50.
42. Nipperdey, *From Napoleon to Bismarck*, 187.
43. Bernhard Löffler, *Die Bayerische Kammer der Reichsräte 1848–1918* (Munich: Beck'sche Verlagsbuchhandlung, 1996), 401.
44. Ibid.
45. Alf Mintzel, "Specificities of Bavarian Political Culture," in Dirk Berg-Schlosser and Ralf Rytlewski, eds., *Political Culture in Germany* (London: Macmillan, 1993), 105.
46. Frank, *Regionale Entwicklungsdisparitäten*, appendix 8, p. 30.
47. Mintzel, "Specificities," 104.
48. Stenographischer Bericht, *Verhandlungen der Bayerischen Kammer der Abgeordneten*, October 18, 1867, 2:60.
49. Ibid., October 21, 1867, 2:50.
50. Similar currents of support and resistance to unification were also clear in Württemberg, where most traditional economic interests resisted closer ties to the north but the Württemberg Manufacturers Association justified their support for unification with the observation that "the movement of Württemberg trade is in the main toward the North Sea . . . a separation from the customs union with Prussia would create the most harmful disturbances in trade." For this group closer ties made sense, but manufacturers were a minority in the Württemberg economy. Indeed, a Prussian general summarized the situation in southern Germany in the 1860s with the optimistic observation, "Even if in South Germany the majority is not for us, the men of intelligence are" (cited by Hamerow, *Social Foundations*, 384).
51. A useful overview of the development of public finance and state building in Prussia with reference to several other German states can be found in Thomas Ertman, *Birth of the Leviathan: Building States and Regimes in Medieval and Early Modern Europe* (Cambridge: Cambridge University Press, 1997), 245–63. According to Ertman, in the eighteenth century, Prussian leaders failed to develop a stable system of public finance that would have required the toleration of representative assemblies. Despite its relatively "modern" bureaucracy, the resulting premodern system of public finance left Prussia vulnerable to military attack and economic bankruptcy.
52. D. E. Schremmer, "Taxation and Public Finance: Britain, France, and Germany," in Peter Mathias and Sidney Pollard, eds., *Cambridge Economic History of Europe*, vol. 8, *The Industrial Economies: The Development of Social Policies* (Cambridge: Cambridge University Press, 1989), 315–548.
53. Tilly, "Political Economy," 493; Ertman, *Birth of the Leviathan*, 262.
54. Dumke, *German Economic Unification*, 27.
55. The bivariate correlation is based on 1850 debt per capita data (debt burden) and population data (state size) of thirty-three German states that eventually joined the Prussian customs union. One interesting state, Bavaria, an outlier with extremely high debt and high population, was excluded from this analysis. If included, the correlation coefficient is still

significant but drops to –0.16. Data for these are drawn from Borchard, "Staatsverbrauch," 91–93.

56. Borchard, "Staatsverbrauch."57. See Dumke, *German Economic Unification*, for a very useful and thorough discussion of Kuehne's (1836) report.

58. Georg von Viebahn (1858) as cited by Dumke, *German Economic Unification*, 34.

59. Dumke, *German Economic Unification*, 30–31.

60. The first state outside of Prussia to join the Zollverein in February 1828 was the relatively small state of Hessen-Darmstadt, which had faced a tax strike in 1818–19, tax conflict in the parliament, and a leader, Ludwig I, who feared a "monarchical-liberal" compromise that would expand the franchise beyond the 988 citizens who could vote out of the population of 650,000 in the state. According to one account, Hessen-Darmstadt was "the most financially troubled state in Germany." With the aim of paying off debts without raising taxes, Prussian proposals that Hessen-Darmstadt be incorporated into the larger union of Prussia made sense. Additionally, Hessen-Darmstadt's largely agricultural economy (58 percent of the population was employed in the agricultural sector) was reliant on Prussian markets. By joining the Prussian customs union, Ludwig I also guaranteed agricultural and manufacturing interests in his state access to larger markets (Hahn, *Wirtschaftliche Integration*, 32).

61. According to estimates of the Prussian government itself, the losses to the Prussian treasury by expanding the Prussian customs union to the other states (between 1834 and 1840) were 1,200,000 thaler a year, approximately 10 percent of the Prussia's total tariff revenues (Prussian government Denkschrift den Einfluss der Zollvereinigungsverträge auf die Preussischen Staats-Einnahmen [1840, p. 87], as cited by Dumke, *German Economic Unification*), part 1, p. 6.

62. Leopold Ranke, *Historische-Politische Zeitschrift*, 2:64, as cited by Dumke, *German Economic Unification*, 7.

63. My analysis counts "abstention" as a vote for Austria, because the actors involved knew that Austria had a majority of the votes and by abstaining, the leaders of Baden, Schaumberg, Lippe, and Reuss jüngere Linie were indirectly though intentionally supporting Austria.

64. The best account of the constitutional crisis remains Eugene Anderson, *The Social and Political Conflict in Prussia, 1858–1864* (Lincoln: University of Nebraska Press, 1954).

65. The electoral victory in the 1861 parliamentary elections of the liberal Progressive Party and left-liberals gave liberals 285 of the 352 parliamentary seats in the Prussian parliament (Nipperdey, *From Napoleon to Bismarck*, 673).

66. Ibid., 681.

67. Ibid., 683.

68. For a summary of post-1859 efforts to reform German Confederation, see Norbert Wehner, *Die deutschen Mittelstaaten auf dem Frankfurter Fürstentag, 1863* (Frankfurt am Main: Peter Lang, 1993).

69. Despite Bismarck's intentions, it is important to note that nationalists and Junkers opposed his 1866 war.

70. Löffler, *Bayerische Kammer der Reichsräte*, 415.

71. See the collected internal correspondence of the Prussian Foreign Ministry, Herbert Michaelis, ed., *Die auswärtige Politik Preussens, 1858–1871*, vol. 8 (Oldenburg: Verlag Gerhard Stalling, 1934). See, for example, "Prinz Reuss an Bismarck, 30 November, 1866," in Michaelis, *Die auswärtige Politik Preussens*, 173–74.

72. See also a discussion of French interpretations of Bavaria's status as the second most powerful German state in Gisela Fay, *Bayern als grösster deutscher Mittelstaat im Kalkel der fränzosischen Diplomatie und im Urteil der Französischen Journalistik, 1859–1866* (Munich: Stadtarchivs München, 1976).

73. Stenographischer Bericht, *Verhandlungen der Bayerischer Kammer der Abgeordneten*, October 21, 1867, no. 33, 2:60.

74. The Bavarian crown was very sensitive of any hints that Prussia sought to undermine Bavarian autonomy. A report from the Bavarian ambassador to Berlin to the crown in Munich made sure to include in his description of the extravagant ceremony that opened the North German Reichstag in February 1867 that the Prussian king began his opening statement with assurances that "the peace treaties of the past year have shaped our relations with our compatriots in the south to assure that we find agreement with them, always with open hands" (*Norddeutsche Allgemeine Zeitung*, February 24, 1867, in Bayerische Gesandschaft Berlin, no. 1036, Bayerisches Staatsarchiv).

75. *Bayerische Zeitung*, no. 20, January 20, 1867.

76. Alexander von Hohenlohe, *Aus meinem Leben* (Frankfurt am Main: Societäts Druckerei, 1925), 285.

CHAPTER FOUR
THE NATIONAL MOMENT IN ITALY: THE DYNAMICS OF REGIONALISM
AND NATIONAL UNIFICATION, 1815–1860

1. The completion of national unification occurred in 1866 when war between Austria and Italy left Italy with the new territory of Venice and also in 1870 with the fall of Napoleon III and the Italian conquest and annexation of Rome.

2. See for example, the important work of Riall, *Sicily and the Unification of Italy*. The paradigmatic example of what might be called the "classic literature" is seen with Benedetto Croce, *Storia d'Italia dal 1871 al 1915* (Bari: G. Laterza, 1928), first published in English as *A History of Italy 1871–1915*, trans. Cecilia M. Ady (Oxford: Clarendon Press, 1929).

3. See, for example, Denis Mack Smith, *Cavour and Garibaldi: A Study in Political Conflict* (Cambridge: Cambridge University Press, 1954).

4. Antonio Gramsci, *Prison Notebooks*, ed. Joseph A. Buttigieg, trans. Joseph A. Buttigieg and Antonio Callari (New York: Columbia University Press, 1992).

5. See Rosario Romeo, *Il Risorgimento in Sicilia* (Bari: Gius. Laterza, 1950), 232.

6. See Raffaele Romanelli, "Political Debate, Social History, and the Italian 'Borghesia': Changing Perspectives in Historical Research," *Journal of Modern History* 63 (1991): 720.

7. Denis Mack Smith, *Victor Emanuel, Cavour and the Risorgimento* (London: Oxford University Press, 1971).

8. Pichler, *Die Wirtschaft Lombardei*.

9. Riall, "Elite Resistance"; Riall, *Sicily*.

10. See, for example, the discussion of powerless resistance of Tuscan aristocracy vis-à-vis Piedmont after the grand duke's departure in Thomas Kroll, *Die Revolte des Patriziats: Der Toskanische Adelsliberalismus im Risorgimento* (Tübingen: Max Niemeyer Verlag, 1999).

11. There were, of course, important peasant revolts against the Kingdom of Two Sicilies in 1820 and 1848. However, though nationalism was sometimes adopted as the idiom of protest, according to the leading scholars of the Risorgimento in Sicily, these movements were "mere agitation without any possibility of further development" (Romeo, *Il Risorgimento in Sicilia*). Nevertheless, as Riall has in particular noted, the center-periphery tensions within the Kingdom of Sicily were decisive in bringing about the unification of Italy (*Sicily*, 17).

12. To date, reliable regional data on membership on Italy's nationalist organizations have not been available. But previously unpublished data on Società Nazionale Italiana membership, by region (1859–63), were generously provided to me by Professor Raymond Grew,

University of Michigan. The data raise some interesting issues on the relationship between economic modernization and support for national unification.

13. It should be noted that in addition to these two hypotheses, another factor that clearly was important in determining the numbers of the SNI in each regional state was the actual policies of each state toward the SNI: In Piedmont, there were essentially no risks in joining; in the Papal States, membership before 1860 could mean a jail sentence, though members of the aristocracy were quite safe, despite the effort by police to penetrate meetings and watch suspected nationalists; in Tuscany, there were also great political freedoms allowed; in Lombardy-Veneto, the Austrian authorities were less draconian, but membership could result in job loss; and in the Kingdom of Two Sicilies, the restrictions on membership were greater than in Lombardy but less than in the Papal States (Raymond Grew, personal correspondence, April 18, 2001, and October 31, 2001).

14. See Robert Putnam, *Making Democracy Work: Civic Traditions in Modern Italy* (Princeton: Princeton University Press, 1993), 137.

15. Before Napoleon's invasion in 1798, Italy's center and north shared a traditional agriculture with Italy's south, though there were some marked and important differences. First, though feudalism had gradually been undermined in north central Italy over several centuries, the tax privileges of southern Italian aristocrats remained much more intact. Second, in contrast to the massive latifundia of Italy's south, the ancient sharecropping system in Italy's north-center was known as *mezzadria*. It was a system in which peasant (*colono*) and landlord each had a half share in produce, though the legal rights of the soil and taxation on the soil belonged to the proprietor. In some regions, the landlord provided most of the capital resources, while in others the peasant did. In either case, the landlord was expected to provide a house and a functioning cultivated piece of land (*podere*). The whole peasant family, living at a subsistence level, participated in the farming of the property and though without formal contract, the peasant and the proprietor shared a secure system in which the relationship of the landlord family and peasant family often existed over many generations. The system was highly unproductive. The benefit of the system, as in Italy's south, was for many landholding aristocrats precisely this stability. For a complete discussion, see Adrian Lyttelton, "Landlords, Peasants, and the Limits of Liberalism," in John A. Davis, ed., *Gramsci and Italy's Passive Revolution* (New York: Barnes and Noble, 1979).

16. According to one scholar of Napoleonic rule in Europe, the two strategies of rule—"direct" and "indirect"—were rooted in how "familiar" French leaders were with the conquered societies. Stuart Woolf writes, "Not only Piedmont, Lombardy, Tuscany, or Holland, but even Savoy, areas of Belgium, and parts of the Rhine left bank where seigneurial rights still survived were societies which the French thought they could 'read' without excessive difficulties . . .which explained more widespread knowledge and permitted more direct and continuous pressure. Southern Italy, Germany, Spain . . . were more distant and less known. At times the reports of the French administrators read as if they were explorers. They identified feudalism as the dominant social systems of [these] regions. . . and recognized with shock that it could not be destroyed at the stroke of a pen" (*Napoleon's Integration of Europe*, 128).

17. My account contrasts with an alternative conceptualization of the impact of French rule articulated by Filippo Sabetti, *The Search for Good Government: Understanding the Paradox of Italian Democracy* (Montreal: McGill-Queen's University Press, 2000), who argues that because of northern Italy's pre-1800 economic advances, the impact of the Napoleonic period was less significant in Italy's north. I believe that the divergent growth in agricultural output between north and south after 1800 attests to the greater impact of the Napoleonic effect in northern Italy than in southern Italy.

18. Hobsbawm, *Age of Revolution*, identifies these two "conditions" as well as the creation of a mobile and free workforce as necessary steps to effectively commercialize agriculture (181).

19. See Anthony Cardoza, *Aristocrats in Bourgeois Italy: The Piedmontese Nobility, 1861–1930* (Cambridge: Cambridge University Press, 1997), 28–29.

20. See Anthony Cardoza, *Agrarian Elites and Italian Fascism: The Province of Bologna, 1901–1921* (Princeton: Princeton University Press, 1982), 29; see also Hobsbawm, *Age of Revolution*, 157.

21. Hobsbawm, *Age of Revolution*, 157. Though Bologna was in the Papal States, the northern provinces of the Papal States had a great deal of institutional autonomy, including taxing autonomy, from Rome.

22. Renato Zangheri, *La propieta terriera e le origini del Risorgimento nel Bolognese* (Bologna: Zanichelli, 1961), 150.

23. Cardoza, *Aristocrats in Bourgeois Italy*, 32.

24. Ibid., 32.

25. Hobsbawm, *Age of Revolution*, 147.

26. See Rosario Romeo, *Risorgimento e capitalismo* (Bari: Laterza, 1959); and Alexander Gerschenkron, "Rosario Romeo and the Original Accumulation of Capital," in *Economic Backwardness in Historical Perspective* (Cambridge: Harvard University Press, 1962), 96, 107–18.

27. In recent years Italian economic historians have provided evidence to make the case that the political unification of Italy was an "economic mistake" that represented the wishful thinking of Italian intellectuals who mistakenly associated economic development with national unification. See, for example, Luciano Cafagna, "La questione delle origini del dualismo economico italiano," in Luciano Cafagna, ed., *Dualismo e sviluppo nella storia d'Italia* (Venice: Marilio, 1989), 187–217; see also Giorgio Mori, "Industrie senza industrializzione: La peninsola italiana dalla fine della dominazione francese all'unita nazionale: 1815–1861," *Studi Storici* 30 (1989): 607. Though this may be true, it does not mean that *perceived* economic interest had no impact on the drive for a "national market." In fact, as the evidence makes clear, though perhaps "wishful thinking," national unification and the creation of a national market were perceived by intellectuals and chambers of commerce throughout Italy's north to be a route to economic development.

28. John Davis, "The South, the Risorgimento, and the Origins of the Southern Problem," in Davis, *Gramsci*, 92.

29. See discussion of data in note 12.

30. See William Keith Hancock, *Ricasoli and the Risorgimento in Tuscany* (London: Faber and Gwyer, 1926), 12.

31. Lyttelton, "Landlords, Peasants," 111.

32. Hancock, *Ricasoli*, 15–16.

33. John Bowring, *Report on the Statistics of Tuscany, Lucca, the Pontifical, and the Lombardo-Venetian States, with a Special Reference to Their Commercial Relations*, Presented to Both Houses of Parliament by Command of Her Majesty (London: Clowes and Sons, 1837), 20.

34. Bowring, *Report on Statistics*, 18–19.

35. Denis Mack Smith, *Cavour* (London: Weidenfeld and Nicolson, 1985), 8.

36. Cardoza, *Aristocrats in Bourgeois Italy*, 50.

37. Cavour's opinion on national unification has been widely debated. Some scholars have argued that national unification was not the most important item on Cavour's political agenda even through 1859–60. It remains nevertheless true that Cavour, like many like-minded Piedmontese, increasingly perceived benefits in a Piedmontese-led national unification. See Mack Smith, *Victor Emanuel*.

38. The best discussion of the pronational and antinational elements within the Piedmontese aristocracy is presented by Anthony Cardoza, *Aristocrats in Bourgeois Italy*, 56–64.

39. Greenfield, *Economics and Liberalism*, 53.

40. Ibid., 58.

41. Ibid., 125–26.

42. The editors of the *Annali* wrote in 1834 the Zollverein in Germany was "a good omen for Italy." See *Annali* 1833, Bulletino, 46, as cited by Greenfield, *Economics and Liberalism*, 209. Greenfield writes, "By 1841, the discussion of an Italian commercial league had gone far enough to bring the Italian public face to face with the crucial difficulty which the presence of Austria on their soil threw in the way of the fulfillment of their desire" (209).

43. Cited by Greenfield, *Economics and Liberalism*, 209.

44. In one typical report as early as 1814, the Milan Chamber of Commerce complained that traffic within Lombardy was deeply constrained as a result of customs policy on the Po River. By the early 1820s, the growing commitment to free trade with other Italian states became increasingly clear in the Milan Chamber of Commerce with the release of several important reports in response to the Austrian government's prohibition of the importation of certain articles. By 1832, the Chamber of Commerce pressed for a reduction or complete abolition of transit duties. See cited reports in Greenfield, *Economics and Liberalism*, 57, 64.

45. Romanelli, "Political Debate"; Adrian Lyttelton, "A New Past for the Mezzogiorno?" *Times Literary Supplement*, October 4, 1991.

46. Judith Chubb, *Patronage, Power, and Poverty in Southern Italy: A Tale of Two Cities* (Cambridge: Cambridge University Press, 1982), 16.

47. Luigi de Rosa, *Iniziative e capitale straniero nell'industria metalmeccanica del mezzogiorno, 1840–1904* (Naples: Giannini, 1968).

48. Davis, "The South, the Risorgimento," 96.

49. Ibid.

50. Davis, "The South, the Risorgimento."

51. Zamagni, *Economic History of Italy*, 14.

52. In her careful analysis of agricultural practices and levels of productivity (ibid., 56), Zamagni notes that "taken as a whole" the south was less productive than the rest of Italy, though certain regions such as Campania and the Marches produced yield per hectare that were above the national average.

53. Davis, "The South, the Risorgimento," 94.

54. Jane Schneider and Peter Schneider, *Culture and Political Economy in Western Sicily* (New York: Academic Press, 1976), 114.

55. Denis Mack Smith, *A History of Sicily after 1713* (London: Chatto and Windus, 1968), 410.

56. Chubb, *Patronage, Power, and Poverty*, 14.

57. Mack Smith, *History of Sicily.*

58. Ibid.

59. Ibid., 345.

60. See Franca Assante, "Le trasformazioni del paesaggio agrario," in Angelo Massafra, ed., *Il mezzogiorno preunitario: Economica, societa, e istituzioni* (Bari: Dedalo, 1988), 29–53; Davis, "The South, the Risorgimento."

61. For examples of the disagreements between Napoleon and Joseph Bonaparte and problems of implementation, see their correspondence, published in Santore, *Modern Naples.*

62. Davis, "The South, the Risorgimento," 73.

63. Hobsbawm, *Age of Revolution*, 157.

64. Davis, "The South, the Risorgimento," 74–75.

65. Ibid.

66. This is a definition of state capacity that resembles the conceptualization offered by Joel Migdal, *Strong Societies and Weak States: State-Society Relations and State Capabilities in the Third World* (Princeton: Princeton University Press, 1988).

67. See discussion in Robert Fried, *The Italian Prefects: A Study in Administrative Politics* (New Haven: Yale University Press, 1963), 52–54.

68. G. Capponi, *Scritti editi ed inediti* (Firenze, 1877), as cited by Hancock, *Ricasoli*, 33.

69. Public finance data on preunification Italian states have been reported in *Archivio Economico dell'Unificazione Italiana* (various issues).

70. Shepard B. Clough, *The Economic History of Modern Italy* (New York: Columbia University Press, 1964), 40.

71. For a thorough discussion of Cavour's motivations during this period, see Rosario Romeo, *Cavour e il suo tempo* (Bari: Laterza, 1984).

72. The size of the Neapolitan military is reported by Binkley, *Realism and Nationalism*, 220; the size of the bureaucracy is reported in my table 4.5; population figures are reported in Zamagni, *Economic History*, 14.

73. See Riall, *Sicily.*

74. Sidney Tarrow, "National Integration, National Disintegration, and Contention: A Paired Comparison of Unlike Cases," in Doug McAdam, Sidney Tarrow, and Charles Tilly, eds., *Dynamics of Contention* (Cambridge: Cambridge University Press, 2001).

CHAPTER FIVE
FROM STRONG REGIONAL LOYALTIES TO A UNITARY SYSTEM: NATIONAL UNIFICATION BY CONQUEST AND THE CASE OF ITALY

1. Cited by Sabetti, *Search for Good Government.*

2. Riker, *Federalism.*

3. Though the concept of "political development" entails a wide range of possible meanings, my use of the term as encompassing these three dimensions of parliamentary, constitutional, and administrative development is one that is especially relevant for nineteenth-century Europe and draws loosely on the classic definition of the term by Samuel Huntington in *Political Order in Changing Societies* (New Haven: Yale University Press, 1968), 93.

4. As this chapter will make clear, there were important variations across the Italian states. While states such as Lombardy-Veneto under Austrian rule and Tuscany experienced higher levels of administrative modernization than other Italian states, the failure to develop parliamentary structures and effective constitutions hampered the institutional effectiveness of even these more institutionally developed states. Additionally, despite the positive revisionist assessments of Neapolitan politics in important recent works, the Neapolitan regime still suffered from problems of institutional incapacity when compared to the southern German states of Baden and Bavaria. For some of these useful more positive assessments, see, for example, Marta Petrusewicz, *Latifundium: Moral Economy and Material Life in European Periphery* (Ann Arbor: University of Michigan Press, 1996); see also Angelantonio Spagnoletti, *Storia del Regno delle Due Sicilie* (Bologna: Il Mulino, 1997).

5. In his important work on state building in Italy, Raffaele Romanelli calls this gap between ideals and political reality the "paradox" of the "liberal project of government." See Raffaele Romanelli, *Il comando impossibile: Stato e società nell'Italia liberale* (Bologna: Il Mulino, 1995), 29.

6. Whereas mass political participation was indirectly restricted in Germany via federalism, in Italy mass participation was *directly* limited by a highly restrictive system of franchise. See Ruth Berins Collier, *Paths toward Democracy* (Cambridge: Cambridge University Press, 1999), 69.

7. The notion of self-reinforcing feedback processes has been most fruitfully discussed with applications for the study of politics by Paul Pierson, "Increasing Returns, Path Dependence, and the Study of Politics," *American Political Science Review* 94 (2000): 251–67. For

a useful discussion of Pierson's conceptualization of path dependence, see Robert Jervis, "Timing and Interaction in Politics: A Comment on Pierson," *Studies in American Political Development* 14 (2000): 93–100.

8. For example, in Piedmont, the restoration of Victor Emanuel I in 1814 led to the elimination of all Napoleonic legislation in a single decree. All public officials, including military officials, hired during the Napoleonic period were purged, and Victor Emanuel's minister Cerruti restored the pre-Napoleonic officials to their posts, using the court almanac of 1798 as a guide and using a hereditary method of hiring to replace officials who had died during the Napoleonic rule. See Alberto Aquarone, "La politica legislative della restaurazione nel regno di Sardegna," *Bollettino Storico—Bibliografico Subalpino* 57 (1959); 21–50, 322–59.

9. For an extremely useful overview in English, see Lucy Riall, *The Italian Risorgimento: State, Society, And National Unification* (London: Routledge, 1994), 11–28.

10. The causal connection between "political development" and "institutional capacity" is based both on my own empirical research and on classic literature on state building. The notion that political development—the creation of constitutions, parliaments, and modern administrative structures—increases both the visibility and legitimacy of the state, thereby increasing the state's reach and effectiveness, finds support among early scholars of state building such as Max Weber and more recently Margaret Levi, *Consent, Dissent, and Patriotism* (Cambridge: Cambridge University Press, 1997), 200–208. Additionally, historians of nineteenth-century Europe have found evidence that the advocates of constitutionalism themselves perceived the creation of parliamentary bodies as necessary for successful bureaucratic consolidation. See, for example, James Sheehan, *German History, 1770–1866* (Oxford: Clarendon Press, 1989), 426.

11. Riall, *The Italian Risorgimento*, 11–28.

12. Ibid., 20–21.

13. For a discussion of the pre- and post-1848 administrative structures of all the Italian regional states, see Luigi Izzo, *La finanza pubblica: Nel primo decennio dell'unita italiana* (Milan: Dott. A Giuffre Editore, 1962), 3–16.

14. See David Laven, "The Age of Restoration," in John Davis, ed., *Italy in the Nineteenth Century* (Oxford: Oxford University Press, 2000).

15. For a discussion of the creation of state ministries before and after 1848, see Izzo, *La finanza pubblica*, 3–16. In 1859, Tuscany had eight ministries, the Kingdom of Two Sicilies had thirteen, Parma six, Modena seven, Papal States seven, and Piedmont eight (Robert Fried, *The Italian Prefects: A Study in Administrative Politics* [New Haven: Yale University Press, 1963], 56).

16. See Silvana Patriarca, *Numbers and Nationhood: Writing Statistics in Nineteenth-Century Italy* (Cambridge: Cambridge University Press, 1996), 85–121.

17. The best English-language description of the administrative structures of the preunification states remains Fried, *The Italian Prefects*, 21–63. As table 5.1 makes clear, the Tuscan, Modena, Lombard-Veneto, and Piedmontese states were the most well developed administratively.

18. See an excellent statement of this in Evan Lieberman, "Payment for Privilege? Race and Space in the Politics of Taxation in South Africa and Brazil," Ph.D. diss., Department of Political Science, University of California, Berkeley. 2000.

19. Izzo, *La finanza pubblica*, 3–4.

20. See for example, the report from Filippo Cordova to Cavour, dated December 23, 1860, on the Sicilian public finance situation. "Relazione del signo Filippo Cordova del 23 dicembre 1860 trasmessa dal Luogotenente generale nelle provincie siciliane al presidente del Considlio dei ministri," *Carteggi di Cavour: La liberazione del Mezzogiorno e la formazione del Regno d'Italie*, vol. 4 (Bologna, 1861), doc. no. 2811, p. 130.

21. An organizational summary of the tax administration structure, including number of personnel for each of the Italian states, is presented by Izzo, *La finanza pubblica*, 513–21.

22. On this point, see both the neo-utilitarian account of Margaret Levi, *Consent, Dissent, and Patriotism*, and the neo-statist account of Peter Evans, *Embedded Autonomy: States and Industrial Transformation* (Princeton: Princeton University Press, 1995).

23. While clearly not exhaustive, *extraction, coercion*, and *regulation* do summarize the most basic work of modern governments in the nineteenth century. My use of these three terms adapts Charles Tilly's similar usage of "extraction, coercion, and control" in "Reflections on the History of European State-Making," in Charles Tilly, ed., *The Formation of Nation States in Western Europe* (Princeton: Princeton University Press, 1975), 50.

24. In measures of state capacity that focus on "taxing capacity," scholars frequently explore the different types of taxes (direct vs. indirect) in seeking to assess the degree of state capacity (see for example Lieberman, "Payment for Privilege?" or Margaret Levi, *Of Rule and Revenue* [Berkeley and Los Angeles: University of California, Press, 1988]). Because of data limitations, I use the admittedly more crude measure of total public revenue per capita.

25. My own measure of conscription rate follows other scholars who have used percentage of the male population in the military as a rough measure of conscription rates. See for example, Margaret Levi, *Consent, Dissent, and Patriotism* (New York: Cambridge University Press, 1997).

26. James Sheehan writes, "To the officials who laid the groundwork for the *Beamtenstaat* there was no more important mission for the state than education. Like military service and taxation, education was one of those new rights and obligations that states conveyed and imposed upon their citizens" (*German History, 1770–1866*, 435).

27. In response to the criticism that the uneven "state capacity" scores of the Italian states might simply reflect underlying differences in regional socioeconomic structure, validity tests suggest that this is not the case. It is instructive, for example, that the correlation between regional GDP per capita and each of my measures of institutional capacity is very low, suggesting that the institutional capacity of the Italian states do not simply reflect underlying socioeconomic differences but have a conceptual weight of their own.

28. For nineteenth-century data on public revenue as percentage of national GDP for other European nation-states, see Peter Flora et al., *State, Economy, and Society in Western Europe, 1815–1975: A Data Handbook*, 2 vols. (Frankfurt: Campus Verlag, 1983). It should be noted that these data on public revenue are constructed solely with "nation-states" as cases and exclude the regional states of Italy and Germany. My data, in this sense, contribute to the existing literature.

29. See Izzo, *La finanza pubblica*, 12–16.

30. Charles Tilly, Louise Tilly, and Richard Tilly, *The Rebellious Century, 1830–1930* (Cambridge: Harvard University Press, 1975), 124.

31. Sheehan, *German History, 1770–1866*.

32. Fried, *The Italian Prefects*, 52.

33. Alberto Caracciolo, *Stato e societa civile* (Turin: Giulio Einaudi, 1960), 119.

34. James C. Albisetti, "Julie Schwabe and the Poor of Naples," paper prepared for presentation at the International Standing Conference for the History of Education (ISCHE) XXIII, Birmingham, England, July 12–15, 2001, 2.

35. See for example, G. John Ikenberry, *After Victory: Institutions, Strategic Restraint, and the Rebuilding of Order after Major Wars* (Princeton: Princeton University Press, 2001); Jay Winik, *April 1865: The Month That Saved America* (New York: HarperCollins, 2001); Herbert Bix, *Hirohito and the Making of Modern Japan* (New York: HarperCollins, 2000).

36. See data reported in J. David Singer and Melvin Small, *National Materials Capabilities Data, 1816–1985* (Ann Arbor, Mich.: Inter-university Consortium for Political and Social Research, 1993), computer file.

37. The negotiations with the French emperor began with an ongoing correspondence with Napoleon's representative, Dr. Conneau. For a description of this correspondence, see A. J. Whyte, *The Political Life and Letters of Cavour, 1848–1861* (London: Oxford University Press, 1930), 254.

38. "Cavour to Victor Emannuel, Baden-Baden, July 24, 1858," cited in Santore, *Modern Naples*, 164.

39. For the text of the treaty, see "Treaty between France and Piedmont, January 1859," in Denis Mack Smith, ed., *The Making of Modern Italy, 1796–1870* (New York: Harper and Row, 1968), 259–60.

40. Three of the best accounts of Cavour during this period remain Mack Smith, *Cavour*, 149–76; Rosario Romeo, *Cavour e il suo tempo* (Roma: Laterza, 1984); and Cafagna, *Cavour*.

41. Santore, *Modern Naples*, 163.

42. After the two-month war broke out in the spring of 1859, the French and Piedmontese defeat of Austria at Magenta and Solferino left Piedmont in a diplomatic position to annex Lombardy directly. Like Bismarck, Cavour sought, above all, the aggrandizement of his own state. Also like Bismarck, a key part of the calculations of how to absorb new states for Cavour was international pressure and the threat of international intervention. Since France assured both Prussia and Piedmont of nonintervention in the early stages (1859 in Italy and 1866 in Germany), they could proceed with direct annexation or unconditional conquest with little need for other calculations. In the Italian case, direct annexation involved France's transfer of Lombardy from its possession to Piedmont according to the stipulations of Villafranca in July 1859. As the German case study will also show (e.g., Hannover in 1866), the domestic dilemma of conquest versus negotiation only becomes relevant when international actors threaten to intervene, making the institutional capacity of the states a relevant factor in determining strategy.

43. As Raymond Grew notes (*Sterner Plan*, 96), however, the National Society committees were less successful in Tuscany than in other states.

44. "Da Carlo Bon Compagni di Mombello," Doc. 380, March 18, 1859, Florence, in Cavour, *Epistolario*, vol. 16 (January–September 1859) (Firenze: Leo S. Olschki Editore, 2000), 352.

45. For a description of the rejection, see Cavour, *Epistolario*, 352. For a description of the status of the "Radicals" led by Giuseppe Dolfi and "Moderates" led by Ricasoli, see Stuart Woolf, *A History of Italy, 1700–1860* (London: Methuen, 1979), 450.

46. "A Carlo Bon Compagni di Mombello," Doc. 780, April 25, 1859, Ministre Sardaigne-Florence, in Cavour, *Epistolario*, 619.

47. See discussion of Fearon, "Domestic Political Audiences," in chapter 1.

48. "Da Carlo Bon Compagni di Mombello," Doc. 800, April 26, 1859, Firenze, in Cavour, *Epistolario*, 628–29.

49. Ibid.

50. "A Carlo Bon Compagni di Mombello," Doc. 805, Ministre Sarde-Florence, April 27, 1859, in Cavour, *Epistolario*, 632–33.

51. A record of the correspondence between Cavour and his envoys to these other states can also be found in Cavour, *Epistolario*.

52. Despite the support for immediate accession in the central Italian states in the summer and fall of 1859, Victor Emanuel was pressured by Napoleon and refused the offers of annexation. See Woolf, *History of Italy*, 453.

53. As we will see in chapter 6, in Germany, Prussia's annexation of the north in 1866 did not prevent accommodations and negotiated peace with southern Germany in 1871.

54. J.A.R. Marriot, *The Makers of Modern Italy* (Oxford: Clarendon Press, 1931), 132.

55. Crispi, *Il Precursore*, August 3, 1860 as cited by Mack Smith, *Cavour and Garibaldi*, 37, 50–51.

56. "Instruzione al conte Ruggero Gabaleone di Salmour, inviato in missione straordinaria presso la corte de Napoli," Doc. 148, Turin, June 1859, in *Il Carteggio Cavour-Salmour*, vol. 10 (Bologna: Nicola Zanichelli, 1961a), 221–28. For all the correspondence and itinerary of Salmour's mission to Naples, see pp. 205–311. The translation of Cavour's message to Salmour comes from Santore, *Modern Naples*, 166–67.

57. Cited by Marriot, *Makers of Modern Italy*, 125–26.

58. See Angelantonio Spagnoletti, *Storia del Regno delle Due Sicilie* (Bologna: Il Mulino, 1997), 271–306.

59. Garibaldi's May 1860 unilateral departure and conquest of Sicily, without explicit consent of the Piedmontese government, has been subject to a great deal of historical analysis. His motivations were multiple, though most historians agree that Cavour's April 26, 1880, cession of Garibaldi's home city of Nice to the French was the proximate impetus that explains the timing of Garibaldi's attack. For a more complete discussion of Garibaldi, see Riall, *Sicily*, 76–107.

60. "Cavour a Nigra," Doc. 823, May 12, 1860, Turin, in *Il carteggio Cavour-Nigra dal 1858 a 1861*, vol. 3 (Bologna: Nicola Zanichelli, 1961), 294.

61. Marriot, *Makers of Modern Italy*, 132.

62. The true attitudes of the Piedmontese king and Cavour during this period have been subject to a wide-ranging debate in the Italian and English-language historiography. See Cafagna, *Cavour*.

63. Brancato, "L'amministrazione garibaldina," as cited by Riall, *Sicily*, 90.

64. *Atti del governo dittatoriale e prodittatoriale*, 171–318, as cited by Riall, *Sicily*, 90.

65. A particularly revealing case is the closure of state statistical offices in Naples, Florence, Modena, and Parma and the elimination of civil servants in these former political capitals and the creation of a central statistical office in Turin, Piedmont, by Piedmontese decree in October 1861. The best English-language description of this can be found in Patriarca, *Numbers and Nationhood*, 95.

66. While the project of "unification by conquest" was driven by a Piedmontese push into the Kingdom of Two Sicilies, in the states of Modena, Parma, and Tuscany and in the northern provinces of the Papal States, the project of "unification by conquest" was also equally driven by the interim leaders who saw Piedmontese intervention as a means of avoiding Papal States and Austrian efforts to reestablish control. For these leaders, the problem of institutional incapacity was also a driving motivation.

67. Mack Smith, *Cavour and Garibaldi*, 12.

68. According to accounts of the war, it was Garibaldi's creative use of guerilla warfare tactics that assured his victory against the superior force of Neapolitan troops (Santore, *Modern Naples*).

69. Though this claim may be difficult to substantiate, a close review of the Mazzini's writings does reveal that what has been called Mazzini's "radical" nationalism, which is typically contrasted with Cavour's "pragmatic" nationalism, is rooted in Mazzini's desire for the "independence" of Italy. Like postcolonial nationalism in the twentieth century, Mazzini's nationalism was rooted in the intellectual linking of "nation" with calls for "independence."

70. For a general discussion of the relationship between the postcolonial situation and revolutionary ideologies, see Reinhard Bendix, *Kings or People: Power and the Mandate to Rule* (Berkeley and Los Angeles: University of California Press, 1978); and Ken Jowitt, *The Leninist Response to National Dependency* (Berkeley: Institute of International Studies, University of California, 1978).

71. Denis Mack Smith, *Mazzini* (New Haven: Yale University Press, 1994), 129–30.

72. This account is based on ibid., 136–38.

73. Riall, *Sicily*, 29.

74. Ibid., 83.

75. Ibid., 106.

76. For a historical treatment of public administration in the Kingdom of Two Sicilies, see Nico Randeraad, *Autorita in cerca di autonomia I prefetti nell'Italia liberale* (Roma: Ministero per i beni culturali e ambientali ufficio per i beni archivistici, 1993), 26–29.

77. Mack Smith, *Cavour and Garibaldi*, 47–48.

78. The notion that this task—winning the approval of the newly annexed public—is a generic feature of nation-state formation that may take on various forms whenever a state expands its borders is also articulated by several classic comparative historical works. George Macaulay Trevelyan compares the union of "north" and "south" Britain in 1707 with the union of "north" and south" Italy in 1860 and makes the point that the two instances of state expansion differ from each other in that the British union was the outcome of careful diplomatic pact, while the Italian union was the outcome of a plebiscite. See George Macaulay Trevelyan, *Garibaldi and the Making of Italy* (London: Longmans, Green, 1914), 263. Similarly Heinrich Treitschke compares the negotiated unification of monarchs in Germany with the revolutionary unification of Italy that found expression in the plebiscite (*Cavour*, 207).

79. Trevelyan, *Garibaldi and the Making of Italy*, 264.

80. Stuart Woolf makes the point that "the myth of universal national patriotism was fired in the furnace of plebiscite" (*History of Italy*, 457).

81. Denis Mack Smith, "Advanced the Southern Question," in Charles F. Delzell, ed., *The Unification of Italy, 1859–1861: Cavour, Mazzini, or Garibaldi?* (New York: Robert E. Krieger, 1965), 67.

82. In this discussion, I focus on the annexation of the Kingdom of Two Sicilies in October 1860 rather than on the annexation of the central and northern Italian states because it was in the contentious relationship between the Kingdom of Two Sicilies—Italy's biggest state—and Piedmont where we could have expected regionalist calls for territorial concessions to generate a federalist impulse. Most historians agree that the terms of the agreement struck between the Kingdom of Two Sicilies and Piedmont beginning in October 1860 were decisive for the future institutional development of Italy (Mack Smith, "Advanced the Southern Question," 67), as in Bavaria, Germany's biggest state after Prussia, where the federalist impulse was strongest.

83. Cited by Mack Smith, *Cavour and Garibaldi*, 294.

84. The following discussion of Ferrara is based on a very useful summary offered by Filippo Sabetti, *The Search for Good Government* (Montreal: McGill University Press, 2000), 43–49.

85. Ferrera, "Brevi note sulla Sicilia," 300–301, as cited by Sabetti, *Search for Good Government*, 45.

86. Ferrara, "Brevi note sulla Sicilia," 304, as cited by Sabetti, *Search for Good Government*, 46.

87. Ferrara, "Brevi note sulla Sicilia," 304, as cited by Sabetti, *Search for Good Government*, 46.

88. Mack Smith, *Cavour and Garibaldi*, 67.

89. Parlamento Sub-Alpino, *Atti Parlamentari*, Acts of the Seventh Legislature, October 2, 1860.

90. Ibid.

91. Ibid.

92. Mack Smith, *Cavour and Garibaldi*, 326,

93. Parlamento Sub-Alpino, *Atti Parlamentari*, Acts of the Seventh Legislature, October 2, 1860.

94. Ibid.

95. See discussion in Mack Smith, *Cavour and Garibaldi.*

96. See John Davis, *Conflict and Control: Law and Order in Nineteenth-Century Italy* (Basingstoke: Macmillan Education, 1988).

97. Mack Smith, *Cavour and Garibaldi*, 344.

98. The best record of this is the multivolume collection of private and diplomatic correspondence collected by the Commissione Editrice dei Carteggi Di Camillo Cavour in Count Camillo di Cavour, *Carteggi di Cavour: La Liberazione del Mezzogiorno e la formazione del Regno d'Italie*, vol. 2 (Bologna, 1961).

99. "F. Cordova a Cavour," August 16, 1860, Doc. no. 639 in Cavour, *Carteggi di Cavour,* 4:94.

100. "Persano a Cavour," August 2, 1860, Doc. no. 528 in Cavour, *Carteggi di Cavour*, 4:8.

101. "Farini a Depretis," August 17, 1860 Doc. no. 647 in Cavour, *Carteggi di Cavour*, 4:99.

102. Riall, *Sicily*, 84.

103. Trevelyan, *Garibaldi and the Making of Italy*, 264.

104. Di Scala, *Italy*, 121.

105. Trevelyan, *Garibaldi and the Making of Italy*, 264.

106. Ibid.

107. See Estratti dai Verbali delle advanze della Commissione Temporare a di Legislazione instituta presso il Consiglio di Stato colla leegga 24. Giugno, 1860, as cited by Fried, *The Italian Prefects.*

108. Ibid.

109. Fried, *The Italian Prefects*, 75.

110. Sabetti, *Search for Good Government*, 49.

CHAPTER SIX
FROM STRONG REGIONAL LOYALTIES TO A FEDERAL SYSTEM:
NATIONAL UNIFICATION BY NEGOTIATION AND THE CASE OF GERMANY

1. Otto von Bismarck, "Konzept eines Erlasses an Goltz-Paris: Instruktion für Haltung zu Frankreich—Bundesreform oder Annexionen, Minimal- und Maximalprogramm," July 9, 1866, in Eberhard Scheler, ed., *Otto von Bismarck: Werke in Auswahl*, vol. 3 (Stuttgart: W. Kohlhammer Verlag, 1965), 755.

2. Some critiques from the period as well as contemporary scholars point out that despite these massive federal concessions, Prussia was the largest state and could dominate the national-level federation. Yet, it is worth noting that not only did the Bundesrat exist as a potential veto point in which states could resist legislation, but even more importantly, once the federation was established after 1871, Prussia often limited itself, anticipating resistance from the states, making the Bundesrat a de facto veto point on Prussian power. For an illustrative example of such an instance, see Margaret Anderson's account of Prussian *Staatsstreich* plans in the 1890s in *Windthorst: A Political Biography* (New York: Oxford University Press, 1981).

3. For a useful English-language overview of the international system facing Prussia in this period, see A.J.P. Taylor, *The Struggle for Mastery in Europe, 1848–1918* (Oxford: Oxford University Press, 1971), 131–200.

4. See, for example, Manfred Rauh, *Föderalismus und Parlamentarismus im Wilhelmischen Reich* (Düsseldorf: Droste Verlag, 1973), 48.

5. See chapter 5 for a more complete discussion of these changes.

6. As my discussion in chapter 5 made clear, my analysis follows Samuel Huntington's lead in focusing on the development of constitutional, parliamentary, and administrative

structures as constituting the core dimensions of "political development." For a more complete discussion of my concept of political development see chapter 5.

7. My claims of "greater" legitimacy, visibility, and capacity are made with specific comparative reference to the Italian states in the same period. But one must be careful not to overstate the German constitutional tradition. The important caveat must be added that the German states differed from the U.S. or French constitutional systems insofar as the German states sustained what scholars have called a "dualistic structure," preserving the "monarchical principle (*monarchische Prinzip*)—that asserted sovereignty comes from the crown and not the people—while allowing room for parliamentary participation (*parlamentarische Mitentscheidung*) within the context of a rule-bound constitutional system. The extent to which these constitutions were more than mere "roadblocks" for absolutist rule has been the subject of much debate. For a discussion of these issues, see Dieter Grimm, *Deutsche Verfassungsgeschichte, 1776–1866* (Frankfurt am Main: Suhrkamp, 1988), 110–22; see also Huber, *Deutsche Verfassungsgeschichte Seit 1789*, 3–26.

8. My estimates of population are from Borchard, "Staatsverbrauch," 91–93. I have excluded the remaining 10 percent of the German Bund's population because this population is spread out over twenty-five miniature states for which it is impossible to collect data. But given that the ten largest states constitute 90 percent of the German population, I believe my analysis is on safe ground both methodologically and substantively.

9. The state of Mecklenburg is exceptional insofar as its *Verfassung* was preabsolutist and is largely regarded by scholars as a premodern state form. For a more on this point, see my own description below.

10. Reinhard Mussgnug, "Die rechtlichen und pragmatischen Beziehungen zwischen Regierung, Parlament, und Verwaltung," in Kurt Jeserich, Hans Pohl, and Georg-Christoph von Unruh, eds., *Deutsche Verwaltungsgeschichte*, vol. 2 (Stuttgart: Deutsche-Verlags Anstalt, 1983), 96.

11. Dieter Grimm, *Deutsche Verfassungsgeschichte, 1776–1866* (Frankfurt am Main: Suhrkamp Verlag, 1988), 112.

12. Huber, *Deutsche Verfassungsgeschichte Seit 1789*, 190.

13. Mussgnug, "Rechtlichen und pragmatischen Beziehungen," 97.

14. Nipperdey, *From Napoleon to Bismarck*, 600.

15. Sheehan, *German History, 1770–1866*, 717.

16. Eckhardt Treichel, "Restaurationssystem und Verwaltungsmodernisierung," in Hans-Peter Ullmann and Clemens Zimmermann, eds., *Restaurationssystem und Reformpolitik: Süddeutschland und Preussen im Vergleich* (Munich: R. Doldenbourg Verlag, 1996), 68, 76–77.

17. Georg-Christoph von Unruh, "Preussen: Die Veränderungen der Preussischen Staatsverfassung durch Sozial- und Verwaltungsreformen," in Jeserich, Pohl, and von Unruh, *Deutsche Verwaltungsgeschichte*, 435–69.

18. Karlheinz Blaschke, "Königreich Sachsen und Thüringische Staaten," in Jeserich, Pohl, and von Unruh, *Deutsche Verwaltungsgeschichte*, 617.

19. For a discussion of the transformation of the fused *Generaldirektorium* into a ministerial system, see Frank-Ludwig Knemeyer, "Beginn der Reorganisation der Verwaltung in Deutschland," in Jeserich, Pohl, and von Unruh, *Deutsche Verwaltungsgeschichte*, 122–23.

20. Treichel, "Restaurationssystem und Verwaltungsmodernisierung," 67.

21. Blaschke, "Königreich Sachsen," 652; and Thomas Klein "Königreich Hannover," in Jeserich, Pohl, and von Unruh, *Deutsche Verwaltungsgeschichte*, 678–714.

22. Walther Hubatsch, "Aufbau, Gliederung und Tätigkeit der Verwaltung in den deutschen Einzelstaaten," in Jeserich, Pohl, and von Unruh, *Deutsche Verwaltungsgeschichte*, 181–84.

23. For review of the "reactionary" crackdown policies of the 1850s, see Hans-Ulrich Wehler, *Deutsche Gesellschaftsgeschicht: Von der Deutschen Doppelrevolution bis zum Beginn des Ersten Weltkrieges*, vol. 3 (Munich: C.H. Beck'sche, 1995), 197–220; see also Theodore Hamerow, *Restoration, Revolution, and Reaction* (Princeton: Princeton University Press, 1958).

24. The only states to abolish their constitutions after the 1849 restoration were the two conservative regimes of Mecklenburg Schwerin and Mecklenburg Strelitz, both of which resorted to eighteenth-century arrangements.

25. The concept of "constitutional waves" is drawn from Dieter Grimm, *Deutsche Verfassungsgeschichte, 1776–1866* (Frankfurt am Main: Suhrkamp Verlag, 1988), 71.

26. The following overview of constitutional developments in the German states draws on Michael Stolleis, *Public Law in Germany, 1800–1914* (New York: Berghahn, 2001), 163–64.

27. Constitutional historians of Germany typically distinguish between two broad types of constitutions and parliaments in this period. In southwest parts of Germany, such as in Bavaria, Baden, and Württemberg, where Napoleonic intervention had disrupted the old *Stände*, constitutions tended to be more progressive, created by civil servants to consolidate state power. In these states, most explicitly in Baden, (1) all citizens who met economic criteria voted for the lower assembly representatives, (2) the two-chamber parliament was to represent the interests of the state rather than specific status groups, and (3) the constitution guaranteed basic rights (*Grundrechte*). By contrast, in northern and central parts of Germany, where Napoleon's indirect rule had left the old social orders intact, for example, in the two Mecklenburg states, the *altständisch* constitutions were conservative documents aimed at defending the old social order. In these constitutions, (1) representatives to both chambers of parliament represented specific social estates, (2) the franchise was limited to specific social status groups, and (3) no basic rights were established for population.

28. As the score for Prussia in table 6.1 indicates, however, the Prussian constitution itself remained such an object of contention and dispute that it was not as effective as Prussian liberals had hoped and eventually gave rise to a deep constitutional conflict between liberals and conservatives. For a useful discussion of the Prussian constitution, leading up to the constitutional conflict, see Eugene Anderson, *The Social and Political Conflict in Prussia, 1858–1864* (Lincoln: University of Nebraska, 1954), 176–240.

29. Wolfgang Siemann, *Vom Staatenbund zum Nationalstaat, Deutschland 1806–1871* (Munich: Verlag C.H Beck, 1995), 29.

30. This argument is made most forcefully by Hans-Peter Ullmann, *Staatsschulden und Reformpolitik. Die Entstehung moderner öffentlicher Schulden in Bayern und Baden, 1780–1820*, vol. 2 (Göttingen: Vandenhöck und Ruprecht, 1986); see also the volume edited by Hans-Peter Ullmann and Clems Zimmermann, *Restaurationssytem und Reformpolitik: Süddeutschland und Preussen im Vergleich* (Munich: Oldenbourg Verlag, 1996).

31. Elisabeth Fehrenbach, "Bürokratische Reform und gesellschaftlicher Wandel: Die badische Verfassung von 1818," in Ernst Otto Bräunche and Thomas Schnabel, eds., *Die Badische Verfassung von 1818* (Ubstadt-Weiher: Verlag Regionalkultur, 1996), 13.

32. Indeed, both quantitative and qualitative evidence supports the argument that institutional reforms reflected the fiscal situation of the German states. First, on average, 16 percent of the total state budgets of the fifteen largest German states even as late as 1851 was consumed by public debts, in contrast the Italian states, where only Piedmont matched this level of debt in the same year, making the need for institutional reforms to develop state capacity more pressing in the German states. Second, those states to adopt constitutions earlier tended to have higher debts. And finally, a great amount of historical evidence suggests that state monarchs and elites proposed constitutions and parliaments precisely with the explicit aim of easing the process of revenue extraction. German data is from Borchard,

"Staatsverbrauch," table 20; Italian data from Shepard B. Clough, *The Economic History of Modern Italy* (New York: Columbia University Press, 1964), 43; and G. Felloni, "La spese effettive e il bilancio degli stati sabaudi dal 1825 al 1860," in *Archivio Economico dell'Unificazione Italiana*, ser. 1, vol. 9 (1959), 5.

33. This argument is made by Bernhard Löffler, *Die Bayerische Kammer der Reichsräte, 1848–1918* (Munich: C.H. Beck, 1996).

34. Though I emphasize the post-1815 period, in his work, Mack Walker makes the important point that this constitutionalism and subnational institutional development in Germany has much older roots and can be traced to the particular structure of the Holy Roman Empire. See Mack Walker, *German Home Towns: Community, State, and General Estate, 1648–1871* (Ithaca: Cornell University Press, 1971), 12–26.

35. Sheehan, *German History, 1770–1866*, 439.

36. See citations in chapter 5.

37. This finding also confirms the regional distribution of civic unrest in Germany in the nineteenth century as reported by Richard Tilly, "Germany," in Tilly, Tilly, and Tilly, *Rebellious Century*, 191–238.

38. For example, James Sheehan writes, "To the officials who laid the groundwork for the *Beamtenstaat* there was no more important mission for the state than education. Like military service and taxation, education was one of those new rights and obligations that states conveyed and imposed upon their citizens" (*German History, 1770–1866*, 435).

39. For a discussion of the socially transforming aims of civil servants throughout Germany in this period, see ibid.

40. The most significant exception to this is Eugen Weber, *Peasants into Frenchmen: The Modernization of Rural France, 1870–1914* (Stanford: Stanford University Press, 1976), 195–220; see also Jeffrey Herbst's important work on state building in Africa. For a systematic and comparative discussion of road density as a measure of state effectiveness, see Jeffrey Herbst, *States and Power in Africa: Comparative Lessons in Authority and Control* (Princeton: Princeton University Press, 2000), 84–87.

41. For an overview of early-nineteenth-century German state-building efforts, see also Borchard, "Staatsverbrauch," 273.

42. The term "a peace by negotiation" is borrowed from Gall, *Bismarck*, 307.

43. For discussion of the king's attitude, see Gordon Craig, *The Politics of the Prussian Army, 1640–1945* (New York: Oxford University Press, 1955), 198.

44. The term "maximalist annexation strategy" comes from a memo from Bismarck to his ambassador to France (Goltz) on July 9, 1866. See Bismarck, *Werke in Auswahl*, 755.

45. Ibid.

46. Craig, *Politics of Prussian Army*, 199.

47. For the terms of the law that stipulated the direct annexation of these states, see Ernst Rudolf Huber, ed., *Dokumente zur Deutschen Verfassungsgeschichte*, vol. 2 (Stuttgart: W. Kohlhammer, 1964), 217.

48. Gall, *Bismarck*, 307.

49. Ibid., 306.

50. For a discussion of technical, tactical, and strategic features of the war, see B. H. Liddell Hart, "Armed Forces and the Art of War: Armies," in J.P.T. Bury, ed., *The New Cambridge Modern History*, vol. 10, *The Zenith of European Power, 1830–1870* (Cambridge: Cambridge University Press, 1960), 305–11, 324–25; see a more recent account by Geoffrey Wawro, *The Austro-Prussian War: Austria's War with Prussia and Italy in 1866* (Cambridge: Cambridge University Press, 1997).

51. "Prince Friedrich Karl to Bismarck, June 15, 1866," in J.A. Ford, ed., *The Correspondence of William I and Bismarck*, vol. 2 (New York: Frederick A. Stokes, 1903), 131.

52. Craig, *Politics of Prussian Army*, 200.

53. Ibid.

54. Ibid., 204.

55. Cited by Irmgard von Barton, *Die preussische Gesandtschaft in München als Instrument der Reichspolitik in Bayern von den Anfängen der Reichsgründung bis zu Bismarcks Entlassung* (Munich: Neue Schriftenreihe des Stadtsarchivs München, 1967), 12–13.

56. Cited by Craig, *Politics of Prussian Army*, 202.

57. Ullner, "Idee des Föderalismus," 102–3.

58. For the text of these treaties, see Huber, *Dokumente zur Deutschen Verfassungsgeschichte*, 212–20.

59. Article 4, Prague Peace Treaty, August 23, 1866, in ibid., 218.

60. Otto von Bismarck, "Schreiben an die Oberbefehlshaber der preussischen Truppen. Richtlinien für die Verwaltung der besetzten Länder, Berlin, June 19, 1866," in *Werke in Auswahl*, 739–40. For the text of the Prussian legislation that approved the annexation of these states, see "Gesetz Betreffend die Vereinigung," September 20, 1866, in Huber, *Dokumente zur Deutschen Verfassungsgeschichte*, 217.

61. Article 4, Prague Peace Treaty, August 23, 1866, in Huber, *Dokumente zur Deutschen Verfassungsgeschichte*, 218.

62. A significant exception, of course, to this negotiated settlement was the total and complete annexation of Hannover, Kurhessen, Nassau, and the city of Frankfurt by Prussia after the war. For the text of the Prussian parliamentary discussions of this outright annexation, see Huber, ibid., 215. For my own discussion of this, see below.

63. The military advantage of Prussia over Austria in 1866 has been the subject of much historical analysis. Most analysts agree that Prussian mobilizational superiority as well as the use of breech-loading rather than muzzle-loading rifles provided a critical tactical advantage that generated three times the losses in life by the Austrians (Hart, "Armed Forces," 325). For a discussion of military plans to cross the Danube, see Craig, *Politics of Prussian Army*, 202–3.

64. See Gall, *Bismarck*.

65. An example from the earlier historiographical tradition can be seen in Treitschke's classic work, *History of Germany in the Nineteenth Century*.

66. The concept of a two-level game as applied to the intersection of domestic and international politics was originally articulated by Robert Putnam, "Diplomacy and Domestic Politics: The Logic of Two-Level Games," *International Organization* 42 (1988): 427–60.

67. This foreign policy problem was heightened by the fact that not only was Bismarck concerned with French perceptions of his actions, but also, from the other end, the French emperor met with the Bavarian monarch in 1867 to warn against excessively warm relations between Bavaria and Prussia. Additionally, unlike the Kingdom of Two Sicilies, which had no where to turn but to Austrian support to prop up the decrepit regime, Bavaria had a realistic "exit" option: The French emperor proposed to the Bavarian king the possibility of forming a *Sudbund* of southern German states that would exist as a French protectorate.

68. "Kaiser Napoleon III an Konig Wilhelm I," Paris, July 4, 1866, no. 174, in the collection of primary documents in Hermann Oncken, ed., *Die Rheinpolitik Kaiser Napoleons III von 1863–1870: Nach den Staatsaken von Österreich, Preussen, und den süddeutschen Mittelstaaten*, vol. 1 (Stuttgart: Deutsche Verlags-Anstalt, 1926), 302.

69. That Saxony was left intact despite its incorporation into the North German Confederation and Hannover was completely annexed can be explained by two factors: First, Hannover was of greater strategic and geographical importance, allowing Prussia to link its western and eastern provinces, creating a "tenable territory." For more on this point, see Stewart Stehlin, *Bismarck and the Guelph Problem, 1866–1890* (The Hague: Martinus Nijhoff, 1973), 34–41. The second reason for the contrasting fates of Saxony and Hannover was that Saxony's independence, unlike Hannover's, was insisted upon by both French and Austrian pow-

ers. See correspondence "Graf Goltz an Bismarck," July 23, 1866, no. 224, in Oncken, *Die Rheinpolitik*, 372–75; see also the discussion in Stehlin, *Bismarck and Guelph Problem*, 40–41.

70. Bismarck, memo to Goltz, *Werke in Auswahl*, 755.

71. Otto von Bismarck, "Rede in der Kommissionssitzung des Abgeordnetenhauses zur Beratung einer Adresse an den Konig vom 17.8 1866," in *Werke in Auswahl*, 799.

72. Otto Becker, *Bismarcks Ringen Um Deutschlands Gestaltung* (Heidelberg: Quelle und Meyer, 1958), 174.

73. Ibid.

74. It was precisely this distrust of a national unification "from below" that had led the Prussian king Friedrich Wilhelm IV to reject the Frankfurt Parliament's 1848–49 offer of the crown of a united Germany. Thomas Nipperdey writes that the Prussian king, "imbued with the position being granted by the grace of God" rejected the 1848 parliament's offer of the crown as a "parliamentary crown of dirt and clay" and as a "dog collar with which people want to chain me to the 1848 revolution" (Nipperdey, *From Napoleon to Bismarck*, 587).

75. This borrows from the insights of organization theory positing that coalitions and networks unite around organizing symbols that give rise to interpretative frameworks. See James March and Johan Olsen, *Rediscovering Institutions: The Organizational Basis of Politics* (New York: Free Press, 1989); for an application of these ideas, see Christopher Ansell, "Symbolic Networks: The Realignment of the French Working Class, 1887–1894," *American Journal of Sociology* 103 (1997): 359–90.

76. Gerhard Lehmbruch, among others, argues that these norms of negotiation and compromise have their roots in the Bismarckian constitution and continue to affect the shape of German federalism today. See Gerhard Lehmbruch, *Parteienwettbewerb im Bundesstaat*, 2nd ed. (Opladen: Westdeutscher Verlag, 1998,); see also Gerhard Lehmbruch, "Der unitarische Bundesstaat in Deutschland: Pfadabhängigkeit und Wandel," Max-Planck-Institut für Gesellschaftsforschung Discussion Paper No. 02/2, 43–46.

77. In fact one common interpretation—for which there is limited evidence—grants Bismarck prescient foresight to argue that the entire complex structure of the 1867 and 1871 constitutions was designed with the intention of assuring his personal power by distributing power between the princes in the Bundesrat, the Reichstag, the Prussian king, and the Prussian *Landtag*. Though the unusual constitutional setup that emerged may have in effect empowered Bismarck, it is a mistake to assume that the origins of the institutions themselves reflect this intention. For a discussion of the broader analytical mistake of assuming that the effects of institutions can explain their *origins,* see Pierson, *Politics in Time*.

78. Erich Kaufmann, *Bismarcks Erbe in der Reichsverfassung* (Berlin: Springer, 1917).

79. For an overview of these debates, see Huber, *Dokumente zur Deutschen Verfassungsgeschichte*, 673–80; see also Peter Caldwell, *Popular Sovereignty and the Crisis of German Constitutional Law* (Durham: Duke University Press, 1997), 25–30; see also Oeter, *Integration und Subsidiarität*, 44–52.

80. In this sense, the notions of "compact" or "contract" might be conceived of as "elaborate codes" that contain an open-endedness in meaning and have less emotive effect than "restrictive codes" but are more effective in bringing diverse interests together. For a discussion of this distinction, see Mary Douglas, *How Institutions Think* (Syracuse: Syracuse University Press, 1986), 22. See also Ansell, "Symbolic Networks," 362–63.

81. Caldwell, *Popular Sovereignty,* 26.

82. Text of treaty in Huber, *Dokumente zur Deutschen Verfassungsgeschichte*, 224–25.

83. For the texts of these treaties, see ibid., 258–76.

84. The discussion of the 1867 and 1871 constitutions is based on the text of the constitutions as presented in Huber, *Dokumente zur Deutschen Verfassungsgeschichte*, 227–40 and 289–305.

85. Max Weber, *Economy and Society*, vol. 3 (New York: Bedminster Press, 1968), 1104–9; Bendix, *Kings or People*, 230.

86. Caldwell, *Popular Sovereignty*, 26.

87. See the complete text of 1849 constitution in Ernst Rudolf Huber, *op.cit.*, (1961), vol. 1, [only vol. 2 is listed in References 304–26; for a useful English language analysis, see Hans Boldt, "Federalism as an Issue in the German Constitutions of 1849 and 1871," in Hermann Wellenreuther, ed., *German and American Constitutional Thought* (New York: Berg, 1990), 260–78.

88. Becker, *Bismarcks Ringen*, 211–24.

89. See, for example, the memoirs of one of these advisors, Max Duncker, *Politischer Briefwechsel aus Seinem Nachlass* (1923; Osnabrück: Biblio Verlag, 1967).

90. The entire text of Max Duncker's proposed constitution is reprinted in Heinrich Triepel, "Zur Vorgeschichte der Norddeutschen Bundesverfassung," in Heinrich Triepel, ed., *Festschrift Otto Gierke zum Siebzigsten Geburtstag* (Weimar: Harmann Boehlaus [Böhlaus?] Nachfolger, 1911), 631–41.

91. Reichstag des Norddeutschen Bundes, *Verhandlunden des Reichstages des Norddeutschen Bundes*, March 9, 1867, 107–9. For a complete collection of all sittings of the Reichstag from 1867, go to http://mdz.bib-bvb.de/digbib/reichstag.

92. Gerhard Lehmbruch, "Unitarische Bundesstaat in Deutschland," 28.

93. Ibid., 35.

94. Thomas Nipperdey, *Deutsche Geschichte, 1866–1918* (Munich: C.H. Beck Verlag, 1992), 182–83.

95. The term "unitary federalism" comes from Konrad Hesse, *Der unitarische Bundesstaat* (Karlsruhe: C.F. Miller, 1962). Despite these developments that suggest a process of political consolidation, it should be noted that during the 1880s, there remained a degree of uncertainty in the Reich's structure prompted by rumors of Bismarck's contemplation of a *Staatsstreich*, which would have been a coup of sorts, doing away with existing constitutional structures. Yet nothing ever did come of this notion. For a detailed account, see John Röhl, "Staatsstreichplan oder Staatsstreichbereitschaft? Bismarcks Politik in der Entlassungskrise," *Historische Zeitschrift* 203 (1966): 610–24.

96. This point is significant for understanding the development of institutions more generally. The point corresponds to Kathleen Thelen's important insight, "Timing and Temporality in the Analysis of Institutional Evolution and Change," *Studies in American Political Development* 14 (2000): 106, "in politics, unlike in the marketplace, losers do not necessarily disappear."

97. Gall, *Bismarck*, 316.

98. For the text of the dictates, see Otto von Bismarck, *Die Gesammelten Werke,* vol. 6, (Berlin: O. Stollberg, 1924), no. 615, October 30, 1866, and no. 616, November 19, 1866.

99. Many scholars such as Huber, *Deutsche Verfassungsgeschichte Seit 1789*, 649–50, cite this quote without reference to its origins. It appears originally in Bismarck, *Die Gesammelten Werke*, no. 615, October 30, 1866.

100. Gall, *Bismarck*, 317.

101. Erich Brandenburg, *Die Reichsgründung* (Leipzig: Quelle und Meyer, 1923), 219.

102. Many parliamentarians and state officials in other states also agreed with this logic in order to protect their spheres of policy jurisdiction. In 1867, the Bavarian Patriots Party leader Jörg looked to constitutional developments in northern Germany and imagined a future in which Bavaria would be absorbed by Prussia. Jörg expressed the sentiment most clearly in a special sitting of the Bavarian parliament: "If you look at articles 3 and 4 [of the North German constitution], you will ask: what stays in our house? Post, telegraph, railway, waterways, social policy, and civil litigation—areas for which we have worked so hard, spent so much time, and money on, would all be wasted [under the North German constitution]."

See transcript of Bavarian parliament, Bayern Landtag, *Verhandlungen der Bayerischen Kammer der Abgeordneten*, October 18, 1867, KDA, [please spell out KDA] 2:61.

103. For a useful overview of the dynamics of this process, see Brandenburg, *Die Reichsgründung*, 215–16.

104. Gall, *Bismarck*, 318.

105. Manfred Rauh, *Föderalismus and Parlamentarismus im Wilhelmischen Reich* (Düsseldorf: Droste, 1973), 47.

106. Peter-Christian Witt, *Die Finanzpolitik des Deutschen Reiches von 1903 bis 1913* (Lübeck: Matthiesen, 1970), 17.

107. The following discussion of the negotiations between December 1866 and February 1867 is based on Becker, *Bismarcks Ringen*, 290–371.

108. Ibid., 291–92.

109. Hans-Otto Binder, *Reich und Einzelstaaten während der Kanzerschaft Bismarcks: 1871–1890* (Tübingen: Mohr, 1971), 48.

110. Becker, *Bismarcks Ringen*, 357.

111. The distribution of the fifty-eight seats, like much about the Bundesrat, was modeled on the 1815 German Bund's counterpart institution, the Bundestag. In the constitution of the North German Confederation and the German Reich, all member states received the same number of seats as they had received in 1815 with two main exceptions. Because of Prussia's annexation of several north German states in 1866, Prussia received more seats, and as part of the negotiations between Bavaria and Prussia in 1871, Bavaria received extra seats. Prussia, though constituting a majority of the German Reich in terms of population, did not have a majority of Bundesrat seats. Some scholars rightly emphasize Prussia's "hegemony" by noting that Prussia could rely on smaller states to help assure a majority if it so desired. Yet other scholars have also noted Prussia's unwillingness to call on them in practice. For a discussion of these issues, see Lehmbruch, "Unitarische Bundesstaat in Deutschland," 40–46.

112. Becker, *Bismarcks Ringen*, 290–371.

113. Ibid., 369.

114. The negotiations that involved the incorporation of the southern German states at the outbreak of war between Germany and France in 1870–71 provided an opportunity for a centralizing reform of Germany's federal system. Indeed, efforts were made by smaller states, even at this juncture, to substitute a Senate-like upper chamber house for the Bundesrat (Binder, *Reich und Einzelstaaten*, 50). But all such efforts were defeated. and the founding of the Reich in 1870–71 only reinforced the negotiated and federal features of the 1867 constitution. In fact, as a result of criticisms and resistance to the North German constitution in southern Germany, special concessions were made to the southern German states, especially Bavaria, granting them their famous "special rights," that is, extra public finance and administrative autonomy (Karl Bosl, "Die Verhandlungen über den Eintritt der süddeutschen Staaten in den Norddeutschen Bund und die Entstehung der Reichsverfassung," in Theodor Schieder, ed., *Reichsgründung 1870/71* [Stuttgart: Seewald Verlag, 1970], 148–63).

CHAPTER SEVEN
CONCLUSION: THE POLITICS OF FEDERALISM AND
INSTITUTION BUILDING IN THE NINETEENTH CENTURY AND BEYOND

1. The term "congealed tastes" draws from William Riker, "Implications from the Disequilibrium of Majority Rule for the Study of Institutions" *American Political Science Review* 74 (1980): 432.

2. The argument that increased economic scale explains the emergence of federations has been made most recently by Rector, "Federations in International Politics."

3. This argument about the relationship between economic and political motivations applies best to the European context. Some scholars of Latin American political development have convincingly argued that the relationship may vary across time and space. For an excellent account that explores the limits of the European-centered state-building models when applied to Latin America, see Sebastian Mazzuca, "Southern Cone Leviathan," manuscript, 2002.

4. Among other excellent accounts of federalist debates in the U.S. case, see Calvin Jillson, *Constitution Making: Conflict and Consensus in the Federal Convention of 1787* (New York: Agathon Press, 1988).

5. A possible research agenda that emerges from this insight is the extent to which a similar dynamic plays itself out within the European Union as that polity expands to incorporate politically much weaker states of east central Europe. For one of the best discussions of EU expansion, see Wade Jacoby, "Tutors and Pupils: International Organizations, Central European Elites, and Western Models," *Governance* (2001): 169–200. If the EU's expansion to southern Europe are any lesson, it is possible that the incorporation of much weaker states results in a dynamic in which the EU intervenes directly in the administration of specific policy areas. For a discussion of this dynamic in southern Europe, see Chris Ansell, Keith Darden, and Craig Parsons, "Dual Networks in European Regional Development Policy," *Journal of Common Market Studies* 35 (1997): 347–75.

6. This analysis is more extensively carried out and the leverage of competing explanations is assessed in Daniel Ziblatt, "The Federal-Unitary Divide," Harvard University Center for European Studies Working Paper, 2005.

7. The methodology used in this section draws on Charles Ragin, *The Comparative Method* (Berkeley and Los Angeles: University of California Press, 1987) as well as, more directly, Chris Ansell and Arthur Burris, "Bosses of the City Unite! Labor Politics and Political Machine Consolidation, 1870–1910," *Studies in American Political Development* 11 (1997): 1–43.

8. J. Denis Derbyshire and Ian Derbyshire, *Political Systems of the World* (New York: St. Martin's Press, 1996), 5. For a recent work that also uses this data on federalism for purposes of cross-national analysis, see Lieberman, "Payment for Privilege?" 340–42.

9. The secondary literature used to code each case is listed by country in appendix B. At the outset, one additional caveat about "founding date" is important. Like the dates 1871 in Germany and 1861 in Italy, I define a "founding moment" as the developmental period in a polity in which the first modern national constitution is written and approved. In some cases, the task of assigning a "founding" date is more difficult than in others. For a discussion of my procedure, see appendix B. One case that deserves special mention is Great Britain, a case of a constantly evolving and unwritten constitution. I have selected 1707 as the founding date for substantive reasons because the incorporation of Scotland that led to the creation of the "United Kingdom" might have given rise to some form of federation in Great Britain. For a discussion of the role of Scotland in the constitutional history of Great Britain, see Linda Colley, *Britons: Forging the Nation, 1707–1837* (New Haven: Yale University Press, 1992).

10. Post-1993 Belgium is exceptional insofar as it is a case of redesigning a constitution for an already-existing polity rather than a case of designing institutions for the first time. For a useful account of the trajectory of institutional reforms in Belgium since 1945, see John Fitzmaurice, *The Politics of Belgium: A Unique Federalism* (Boulder, Colo.: Westview Press, 1996).

11. In all of these cases, there were regional-level parliaments, constitutions, and systems of administration in most of the constituent states. For a more detailed description of these cases see appendix B. For literature on these cases, see Thomas Maissen, "The 1848 Conflicts

and Their Significance in Swiss Historiography," in Michael Butler, Malcolm Pender, and Joy Charnley, eds., *The Making of Modern Switzerland, 1848–1998* (London: Macmillan, 2000), 3–34; and Wilhelm Brauneder, *Deutsch-Österreich 1918* (Vienna: Amalthea, 2000).

12. Widespread and elite support of federalism in Italy has already been demonstrated. It is interesting to note that in the Netherlands in 1798, a series of important and serious proposals for a federally organized Netherlands shaped the political debate among key political actors. For a discussion of these debates, see J. Roegiers and N.C.F. van Sas, "Revolution in the North and the South, 1780–1830," in J.C.H. Blom and E. Lamberts, eds., *History of the Low Countries* (New York: Berghahn, 1999), 278–82.

13. Though neither the Italian nor the Dutch constituent states had well-developed internal structures, the trajectories of state formation were different in these two cases: While in Italy the independent states aside from Piedmont never were rationalized political structures, in the Netherlands, the long-standing effective and consolidated provinces of the Dutch Confederation were entirely dismantled between 1798 and 1815 by the particularly intrusive rule of Napoleon. For a discussion of the Dutch case, see ibid.

14. John Ruggie, "Territoriality and Beyond: Problematizing Modernity in International Relations," *International Organization* 47 (1993): 151.

15. My use of the terms "layering" and "conversion" refines the original formulation by Kathleen Thelen, "How Institutions Evolve," 226–28.

Appendix B
Origins of Federalism Data on Seventeen
Largest West European Nation-States

1. The date 1707 is selected despite the constantly evolving and unwritten nature of the British constitution because like 1861 in Italy and 1871 in Germany, 1707 represents the date when territory was incorporated (Scotland) giving birth to the modern polity of Great Britain. See discussion in chapter 7, note 9.

REFERENCES

Afonso, Jose, and Luiz de Mello. "Brazil: An Evolving Federation." Paper presented to the Conference on Fiscal Decentralization, International Monetary Fund, Fiscal Affairs Department, November 20–21, 2000.

Albisetti, James C. "Julie Schwabe and the Poor of Naples." Paper prepared for presentation at the International Standing Conference for the History of Education (ISCHE) XXIII, Birmingham, England, July 12–15, 2001.

Anderson, Eugene. *The Social and Political Conflict in Prussia, 1858–1864.* Lincoln: University of Nebraska Press, 1954.

Anderson, Margaret. *Windthorst: A Political Biography.* New York: Oxford University Press, 1981.

Andrey, Georges. "Auf der Suche nach dem neuen Staat, 1798–1848." In Beatrix Mesner, ed., *Geschichte der Schweiz und der Schweizer.* 2nd ed. Basel: Helbing and Lichtenhahn, 1983. 527–637.

Ansell, Christopher. "Symbolic Networks: The Realignment of the French Working Class, 1887–1894." *American Journal of Sociology* 103 (1997): 359–90.

Ansell, Chris, and Arthur Burris. "Bosses of the City Unite! Labor Politics and Political Machine Consolidation, 1870–1910." *Studies in American Political Development* 11 (1997): 1–43.

Ansell, Chris, Keith Darden, and Craig Parsons. "Dual Networks in European Regional Development Policy." *Journal of Common Market Studies* 35 (1997): 347–75.

Applegate, Celia. *A Nation of Provincials: The German Idea of Heimat.* Berkeley and Los Angeles: University of California Press, 1990.

Aquarone, Alberto. "La politica legislative della restaurazione nel regno di Sardegna." *Bollettino Storico-Bibliografico Subalpino* 57 (1959): 21–50, 322–59.

Arrow, Kenneth. *Social Choice and Individual Values.* New Haven: Yale University Press, 1951.

Assante, Franca. "Le trasformazioni del paesaggio agrario." In Angelo Massafra, ed., *Il mezzogiorno preunitario: Economica, societa, e istituzioni.* Bari: Dedalo, 1988. 29–53.

Bairoch, Paul. *Révolution industrielle et sous-développement.* Paris: Societe d'edition d'enseignement superieur, 1963.

Barzini, Luigi. *The Europeans.* New York: Penguin, 1983.

Bayerische Zeitung, January 20, 1867, Bayerisches Hauptstaatsarchiv, Munich, Abteilung 1.

Bayern Landtag. *Verhandlungen der Bayerischer Kammer der Abgeordneten,* 1866–1867. Bayerisches Hauptstaatsarchiv, Munich, Abteilung 2, Neuere Bestände 19./20. Jahrhundert.

Becker, Otto. *Bismarcks Ringen Um Deutschlands Gestaltung.* Heidelberg: Quelle und Meyer, 1958.

Bednar, Jenna. "Formal Theories of Federalism." *Newsletter of the Comparative Politics Section, American Political Science Association* 11, no. 1 (2000): 19–23.

Bendix, Reinhard. *Kings or People: Power and the Mandate to Rule.* Berkeley and Los Angeles: University of California Press, 1978.

———. *Max Weber: An Intellectual Portrait.* Berkeley and Los Angeles: University of California Press, 1977.

Berger, Suzanne. *The French Political System.* New York: Random House, 1974.

Bermeo, Nancy. "The Merits of Federalism." In Nancy Bermeo and Ugo Amoretti, eds., *Federalism and Territorial Cleavages.* Baltimore: Johns Hopkins University Press, 2004. 457–82.

Best, Heinrich. *Interessenpolitik und nationale Integration 1848/1849. Handelspolitische Konflikte im frühindustriellen Deutschland.* Göttingen: Vandenhöck und Ruprecht, 1980.

Biefang, Andreas. *Politisches Bürgertum in Deutschland, 1857–1868. Nationale Organisationen und Eliten.* Düsseldorf: Droste Verlag, 1994.

Binder, Hans-Otto. *Reich und Einzelstaaten während der Kanzerschaft Bismarcks: 1871–1890.* Tübingen: Mohr, 1971.

Binkley, Robert. *Realism and Nationalism, 1852–1871.* New York: Harper and Row, 1935.

Bismarck, Otto, Furst von. *Die Gesammelten Werke.* Vol. 6. Berlin: O. Stollberg, 1924.

———. *Werke in Auswahl.* Ed. Eberhard Scheler. Vol. 3. Stuttgart: W. Kohlhammer Verlag, 1965.

Bix, Herbert. *Hirohito and the Making of Modern Japan.* New York: HarperCollins, 2000.

Blaschke, Karlheinz. "Königreich Sachsen und Thüringische Staaten." In Kurt Jeserich, Hans Pohl, and Georg-Christoph von Unruh, eds., *Deutsche Verwaltungsgeschichte.* Vol. 2. Stuttgart: Deutsche Verlags-Anstalt, 1983. 608–45.

Blom, J.C.H., and E. Lamberts, eds. *History of the Low Countries.* New York: Berghahn, 1994.

Böhme, Helmut. *Deutschlands Weg Zur Grossmacht.* 1966; Cologne: Kiepenheuer und Witsch, 1972.

Boix, Carles. "Setting the Rules of the Game: The Choice of Electoral Systems in Advanced Democracies." *American Political Science Review* 93 (2000): 609–24.

Boldt, Hans. "Federalism as an Issue in the German Constitutions of 1849 and 1871." In Wellenreuther, Hermann, ed., *German and American Constitutional Thought.* New York: Berg, 1990. 260–78.

Borchard, Karl. "Staatsverbrauch und Öffentliche Investitionen in Deutschland, 1780–1850." Dissertation, Wirtschafts und Sozialwissenschaftlichen Fakultät, Göttingen, 1968.

Bosl, Karl. "Die Verhandlungen über den Eintritt der süddeutschen Staaten in den Norddeutschen Bund und die Entstehung der Reichsverfassung." In Theodor Schieder, ed., *Reichsgründung 1870/71.* Stuttgart: Seewald Verlag, 1970. 148–64.

Bowring, John. *Report on the Statistics of Tuscany, Lucca, the Pontifical, and the Lombardo-Venetian States, with a Special Reference to Their Commercial Rela-*

tions. Presented to Both Houses of Parliament by Command of Her Majesty. London: Clowes and Sons, 1837.

Brandenburg, Erich. *Die Reichsgründung.* 2nd ed. Vol. 2. Leipzig: Quelle und Meyer, 1923.

Brandt, Harm-Hinrich. *Deutsche Geschichte, 1850–1870. Entscheidung über die Nation.* Stuttgart: Kohlhammer, 1999.

Brauneder, Wilhelm. *Deutsch-Österreich 1918.* Vienna: Amalthea, 2000.

Brose, Eric Dorn. *German History, 1789–1871.* Providence: Berghahn, 1997.

Bull, Hedley. *The Anarchical Society: A Study of Order in World Politics.* New York: Columbia University Press, 1977.

Burgess, Michael. "The European Tradition of Federalism: Christian Democracy and Federalism." In Michael Burgess and A. G. Gagnon, eds., *Comparative Federalism and Federation.* Toronto: University of Toronto Press, 1993. 138–53.

Cafagna, Luciano. *Cavour.* Bologna: Il Mulino, 1999.

———. "La questione delle origini del dualismo economico italiano." In Luciano Cafagna, ed., *Dualismo e sviluppo nella storia d'Italia.* Venice: Marilio, 1989. 187–217.

Caldwell, Peter. *Popular Sovereignty and the Crisis of German Constitutional Law.* Durham: Duke University Press, 1997.

Caracciolo, Alberto. *Stato e società civile.* Turin: Giulio Einaudi, 1960.

Cardoza, Anthony. *Agrarian Elites and Italian Fascism: The Province of Bologna, 1901–1921.* Princeton: Princeton University Press, 1982.

———. *Aristocrats in Bourgeois Italy: The Piedmontese Nobility, 1861–1930.* Cambridge: Cambridge University Press, 1997.

Carr, Raymond. *Spain, 1808–1975.* Oxford: Clarendon Press, 1982.

Cavour, Count Camillo di. *Carteggi di Cavour: Il carteggio Cavour-Salmour.* Vol. 10. Bologna: Nicola Zanichelli, 1961.

———. *Carteggi di Cavour: Il carteggio Cavour-Nigra dal 1858 a 1861* Vol. 3. Bologna: Nicola Nicola Zanichelli, 1961.

———. *Carteggi di Cavour: La liberazione del mezzogiorno e la formazione del regno d'Italie.* Vol. 4. Bologna: Nicola Zanichelli, 1961.

———. *Epistolario.* Vol. 16 (January–September 1859). Firenze: Leo S. Olschki Editore, 2000.

Chubb, Judith. *Patronage, Power, and Poverty in Southern Italy: A Tale of Two Cities.* Cambridge: Cambridge University Press, 1982.

Clogg, Richard. *A Concise History of Greece.* Cambridge: Cambridge University Press, 2002.

———, ed. *Balkan Society in the Age of Greek Independence.* Totowa, N.J.: Barnes and Noble, 1981.

Clough, Shepard B. *The Economic History of Modern Italy.* New York: Columbia University Press, 1964.

Colley, Linda. *Britons: Forging the Nation, 1707–1837.* New Haven: Yale University Press, 1992.

Collier, David. "Letter from the President: Comparative Methodology in the 1990s." *APSA-Comparative Politics Newsletter* 9, no. 1 (1998): 1–5.

Collier, David, and Robert Adcock. "Measurement Validity: A Shared Standard for Qualitative and Quantitative Research." *American Political Science Review* 95 (2001): 529–46.

Collier, David, and James E. Mahon. "Conceptual Stretching Revisited: Adapting Categories in Comparative Analysis." *American Political Science Review* 87 (1993): 845–55.

Collier, Ruth Berins. *Paths toward Democracy.* Cambridge: Cambridge University Press, 1999.

Collier, Ruth Berins, and David Collier. *Shaping the Political Arena: Critical Junctures, the Labor Movement, and Regime Dynamics in Latin America.* Princeton: Princeton University Press, 1991.

Confino, Alon. "Federalism and the Heimat Idea in Imperial Germany." In Maiken Umbach, ed., *German Federalism: Past, Present, and Future.* London: Palgrave, 2002. 70–90.

———. *The Nation as a Local Metaphor: Württemberg, Imperial Germany, and National Memory, 1871–1917.* Chapel Hill: University of North Carolina Press, 1997.

Coppa, Frank. *Cardinal Giacomo Antonelli and Papal Politics in European Affairs.* Albany: State University of New York, 1990.

Craig, Gordon. *The Politics of the Prussian Army, 1640–1945.* New York: Oxford University Press, 1955.

Croce, Benedetto. *A History of Italy, 1871–1915.* Oxford: Clarendon Press, 1929.

———. *Storia d'Italia dal 1871 al 1915.* Bari: G. Laterza, 1928.

Davis, John. *Conflict and Control: Law and Order in Nineteenth-Century Italy.* Basingstoke: Macmillan Education, 1988.

———. "The South, the Risorgimento, and the Origins of the Southern Problem." In John Davis, ed., *Gramsci and Italy's Passive Revolution.* New York: Barnes and Noble, 1979. 67–103.

De Cesare, Raffaele. *The Last Days of Papal Rome.* Boston: Houghton Mifflin 1909.

de Figueiredo, Rui, and Barry Weingast. "Self Enforcing Federalism." Manuscript, Hoover Institution, 2002.

de Rosa, Luigi. *Iniziative e capitale straniero nell'industria metalmeccanica del mezzogiorno, 1840–1904.* Naples: Giannini, 1968.

Derbyshire, J. Denis, and Ian Derbyshire. *Political Systems of the World.* 2nd ed. New York: St. Martin's Press, 1996.

Di Scala, Spencer. *Italy: From Revolution to Republic.* Boulder, Colo.: Westview Press, 1995.

Diefendorf, Jeffry M. *Businessmen and Politics in the Rhineland, 1789–1834.* Princeton: Princeton University Press, 1980.

Douglas, Mary. *How Institutions Think.* Syracuse: Syracuse University Press, 1986.

Duchacek, Ivo. *Comparative Federalism: The Territorial Dimension of Politics.* New York: Holt, Rinehart, and Winston, 1970.

Dumke, Rolf. "Anglo-deutscher Handel und Freuhindustrialisierung in Deutschland, 1822–1865." *Geschichte und Gesellschaft* 5 (1979): 175–200.

———. *German Economic Unification in the Nineteenth Century: The Political Economy of the Zollverein.* Munich: University of the Bundeswehr, 1994.

Duncker, Max. *Politischer Briefwechsel aus Seinem Nachlass.* 1923; Osnabrück: Biblio Verlag, 1967.

Eckhardt, Albrecht. "Der konstitionelle Staat (1848–1918)." In Eckhardt, Albrecht, ed., *Geschichte des Landes Oldenburg: Ein Handbuch.* Oldenburg: Heinz Holzberg Verlag, 1988. 333–402.

Eisenhart, Rothe von, and A. W. Ritthaler, eds. *Vorgeschichte und Begründung des Deutschen Zollvereins 1815–1834.* Berlin: Verlag von Reimar Hobbing, 1934.

Ertman, Thomas. *Birth of the Leviathan: Building States and Regimes in Medieval and Early Modern Europe.* Cambridge: Cambridge University Press, 1997.

Esposto, Alfredo. "Estimating Regional Per Capita Income: Italy, 1861–1914." *Journal of European Economic History* 26 (1997): 585–604.

Evans, Peter. *Embedded Autonomy: States and Industrial Transformation.* Princeton: Princeton University Press, 1995.

Evans, Peter, Dietrich Rueschemeyer, and Theda Skocpol, eds. *Bringing the State Back In.* Cambridge: Cambridge University Press, 1985.

Faber, Hanns. *Modena-Austria: Das Herzogtum und das Kassereich von 1814 bis 1867.* Frankfurt am Main: Peter Lang, 1996.

Fay, Gisela. *Bayern als grösster deutscher Mittelstaat im Kalkel der fränzosischen Diplomatie und im Urteil der Französischen Journalistik, 1859–1866.* Munich: Stadtarchivs München, 1976.

Fearon, James. "Domestic Political Audiences and the Escalation of International Disputes." *American Political Science Review* 88 (1994): 577–92.

Fehrenbach, Elisabeth. "Bürokratische Reform und gesellschaftlicher Wandel: Die badische Verfassung von 1818." In Ernst Otto Bräunche and Thomas Schnabel, eds. *Die Badische Verfassung von 1818.* Ubstadt-Weiher: Verlag Regionalkultur, 1996. 13–24.

Felloni, G. "La Spese Effettive e Il Bilancio degli Stati Sabaudi dal 1825 al 1860." In *Archivio Economico dell'Unificazione Italiana,* ser. 1, vol. 9 (1959): 1–78.

Fischer, Wolfram. *Wirtschaft und Gesellschaft im Zeitalter der Industrialisierung.* Göttingen: Vandenhöck und Ruprecht, 1964.

Fitzmaurice, John. *The Politics of Belgium: A Unique Federalism.* Boulder, Colo.: Westview Press, 1996.

Flora, Peter, et al. *State, Economy, and Society in Western Europe, 1815–1975: A Data Handbook.* 2 vols. Frankfurt am Main: Campus Verlag, 1983.

Ford, J. A., ed. *The Correspondence of William I and Bismarck.* Vol. 2. New York: Frederick A. Stokes, 1903.

Frank, Harald. *Regionale Entwicklungsdisparitäten im deutschen Industrialisierungsprozess, 1849–1939.* Münster: Lit Verlag, 1996.

Fried, Robert. *The Italian Prefects: A Study in Administrative Politics.* New Haven: Yale University Press, 1963.

Friedrich, Carl. *Trends of Federalism in Theory and Practice.* New York: Praeger, 1968.

Gall, Lothar. *Bismarck: The White Revolutionary.* London: Allen and Unwin, 1986.

———. *Der Liberalismus als regierende Partei. Das Grossherzogtum Baden zwischen Restauration and Reichsgründung.* Wiesbaden: F. Steiner, 1968.

Gall, Lothar, and Dieter Langewiesche, eds. *Liberalismus und Region*. Munich: R. Oldenbourg Verlag, 1995.

Garman, Christopher, Stephen Haggard, and Eliza Willis. "Fiscal Decentralization: A Political Theory with Latin American Cases." *World Politics* 53 (2001): 205–34.

Gellner, Ernest. *Nations and Nationalism*. Oxford: Oxford University Press, 1983.

Gerschenkron, Alexander. *Economic Backwardness in Historical Perspective*. Cambridge: Harvard University Press, 1962.

Gibson, Edward L., and Tulia Falleti. "Unity by the Stick: Regional Conflict and the Origins of Argentine Federalism." In Edward L. Gibson, ed., *Federalism and Democracy in Latin America*. Baltimore: Johns Hopkins University Press, 2003. 226–54.

Gould, Andrew C. "Conflicting Imperatives and Concept Formation." *Review of Politics* 61 (1999): 439–63.

Gourevitch, Peter. *Politics in Hard Times*. Ithaca: Cornell University Press, 1986.

Gramsci, Antonio. *Prison Notebooks*. New York: Columbia University Press, 1992.

Greenfeld, Liah. *Nationalism: Five Roads to Modernity*. Cambridge: Harvard University Press, 1992.

Greenfield, Kent. *Economics and Liberalism in the Risorgimento: A Study of Nationalism in Lombardy, 1814–1848*. Baltimore: Johns Hopkins Press, 1965.

Grew, Raymond. "How Success Spoiled the Risorgimento." *Journal of Modern History* 34, no. 3 (1962): 239–53.

———. *A Sterner Plan for Italian Unity: The Italian National Society in the Risorgimento*. Princeton: Princeton University Press, 1963.

Grimm, Dieter. *Deutsche Verfassungsgeschichte, 1776–1866*. Frankfurt am Main: Suhrkamp, 1988.

Haas, Ernst. *Nationalism, Liberalism, and Progress*. Ithaca: Cornell University Press, 1997.

Hahn, Hans-Werner. *Wirtschaftliche Integration im 19. Jahrhundert: Die hessischen Staaten und der Deutsche Zollverein*. Göttingen: Vandenhöck und Ruprecht, 1982.

Hamerow, Theodore S. *Restoration, Revolution, and Reaction*. Princeton: Princeton University Press, 1958.

———. *The Social Foundations of German Unification, 1858–1871*. Princeton: Princeton University Press, 1969.

Hancock, William Keith. *Ricasoli and the Risorgimento in Tuscany*. London: Faber and Gwyer, 1926.

Hansen, Hal. "Caps and Gowns." Ph.D. diss., University of Wisconsin–Madison, 1997.

Hart, B. H. Liddell. "Armed Forces and the Art of War: Armies." In J.P.T. Bury, ed., *The New Cambridge Modern History*. Vol. 10, *The Zenith of European Power, 1830–1870*. Cambridge: Cambridge University Press, 1960. 302–30.

Hechter, Michael. *Containing Nationalism*. Oxford: Oxford University Press, 2000.

Henderson, W. O. *The Zollverein*. Cambridge: Cambridge University Press, 1939.

Herbst, Jeffrey. *States and Power in Africa: Comparative Lessons in Authority and Control*. Princeton: Princeton University Press, 2000.

Herrigel, Gary. *Industrial Constructions: The Sources of German Industrial Power.* Cambridge: Cambridge University Press, 1996.

Hesse, Konrad. *Der unitarische Bundesstaat.* Karlsruhe: C. F. Miller, 1962.

Hintze, Otto. "The State in Historical Perspective." In Reinhard Bendix, ed., *State and Society: A Reader in Comparative Political Sociology.* Berkeley and Los Angeles: University of California Press, 1968. 154–69.

Hobsbawm, E. J. *The Age of Revolution: Europe, 1789–1848.* London: Weidenfeld and Nicolson, 1962.

Hope, Nicholas Martin. *The Alternative to German Unification: The Anti-Prussian Party, Frankfurt, Nassau, and the Two Hessens, 1859–1867.* Wiesbaden: F. Steiner Verlag, 1973.

Howard, Marc Morje. "The Weakness of Postcommunist Civil Society." *Journal of Democracy* 13, no. 1 (2002): 157–69.

Hubatsch, Walter. "Aufbau, Gliederung und Tätigkeit der Verwaltung in den deutschen Einzelstaaten." In Kurt Jeserich, Hans Pohl, and Georg-Christoph von Unruh, eds., *Deutsche Verwaltungsgeschichte.* Vol. 2. Stuttgart: Deutsche Verlags-Anstalt, 1983. 166–98.

Huber, Ernst Rudolf. *Deutsche Verfassungsgeschichte Seit 1789.* Vol. 3. Stuttgart: W. Kohlhammer Verlag, 1963.

———, ed. *Dokumente zur Deutschen Verfassungsgeschichte.* Vol. 2. Stuttgart: W. Kohlhammer Verlag, 1964.

Huntington, Samuel. *Political Order in Changing Societies.* New Haven: Yale University Press, 1968.

Ikenberry, G. John. *After Victory: Institutions, Strategic Restraint, and the Rebuilding of Order after Major Wars.* Princeton: Princeton University Press, 2001.

Izzo, Luigi. *La finanza pubblica: Nel primo decennio dell'unita italiana.* Milan: Dottore a Giuffre Editore, 1962.

Jacob, Herbert. *German Administration since Bismarck.* New Haven: Yale University Press, 1963.

Jacoby, Wade. "Tutors and Pupils: International Organizations, Central European Elites, and Western Models." *Governance* 14, no. 2 (2001): 169–200.

Jervis, Robert. "Timing and Interaction in Politics: A Comment on Pierson." *Studies in American Political Development* 14, no. 1 (2000): 93–100.

John, Michael. "The Napoleonic Legacy and Problems of Restoration in Central Europe: The German Confederation." In David Laven and Lucy Riall, eds., *Napoleon's Legacy: Problems of Government in Restoration Europe.* Oxford: Berg, 2000. 83–96.

Jones, W. Glyn. *Denmark: A Modern History.* London: Croom Helm, 1986.

Jowitt, Ken. *The Leninist Response to National Dependency.* Berkeley: Institute of International Studies Research, University of California, 1978.

———. "Nation-Building as Amalgam of State, Civic, and Ethnicity." Manuscript, University of California, Berkeley, 2001.

Jussila, Osmo. *From Grand Duchy to Modern State: A Political History of Finland since 1809.* London: Hurst, 1999.

Kammer der Reichsräthe. *Verhandlungen der Kammer der Reichsräthe des Königreiches Bayerns,* 1870/1871, 24. Landtag. Bayerisches Hauptstaatsarchiv, Munich, Abteilung 2, Neuere Bestände 19./20. Jahrhundert.

Karlsson, Gunnar. *History of Iceland.* Minneapolis: University of Minnesota Press, 2000.

Kaufmann, Erich. *Bismarcks Erbe in der Reichsverfassung.* Berlin: Springer, 1917.

Kern, Robert. *A Historical Dictionary of Modern Spain, 1700–1988.* New York: Greenwood Press, 1990.

Kiesewetter, Hubert. *Industrialisierung und Landwirtschaft. Sachsens Stellung im regionalen Industrialisierungsprozess Deutschlands im 19. Jahrhundert.* Cologne: Böhlau Verlag, 1988.

King, Gary, Robert Keohane, and Sidney Verba. *Designing Social Inquiry: Scientific Inference in Qualitative Research.* Princeton: Princeton University Press, 1994.

Klein, Thomas. "Königreich Hannover." In Kurt Jeserich, Hans Pohl, and Georg-Christoph von Unruh, eds., *Deutsche Verwaltungsgeschichte.* Vol. 2. Stuttgart: Deutsche Verlags-Anstalt, 1983. 678–714.

———. "Hessische Staaten." In Kurt Jeserich, Hans Pohl, and Georg-Christoph von Unruh, eds., *Deutsche Verwaltungsgeschichte.* Vol. 2. Stuttgart: Deutsche Verlags-Anstalt, 1983. 645–77.

Knemeyer, Frank-Ludwig. "Beginn der Reorganisation der Verwaltung in Deutschland." In Kurt Jeserich, Hans Pohl, and Georg-Christoph von Unruh, eds., *Deutsche Verwaltungsgeschichte.* Vol. 2. Stuttgart: Deutsche Verlags-Anstalt, 1983. 122–54.

Kocka, Jürgen. "Germany." In Ira Katznelson and Aristide Zolberg, eds., *Working-Class Formation.* Princeton: Princeton University Press, 1986. 279–351.

Köllmann, Wolfgang, ed. *Quellen zur Bevölkerungs-, Sozial- und Wirtschaftsstatistik, 1815–1875.* Vol. 1. Boppard am Rhein: Harald Boldt Verlag, 1980.

Kossman, E. H. *The Low Countries, 1780–1940.* New York: Oxford University Press, 1978.

Krieger, Joel, ed. *The Oxford Companion to Politics of the World.* 2nd ed. Oxford: Oxford University Press, 2001.

Kroll, Thomas. *Die Revolte des Patriziats: Der Toskanische Adelsliberalismus im Risorgimento.* Tübingen: Max Niemeyer Verlag, 1999.

Langewiesche, Dieter. "Föderativer Nationalismus als Erbe der deutschen Reichsnation: Über Föderalismus und Zentralismus in der deutschen Nationalgeschichte." In Dieter Langewiesche and G. Schmidt, eds., *Föderative Nation: Deutschlandkonzepte von der Reformation bis zum Ersten Weltkrieg.* Munich: Oldenbourg Verlag, 2000. 215–42.

Laven, David. "The Age of Restoration." In John Davis, ed., *Italy in the Nineteenth Century.* Oxford: Oxford University Press, 2000. 51–73.

Laven, David, and Lucy Riall, eds. *Napoleon's Legacy: Problems of Government in Restoration Europe.* Oxford: Berg, 2000.

Lehmbruch, Gerhard. *Parteienwettbewerb im Bundesstaat.* 2nd ed. Opladen: Westdeutscher Verlag, 1998.

———. "Der unitarische Bundesstaat in Deutschland: Pfadabhängigkeit und Wandel." Max-Planck-Institut für Gesellschaftsforschung Discussion Paper No. 02/2, 2002.

Luebbert, Gregory. *Liberalism, Fascism, or Social Democracy.* Oxford: Oxford University Press, 1991.

Levi, Margaret. *Consent, Dissent, and Patriotism.* Cambridge: Cambridge University Press, 1997.

———. *Of Rule and Revenue.* Berkeley and Los Angeles: University of California Press, 1988.

Levy, Jonah. *Tocqueville's Revenge: State, Society, and Economy in Post-Dirigiste France.* Cambridge: Harvard University Press, 1999.

Lieberman, Evan. "Causal Inference in Historical Institutional Analysis: A Specification of Periodization Strategies." *Comparative Political Studies* 34 (2001): 1011–35.

———. "Payment for Privilege? Race and Space in the Politics of Taxation in South Africa and Brazil." Ph.D. diss., Department of Political Science, University of California, Berkeley, 2000.

Lijphart, Arend. "Comparative Politics and the Comparative Method." *American Political Science Review* 65 (1971): 682–93.

———. *Patterns of Democracy.* New Haven: Yale University Press, 1999.

Lipset, Seymour Martin, and Stein Rokkan, eds. *Party System and Voter Alignment.* New York: Free Press, 1967.

Löffler, Bernhard. *Die Bayerische Kammer der Reichsräte 1848–1918.* Munich: Beck'sche Verlagsbuchhandlung, 1996.

Lovett, Clara. *Carlo Cattaneo and the Politics of the Risorgimento, 1820–1860.* The Hague: Martinus Nijhoff, 1972.

Lyttelton, Adrian. "Landlords, Peasants, and the Limits of Liberalism." In John A. Davis, ed., *Gramsci and Italy's Passive Revolution.* New York: Barnes and Noble, 1979. 104–35.

———. "A New Past for the Mezzogiorno?" *Times Literary Supplement,* October 4, 1991.

Mack Smith, Denis. "Advanced the Southern Question." In Charles F. Delzell, ed., *The Unification of Italy, 1859–1861: Cavour, Mazzini, or Garibaldi?* New York: Robert E. Krieger, 1965. 66–69.

———. *Cavour.* London: Weidenfeld and Nicolson, 1985.

———. *Cavour and Garibaldi: A Study in Political Conflict.* Cambridge: Cambridge University Press, 1954.

———. *A History of Sicily after 1713.* London: Chatto and Windus, 1968.

———. *Italy: A Modern History.* Ann Arbor: University of Michigan Press, 1969.

———. *Mazzini.* New Haven: Yale University Press, 1994.

———. *Victor Emanuel, Cavour and the Risorgimento.* London: Oxford University Press, 1971.

———, ed. *The Making of Modern Italy, 1796–1870.* New York: Harper and Row, 1968.

Mahoney, James, and Dietrich Rueschemeyer. "Comparative Historical Analysis: Achievements and Agendas." In James Mahoney and Dietrich Rueschemeyer, eds., *Comparative Historical Analysis in the Social Sciences.* Cambridge: Cambridge University Press, 2003. 3–40.

Maier, Charles. "Consigning the Twentieth Century to History: Alternative Narratives for the Modern Era." *American Historical Review* 105 (2000): 807–31.

———. "Transformations of Territoriality, 1600–2000." Manuscript, Harvard University, September 12, 2002.

Maissen, Thomas. "The 1848 Conflicts and Their Significance in Swiss Historiography." In Michael Butler, Malcolm Pender, and Joy Charnley, eds., *The Making of Modern Switzerland, 1848–1998*. London: Macmillan, 2000. 3–34.

Mann, Michael. *The Sources of Social Power*. Vol. 2. Cambridge: Cambridge University Press, 1993.

March, James, and Johan Olsen. *Rediscovering Institutions: The Organizational Basis of Politics*. New York: Free Press, 1989.

Marriott, J.A.R. *The Makers of Modern Italy*. Oxford: Clarendon Press, 1931.

Mazzuca, Sebastian. "Southern Cone Leviathan." Manuscript, University of California, Berkeley, 2002.

McKay, David. *Federalism and the European Union*. Oxford: Oxford University Press, 1999.

———. "William Riker on Federalism: Sometimes Wrong but More Right Than Anyone Else." Paper presented to the William Riker Conference on Constitutions, Voting and Democracy, Washington University, December 7–8, 2001.

Mendels, Franklin F. "Proto-industrialization: The First Phase of the Industrialization Process." *Journal of Economic History* 32 (1972): 241–61.

Michaelis, Herbert, ed. *Die auswärtige Politik Preussens, 1858–1871*. Vol. 8. Oldenburg: Verlag Gerhard Stalling, 1934.

Migdal, Joel. *Strong Societies and Weak States: State-Society Relations and State Capabilities in the Third World*. Princeton: Princeton University Press, 1988.

Mill, John Stuart. "Two Methods of Comparison." In Amatai Etzioni and Frederic L. DuBow, eds., *Comparative Perspectives: Theories and Methods*. Boston: Little, Brown, 1970. 205–13.

Milner, Helen. *Resisting Protectionism: Global Industries and the Politics of International Trade*. Princeton: Princeton University Press, 1988.

Mintzel, Alf. "Specificities of Bavarian Political Culture." In Dirk Berg-Schlosser and Ralf Rytlewski, eds., *Political Culture in Germany*. London: Macmillan, 1993. 105.

Mitchell, B. R. *International Historical Statistics: Europe, 1750–1993*. London: Macmillan, 1998.

Moore, Barrington. *Injustice: The Social Bases of Obedience and Revolt*. White Plains, N.Y.: M. E. Sharpe, 1978.

———. *Social Origins of Dictatorship and Democracy: Lord and Peasant in the Making of the Modern World*. Boston: Beacon Press, 1966.

Mori, Giorgio. "Industrie senza industrializzione: La peninsola italiana dalla fine della dominazione francese all'unita nazionale: 1815–1861." *Studi Storici* 30 (1989): 603–35.

Mussgnug, Reinhard. "Die rechtlichen und pragmatischen Beziehungen zwischen Regierung, Parlament, und Verwaltung." In Kurt Jeserich, Hans Pohl, and Georg-Christoph von Unruh, eds., *Deutsche Verwaltungsgeschichte*. Vol. 2. Stuttgart: Deutsche-Verlags Anstalt, 1983. 95–121.

Nipperdey, Thomas. *Deutsche Geschichte, 1866–1918*. Munich: C. H. Beck Verlag, 1992.

———. *Germany from Napoleon to Bismarck, 1800–1866*. Princeton: Princeton University Press, 1996.

Norddeutsche Allgemeine Zeitung. February 24, 1867, in Bayerische Gesandschaft Berlin, no. 1036. Bayerisches Hauptstaatsarchiv, Munich, Abteilung 1 and 2.

Nordstrom, Byron. *The History of Sweden.* Minneapolis: University of Minnesota Press, 2002.

———. *Scandinavia since 1500.* Minneapolis: University of Minnesota Press, 2000.

Oeter, Stefan. *Integration und Subsidiarität im deutschen Bundesstaatsrecht: Untersuchungen zu Bundesstaatstheorie unter dem Grundgesetz.* Tübingen: Mohr Siebeck, 1998.

Oncken, Hermann, ed. *Die Rheinpolitik Kaiser Napoleons III. Von 1863 Bis 1870 und der Ursprung des Krieges von 1870/1871.* Stuttgart: Deutsche Verlags-Anstalt, 1926.

Ordeshook, Peter. "Federal Institutional Design: A Theory of Self-Sustainable Federal Government." Manuscript, California Institute of Technology, 2001.

Parlamento Sub-Alpino. *Atti Parlamentari,* Acts of the 1st–7th Legislatures, 1848–61.

Patriarca, Silvana. *Numbers and Nationhood: Writing Statistics in Nineteenth-Century Italy.* Cambridge: Cambridge University Press, 1996.

Petrusewicz, Marta. *Latifundium: Moral Economy and Material Life in a European Periphery.* Ann Arbor: University of Michigan Press, 1996.

Pichler, Rupert. *Die Wirtschaft Lombardei als Teil Österreichs.* Berlin: Duncker und Humblot, 1996.

Pierson, Paul. "Increasing Returns, Path Dependence, and the Study of Politics." *American Political Science Review* 94 (2000): 251–67.

———. "Not Just What, but *When*: Issues of Timing and Sequence in Political Processes." *Studies in American Political Development* 14, no. 1 (2000): 73–93.

———. *Politics in Time: History, Institutions, and Social Analysis.* Princeton: Princeton University Press, 2004.

Plumb, J. H. *England in the 18th Century.* Middlesex: Penguin, 1950.

Polanyi, Karl. *The Great Transformation.* New York: Farrar and Rinehart, 1944.

Pollard, Sidney. *Peaceful Conquest: The Industrialization of Europe, 1760–1970.* Oxford: Oxford University Press, 1981.

Price, Arnold. *The Evolution of the Zollverein: A Study of the Ideas and Institutions Leading to German Economic Unification between 1815 and 1833.* New York: Octagon, 1973.

Przeworski, Adam, and Henry Teune. *The Logic of Comparative Social Inquiry.* New York: Wiley Interscience, 1970.

Putnam, Robert. "Diplomacy and Domestic Politics: The Logic of Two-Level Games." *International Organization* 42 (1988): 427–60.

———. *Making Democracy Work: Civic Traditions in Modern Italy.* Princeton: Princeton University Press, 1993.

Ragin, Charles. *The Comparative Method: Moving beyond Qualitative and Quantitative Strategies.* Berkeley and Los Angeles: University of California Press, 1987.

Rall, Hans. "Die politische Entwicklung von 1848 bis zur Reichsgründung 1871." In Max Spindler, ed., *Handbuch der Bayerischen Geschichte, 1800–1870,* Vol. 4. Munich: C. H. Beck'sche Verlagsbuchhandlung, 1974. 224–82.

Randeraad, Nico. *Autorita in cerca di autonomia I prefetti nell'Italia liberale.* Rome: Ministero per i beni culturali e ambientali ufficio per i beni archivistici, 1993.

Ranelagh, John. *A Short History of Ireland.* 2nd ed. Cambridge: Cambridge University Press, 1994.

Rauh, Manfred. *Föderalismus und Parlamentarismus im Wilhelmischen Reich.* Düsseldorf: Droste Verlag, 1973.

Rector, Chad. "Federations in International Politics." Ph.D. diss., Department of Political Science, University of California, San Diego, May 2003.

———. "Political Confederations: The Limits of International Organizations and the 1901 Choice for Australia." Paper presented to the American Political Science Association Convention, September 2002.

Reichstag des Norddeutschen Bundes. *Verhandlunden des Reichstages des Norddeutschen Bundes,* 1867–1870. Vols. 1–19, Bayerische Staatsbibliothek, Munich. http://mdz.bib-bvb.de/digbib/reichstag.

Riall, Lucy. "Elite Resistance to State Formation: The Case of Italy." In Mary Fulbrook, ed., *National Histories and European History.* Boulder, Colo.: Westview Press, 1993. 46–68.

———. *The Italian Risorgimento: State, Society, and National Unification.* London: Routledge, 1994.

———. *Sicily and the Unification of Italy: Liberal Policy and Local Power, 1850–1866.* Oxford: Clarendon Press, 1998.

Riker, William. *Federalism: Origins, Operation, Significance.* New York: Little, Brown, 1964.

———. "Implications from the Disequilibrium of Majority Rule for the Study of Institutions." *American Political Science Review* 74 (1980): 432–46.

Robinson, R.A.H. *Contemporary Portugal: A History.* London: Unwin, 1979.

Rodden, Jonathan. "The Dilemma of Fiscal Federalism: Grants and Fiscal Performance around the World." *American Journal of Political Science* 46 (2002): 670–87.

———. "Reviving Leviathan: Fiscal Federalism and the Growth of Government." *International Organization* 57 (2003): 695–729.

Rodden, Jonathan, and Erik Wibbels. "Beyond the Fiction of Federalism: Macroeconomic Management in Multitiered Systems." *World Politics* 54 (2002): 494–531.

Roegiers, J., and N.C.F. van Sas. "Revolution in the North and the South, 1780–1830." In J.C.H. Blom and E. Lamberts, eds., *History of the Low Countries.* New York: Berghahn, 1999. 269–310.

Rogosch, Detlef. *Hamburg im Deutschen Bund 1859–1866: Zur Politik eines Kleinstaates in einer mitteleuropaischen Föderativordnung.* Hamburg: R. Kramer, 1990.

Röhl, John. "Staatsstreichplan oder Staatsstreichbereitschaft? Bismarcks Politik in der Entlassungskrise." *Historische Zeitschrift,* December 1966, 610–24.

Romanelli, Raffaele. *Il comando impossibile: Stato e società nell'Italia liberale.* Bologna: Il Mulino, 1988.

———. "Political Debate, Social History, and the Italian 'Borghesia': Changing Perspectives in Historical Research." *Journal of Modern History* 63 (1991): 717–39.

———, ed. *Storia dello stato italiano dall'Unita a oggi.* Bologna: Il Mulino, 1995.

Romeo, Rosario. *Cavour e il suo tempo.* 3rd ed. Rome: Laterza, 1984.

———. *Risorgimento e capitalismo.* Bari: Laterza, 1959.

———. *Il Risorgimento in Sicilia.* Bari: Gius. Laterza, 1950.

Ruggie, John. "Territoriality and Beyond: Problematizing Modernity in International Relations." *International Organization* 471 (1993): 139–74.

Sabetti, Filippo. "The Liberal Idea in Nineteenth-Century Italy." Paper presented to the Annual Meeting of the American Political Science Association, August 2001.

———. *The Search for Good Government: Understanding the Paradox of Italian Democracy.* Montreal: McGill-Queen's University Press, 2000.

Sachsen-Coburg-Gotha, Ernst II, Herzog von. *Aus meinem Leben und aus meiner Zeit.* Vol. 3. Berlin: Verlag von Wilhelm Herz, 1889.

Salomone, William. *Italy in the Giolittian Era: Italian Democracy in the Making, 1900–1914.* Philadelphia: University of Pennsylvania Press, 1960.

Santore, John. *Modern Naples: A Documentary History, 1799–1999.* New York: Italica Press, 2001.

Sartori, Giovanni. "Concept Misformation in Comparative Research." *American Political Science Review* 64 (1970): 1033–53.

Schambeck, Herbert. *Föderalismus und Parlamentarismus in Österreich.* Vienna: Verlag der Österreichischen Staatsdruckerei, 1992.

Schickler, Eric. "Institutional Change in the House of Representatives, 1867–1998: A Test of Partisan and Ideological Power Balance Models." *American Political Science Review* 94 (2000): 269–88.

Schneider, Jane, and Peter Schneider. *Culture and Political Economy in Western Sicily.* New York: Academic Press, 1976.

Schremmer, D. E. "Taxation and Public Finance: Britain, France, and Germany." In Peter Mathias and Sidney Pollard, eds., *Cambridge Economic History of Europe.* Vol. 8, *The Industrial Economies: The Development of Social Policies.* Cambridge: Cambridge University Press, 1989. 315–548.

Schwarz, Peter Klaus. *Nationale und Soziale Bewegung in Oldenburg im Jahrzehnt von der Reichsgründung.* Oldenburg: Heinz Holzberg Verlag, 1979.

Schwarzwälder, Herbert. *Geschichte der Freien Hansestadt Bremen.* Vol. 2. Bremen: Verlag Friedrich Röver, 1976.

Scirocco, Alfonso. *L'Italia del Risorgimento.* Bologna: Il Mulino, 1990.

Scott, Samuel, and Barry Rothaus, eds. *Historical Dictionary of the French Revolution, 1789–1799.* Westport, Conn.: Greenwood Press, 1985.

Sheehan, James. *German History, 1770–1866.* Oxford: Clarendon Press, 1989.

Shefter, Martin. *Political Parties and the State: The American Historical Experience.* Princeton: Princeton University Press, 1994.

Siemann, Wolfram. *Vom Staatenbund zum Nationalstaat: Deutschland 1806–1871.* Munich: Beck, 1995.

214 REFERENCES

Singer, J. David, and Melvin Small. *National Material Capabilities Data, 1816–1985.* Computer file. Ann Arbor: Inter-university Consortium for Political and Social Research, 1993.

Skocpol, Theda. "How Americans Became Civic." In Theda Skocpol and Morris P. Fiorina, eds., *Civic Engagement in American Democracy.* Washington, D.C.: Brookings Institution Press and the Russell Sage Foundation, 1999. 27–80.

Skocpol, Theda, and Margaret Somers. "The Uses of History in Macrosocial Inquiry." *Comparative Studies in Society and History* 22, no. 2 (1980): 174–97.

Snyder, Richard. "Scaling Down: The Subnational Comparative Method." *Studies in Comparative International Development* 36, no. 1 (2001): 93–110.

Spagnoletti, Angelantonio. *Storia del Regno delle Due Sicilie.* Bologna: Il Mulino, 1997.

Speck, W. A. *A Concise History of Britain, 1707–1975.* Cambridge: Cambridge University Press, 1993.

Sperber, Jonathan. *Rhineland Radicals: The Democratic Movement and the Revolution of 1848–1849.* Princeton: Princeton University Press, 1991.

Stehlin, Stewart, *Bismarck and the Guelph Problem, 1866–1890.* The Hague: Martinus Nijhoff, 1973.

Stenographischer Bericht. *Verhandlungen der Bayerischen Kammer der Abgeordneten.*

Stepan, Alfred. "Toward a New Comparative Politics of Federalism, Multinationalism, and Democracy: Beyond Rikerian Federalism." In *Arguing Comparing Politics.* Oxford: Oxford University Press, 2001. 315–61.

Stjernquist, Nils. "The Creation of the 1809 Constitution." In Steven Koblik, ed., *Sweden's Development from Poverty to Affluence, 1750–1970.* Minneapolis: University Minnesota Press, 1975.

Stolleis, Michael. *Public Law in Germany, 1800–1914.* New York: Berghahn, 2001.

Tarrow, Sidney. *Between Center and Periphery: Grassroots Politicians in Italy and France.* New Haven: Yale University Press, 1977.

———. "National Integration, National Disintegration, and Contention: A Paired Comparison of Unlike Cases." In Doug McAdam, Sidney Tarrow, and Charles Tilly, eds., *Dynamics of Contention.* Cambridge: Cambridge University Press, 2001. 176–204.

Taylor, A.J.P. *The Struggle for Mastery in Europe, 1848–1918.* Oxford: Oxford University Press, 1971.

Thelen, Kathleen. "How Institutions Evolve: Insights from Comparative Historical Analysis." In James Mahoney and Dietrich Rueschemeyer, eds., *Comparative Historical Analysis in the Social Sciences.* Cambridge: Cambridge University Press, 2003. 208–40.

———. "Timing and Temporality in the Analysis of Institutional Evolution and Change." *Studies in American Political Development* 14 (spring 2000): 101–8.

Tilly, Charles. "Reflections on the History of European State-Making." In Charles Tilly, ed., *The Formation of National States in Western Europe.* Princeton: Princeton University Press, 1975. 3–83.

Tilly, Charles, Louise Tilly, and Richard Tilly. *The Rebellious Century, 1830–1930.* Cambridge: Harvard University Press, 1975.

Tilly, Richard. "The Political Economy of Public Finance and the Industrialization of Prussia, 1815–1866." *Journal of Economic History* 26 (1966): 484–97.

Treichel, Eckhardt. "Restaurationssystem und Verwaltungsmodernisierung." In Hans-Peter Ullmann and Clemens Zimmermann, eds., *Restaurationssystem und Reformpolitik: Süddeutschland und Preussen im Vergleich*. Munich: R. Doldenbourg Verlag, 1996. 65–84.

Treitschke, Heinrich. *Cavour: Der Wegbereiter des neuen Italiens*. Leipzig: Wilhelm Langeweische-Brandt, 1942.

———. *Historische und Politische Aufsätze*. Leipzig: Verlag von Hirzel, 1867.

———. *History of Germany in the Nineteenth Century*. Trans. Eden Paul and Cedar Paul. London: Jarrold and Sons, 1918.

Trevelyan, George Macaulay. *Garibaldi and the Making of Italy*. London: Longmans, Green, 1914.

Triepel, Heinrich. "Zur Vorgeschichte der Norddeutschen Bundesverfassung." In Heinrich Triepel, ed., *Festschrift Otto Gierke zum Siebzigsten Geburtstag*. Weimar: Harmann Böhlaus Nachfolger, 1911. 589–630.

Ullmann, Hans-Peter. *Staatsschulden und Reformpolitik. Die Entstehung moderner öffentlicher Schulden in Bayern und Baden, 1780–1820*. Vol. 2. Göttingen: Vandenhöck und Ruprecht, 1986.

Ullmann, Hans-Peter, and Clems Zimmermann, eds. *Restaurationssytem und Reformpolitik: Süddeutschland und Preussen im Vergleich*. Munich: Oldenbourg Verlag, 1996.

Ullner, Rudolf. "Die Idee des Föderalismus in Jahrzehnt der deutschen Einigungskriege." *Historischen Studien* 393 (1965): 5–164.

Umbach, Maiken. *Federalism and Enlightenment in Germany, 1740–1806*. London: Hambledon Press, 2000.

Vitense, Otto. *Geschichte von Mecklenburg*. Gotha: Friedrich Andreas Perthes, 1920.

von Barton, Irmgard. *Die preussische Gesandtschaft in München als Instrument der Reichspolitik in Bayern von den Anfängen der Reichsgründung bis zu Bismarcks Entlassung*. Munich: Neue Schriftenreihe des Stadtarchivs München, 1967.

von Hohenlohe, Alexander. *Aus meinem Leben*. Frankfurt am Main: Societäts Druckerei, 1925.

von Unruh, Georg-Christoph. "Preussen: Die Veränderungen der Preussischen Staatsverfassung durch Sozial- und Verwaltungsreformen." In Kurt Jeserich, Hans Pohl, and Georg-Christoph von Unruh, eds., *Deutsche Verwaltungsgeschichte*. Vol. 2. Stuttgart: Deutsche-Verlags Anstalt, 1983. 435–69.

Walker, Mack. *German Home Towns: Community, State, and General Estate, 1648–1871*. Ithaca: Cornell University Press, 1971.

Watts, Ronald L. "Federalism, Federal Political Systems, and Federations." *Annual Review of Political Science* 1 (1998): 117–37.

Wawro, Geoffrey. *The Austro-Prussian War: Austria's War with Prussia and Italy in 1866*. Cambridge: Cambridge University Press, 1997.

Weber, Eugen. *Peasants into Frenchmen: The Modernization of Rural France, 1870–1914*. Stanford: Stanford University Press, 1976.

Weber, Max. *Economy and Society*. Ed. Guenther Roth and Claus Wittich. Trans. Ephraim Fischoff et al. Vol. 3. New York: Bedminster Press, 1968.

Wehler, Hans-Ulrich. *Deutsche Gesellschaftsgeschicht: Von der Deutschen Doppelrevolution bis zum Beginn des Ersten Weltkrieges.* Vol. 3. Munich: C. H. Beck'sche, 1995.

Wehner, Norbert. *Die deutschen Mittelstaaten auf dem Frankfurter Fürstentag, 1863.* Frankfurt am Main: Peter Lang, 1993.

Weingast, Barry. "The Economic Role of Political Institutions: Market-Preserving Federalism and Economic Development." *Journal of Law, Economics, and Organization* 11, no. 1 (1995): 1–31.

Wellenreuther, Hermann, ed. *German and American Constitutional Thought.* New York: Berg, 2000.

Wheare, K. C. *Federal Government.* New York: Oxford University Press, 1964.

Wheeler, Douglas. *Historical Dictionary of Portugal.* London: Scarecrow Press, 1993.

Whyte, A. J. *The Political Life and Letters of Cavour, 1848–1861.* London: Oxford University Press, 1930.

Winik, Jay. *April 1865: The Month That Saved America.* New York: HarperCollins, 2001.

Witt, Peter-Christian. *Die Finanzpolitik des Deutschen Reiches von 1903 bis 1913.* Lübeck: Matthiesen, 1970.

Woolf, Stuart. *A History of Italy, 1700–1860.* London: Methuen, 1979.

———. *The Italian Risorgimento.* New York: Barnes and Noble, 1969.

———. *Napoleon's Integration of Europe.* New York: Routledge, 1991.

Zamagni, Vera. *The Economic History of Italy, 1860–1990.* Oxford: Clarendon Press, 1993.

Zangheri, Renato. *La propieta terriera e le origini del Risorgimento nel Bolognese.* Bologna: Zanichelli, 1961.

Ziblatt, Daniel. "The Federal-Unitary Divide." Harvard University Center for European Studies Working Paper, 2005.

Ziblatt, Daniel, "Rethinking the Origins of Federalism: Puzzle, Theory, and Evidence from Nineteenth Century Europe" *World Politics* 57 (October 2004), 70–98.

INDEX

Aachen, 35, 37, 38
Absolutism: in Germany, 113–14; in Italy, 83–84
Alfieri, Cesare, 66
Arnsberg, 35, 41
Associazione Nazionale. See Nationalist organizations
Austria: relationship with Prussia, 51–54, 122; war with Piedmont, 90

Baden, 39, 55, 111, 114–17, 122–24, 130, 155n.5, 180n.63, 193n.27
Balbo, Cesare, 10, 67
Bavaria, 19–20, 22, 30, 39, 41, 77, 111, 127; economic developments in, 42–43; and parliamentary and constitutional developments after 1815, 114–17; political developments in: 43, 55–56; and resistance to national unification, 42–45, 55–56
Beckerath, Hermann von, 37
Bendix, Reinhard, 131
Bentham, Jeremy, 66
Bermeo, Nancy, 3
Binkley, Robert, 8
Bismarck, Otto von, xi, 7, 8, 32, 111, 137–38, 176n.2, 177n.21; correspondence and speeches of, 109, 111, 122–24, 126–27, 135, 194n.44; parallels with Count Cavour, 75–76, 89, 92–93, 188n.42; and Prussian politics, 53–55
Bonaparte, Joseph, 62, 71
Boncompagni, Carlo, 91
Borchard, Karl, 48
Bourgeoisie, 57, 59; weakness in southern Italy and, 58
Bremen, 30, 35, 44–45, 138, 155n.4
British Parliament, 46
Bucher, Lothar, 133
Bund. *See* German Confederation
Bundesrat, 110, 129–30, 136–38, 198n.111
Burgess, Michael, 5, 8

Calhoun, John, 129
Camphausen, Ludolf, 37
Catholicism. *See* Religious divisions

Cattaneo, Carlo, 9, 59, 65, 67, 79, 101, 106
Cavour, Camillo di, xi, 7, 57, 59, 65, 66, 72; as advocate of decentralization, 10; as advocate of agricultural reform, 66; as architect of Italian unification, 89–105; correspondence with, 85, 90, 91, 93–94; and Piedmontese politics, 75–77, 111, 122, 125, 135
Chambers of Commerce: support for national market in German states, 38, 40; support for and opposition to national market in Italian states, 67–68, 184n.44
Charles Albert of Piedmont (King), 74
Chubb, Judith, 68
Clough, Sheperd, 75
Coercive capacity, 86–87, 118. *See also* Conscription rates
Commercialization: definition of, 173n.7; in German states, 21, 24, 34–37, 39–43; in Italian states, 62–63, 65–67; and relationship to industrialization, 63; weakness of, in southern Italy, 68–69, 70–72
Comparative historical method, 14–16
Confino, Alon, 10
Conscription rates, 87, 118–19
Constitutional developments: in German Reich in 1866–67, 132–38; in German states before 1866, 112–18, 192n.7, 193n.27; in Italian states before 1860, 83–85
Constitutional thought: in Germany, 129–31; in Italy, 101–2. *See also* Constitutional developments
Crefeld, 35–36

Decentralization: proposals for, in Italy, 105–7
Depretis, Agostino, 104
Di Scala, Spencer, 105
Dumke, Rolf, 49–50
Duncker, Max, 133–34
Düsseldorf, 35, 40

Educational reform, 87–88
Emilia, 62, 81, 85
Extractive capacity, 86–87, 118–19